J M Fourier.
1985.

THE LIBERATION
OF
THE CHURCH

The role of basic Christian groups
in
a new re-formation

DAVID CLARK

The National Centre for Christian Communities and Networks

1984.

First published in 1984 by
The National Centre for Christian Communities
and Networks
Westhill College
Selly Oak
Birmingham B29 6LL

© by David Clark

Printed in Great Britain by
Cambray Printing Services Ltd.
Cheltenham

British Library Cataloguing in Publication Data

Clark, David, 1934 —
    The Liberation of the Church.
    1. Church renewal — Great Britain
    I. Title
    262'.0017   BV600

ISBN 0-946185-05-0

THE LIBERATION OF THE CHURCH

The role of basic Christian groups in a new re-formation

To Sue,
Peter and Kirsten

CONTENTS

PREFACE

I am grateful to all those who, directly or indirectly, have made the writing and publication of this book possible.

The manuscript has gone through numerous drafts and revisions in the light of helpful criticisms made by those kind enough to read all or part of it. My thanks go in particular to Rupert Davies, Peter Houghton, Michael Hornsby-Smith, Chris Lawson, Leslie Paul and John Todd. Sue, my wife, has greatly helped in enabling me to clarify certain parts of the text.

The quotations used at the head of some chapters are taken from taped interviews with lay people active in the life of Birmingham. Their comments confirm me in my belief that many laity have an astute grasp of the situation in which the church now finds itself.

I am most appreciative of the efficient way in which my untidy script has been sorted out and typed by Pat Priestley and Pat Weaver.

I am also very grateful to Valerie Knight who over the years has kept the files of the National Centre, on which I have frequently drawn for information, in such good order.

My thanks go to the National Centre for Christian Communities and Networks for being willing to sponsor this publication.

Nonethless, I write in a personal capacity and neither those who read the manuscript nor those administering the affairs of the National Centre would necessarily share all my views. The responsibility for what follows is mine alone.

I am only too aware that if I had waited for another ten, or even five, years, the shape of things to come would have been a good deal clearer. But I believe that the direction of ecclesiastical developments in the United Kingdom is already being set for many years, if not many decades, to come. Thus what basic Christian groups are doing, and how they can be catalysts for change in the life of the church, need to be widely recognised at this point in time. To leave the basic Christian community movement out of the debate about the future would be to neglect an immensely encouraging sign of hope.

David Clark
Birmingham
April 1984

INTRODUCTION

'The Liberation of the Church' is an audacious title to give a book. It was not the one I began with. But as the chapters were written — and re-written — I became convinced that it was the only title that would do.

This was in part because what follows is not just about the church 'out there' — it is about my own life; my own calling as a Methodist minister and my own hopes for the church, my own attempts at making the gospel real, my own frustrations, but above all my own sense of captivity and my own search for liberation. So I begin with a word about myself and how this book came to be written.

I was born in 1934. I was brought up in a home in which Methodism permeated the very air we breathed. I owe an immense amount to my family — but also to my church. Methodism showed me what Christian community (the old fashioned word was 'fellowship') was all about. Methodism taught me the meaning of passion for the things of God — I was converted at fifteen at a service led by William Gowland who inspired me then, and has done so ever since, by his evangelical zeal and by his deep desire to preach a gospel relevant to the needs of the modern world.

From Methodism I learnt the meaning of 'the priesthood of all believers'; of a church wherein all members, be they enlightened or not, are allowed to have their say. As a consequence I have had little trouble with the idea, apparently still strange to many, that the church is in practice, and not just in theory, the whole people of God.

My home, my church, my conversion, in fact my world at that time, propelled me at an early age into seeing ordination as a natural vocation. It was an intention which remained constant over the next decade. I did national service. I studied history at Oxford, where the John Wesley Society early on showed me the strength to be gained from basic Christian groups. Then I undertook a diploma year in the social sciences — it was the gospel applied to life that still interested me.

In 1959 I went to Handsworth College, Birmingham, to prepare for the Methodist ministry. It was a time of great 'fellowship' with other ordinands, but, though a caring community, I felt it to be a somewhat narrow society shaped by the past rather than the challenge of the future.

Two years later I experienced one of the most liberating times of my life — a final twelve months of study spent at the William Temple College, Rugby, under its dynamic Principal, Mollie Batten (the only woman I ever saw smoking a pipe!). There for the first time I discovered what it was to make the concerns of lay people — especially daily work — a top priority on the church's agenda. At the William Temple College

I learnt that Christians need to engage with a secular society with all the resources — of mind as well as heart — at their disposal. Intellectual openness, honesty and rigour were the order of the day. For the first time, too, I had a taste of true ecumenism in operation — and came in particular to respect the traditions and ways of worship of my fellow Anglicans.

In 1962, with Sue my wife, I moved to begin my Methodist ministry in Woodhouse, near Sheffield. Woodhouse had once been a thriving farming, then a mining, village. By the time we arrived it was a declining working class, and largely neglected, suburb on the outskirts of the city. Nevertheless, I learnt in Woodhouse a good deal more about the qualities of a close-knit community. I learnt how the members of my churches could care for one another, could have great fun together, could support the sick, could look after the elderly, could share the sorrows of the bereaved, could care for the church building as if it were their own home, could give of their money with generosity. But I also learnt how inward looking such a community could be. I found those who could be stubbornly possessive about church offices, who under no circumstances would permit two of my congregations worshipping within a few hundred yards of each other to come closer together, who disliked newcomers to the area and made little attempt to open the church to them, whose domestic concerns took priority over the problems of the wider world — in short, who were helping the church to sign and seal its own death warrant.

Yet I still admired what the residents of Woodhouse had achieved in times past, and their many qualities in the present. So much so that I made the comparison of Woodhouse past and present the subject of my doctorate in sociology at Sheffield University. However, one thing became clear. There was little hope that my vision of what the church should be could in the Woodhouse of the mid sixties be made a reality.

In 1967 I moved with my wife, and now two children, to West Greenwich, London — to a church with fifty members, where it had once had five hundred. I was sent into this situation by the Methodist Home Mission Department who believed that, as a sociologist, I might have some useful reflections to offer concerning the future of the church in the inner city. After only eighteen months it was obvious that the small Methodist society of which I was now minister could not survive much longer. We closed, and with most of our congregation moved to St. Mark's, a very hospitable Presbyterian church across the road. We there formed the first united Methodist-Presbyterian Church in England.

It was a great opportunity to put ideals into practice — a live, though still small, combined congregation and two ministers. We tried everything we knew — liturgical changes, an imaginative extended

3

Sunday school programme, house groups, a well produced magazine, exciting posters outside the church, the extension of the student chaplaincy work, the establishment of an active council of churches, house to house visitation, a scheme of neighbourhood care linked in with the social services, play groups, youth groups and numerous other activities. It kept the church very much alive — and it has remained so ever since. We attracted some 'new blood'. We became a small sign of what a vigorous inner city church could be. But we remained captive to circumstances beyond our control — a secular society which saw us as largely irrelevant, a neighbourhood-based operation which could minister to the domestic concerns of people but had little impact on their public lives, and a church still inevitably 'competing' for scarce resources with other denominations just around the corner.

Meanwhile during this period of the late 'sixties, western society was fortifying its defences to ward off what it saw as dangerous threats from the civil rights movement, flower power and student revolts; whilst conservative forces within the mainstream churches decided that the people of God could not yet be trusted with Christian unity.

For me time was beginning to run out. I had done eleven years in Methodist circuit work and was nearly forty. As a young person I had been inspired by the vision of a socially caring and concerned church, a vision widened and enriched by my experience at the William Temple College, as well as by the vigorous debate going on throughout the 'sixties about the new shape of a missionary church. But, with the institutional church as immovable as ever, there seemed no hope of making that vision come true — least of all by moving to affluent suburbia in which direction Methodism was gently pushing me. The only way forward was to break with the structures as they existed and seek to find a way out of the impasse by another route. Thus in 1973 I applied for, and gained the cautious permission of Methodism to take up, a post of lecturer in community and youth work at Westhill College, Birmingham.

Westhill enlarged my experience in a number of important ways. First, the department in which I worked introduced me at first-hand to those, staff and students, with a deep desire to bring more humanity to, and work for greater justice within, an often uncaring social system. I began, late in the day, to appreciate what politics was really about. Secondly, Westhill as part of the Selly Oak Colleges Federation, gave me the chance to meet Christians from all parts of the world — it was a veritable ecclesiastical 'united nations'. I came to want to know much more about the world church, a wish partly fulfilled by a visit to South Africa in 1982 and to the Sixth Assembly of the World Council of Churches in Vancouver in 1983.

But Westhill also gave me the opportunity to pursue my search for ways in which the church might be freed from its preoccupation with

4

closed ideologies and restrictive organisational forms and find a message, a dynamism and a structure able to meet the challenges of a modern world.

Throughout the 'sixties I had been a keen member of the Methodist Renewal Group. In 1970 this joined up with other similar bodies to form 'One for Christian Renewal', on whose council I served for a decade. But One for Christian Renewal, though giving me considerable personal support and being instrumental in helping to launch a number of important new initiatives in ministry and mission, seemed itself too tied to the fortunes of the mainsteam churches to be able to make a real breakthrough.

However, other signs of life were beginning to appear on the horizon. Back in 1962 I had paid a brief visit to the Taizé community in central France and had been deeply impressed by what was happening there. In 1970 I had been invited to lecture on Iona and had been inspired by the dedication, enthusiasm and work of the Iona Community. Towards the end of my stay in London, I had begun to come across other Christian groups (the Blackheath Commune was a few hundred yards away from our manse) exploring new ways of living out their faith in a secular society. Such groups as these, springing up in many different parts of the country, seemed a very different proposition from anything I had encountered before. They were intent on discovering fresh ways of making the gospel work which did not depend on existing ecclesiastical structures, indeed often challenged them in the name of a deeper understanding of faith and of Christian community.

My situation at Westhill College gave me the chance to see what was going on for myself. During a number of college vacations between 1974 and 1976, with my long-suffering family in tow, I visited a wide variety of Christian groups in all parts of the United Kingdom — we slept everywhere from floor-boards in crumbling old Victorian houses to feather beds in the homes of the nobility. But invariably we received a warm welcome and generous hospitality. These journeys culminated in 1976 with a visit to the States to look at similar things happening over there.

At the same time, through the medium of the magazine 'Community', which I had started in late 1971, I was attempting to share with a wider audience something of what the groups I visited were doing and saying. In 1977 I wrote a full account of what I had found in my book 'Basic Communities — towards an alternative society' (SPCK). (If readers wish to learn more about the life and activities of what I now prefer to call 'basic Christian groups' — as while some are residential communities, others by choice are not — it is to that volume that they should refer. Some details are now rather dated but the meaning and message of the groups' endeavours still remain much as I described them.)

My travels brought me into contact with many fine people. They also

enabled me for the first time to meet members of the religious orders —
Anglican and Roman Catholic — about whom I then knew next to
nothing. I was greatly impressed — and have remained so since — by
what the religious have to offer, not only to younger Christian groups, but
to the life of the whole church. I owe much in this respect to Father Alan
Harrison, Secretary of the Anglican Communities Consultative Council,
and to Sister Catherine Hughes, Provincial of the Sisters of Notre Dame.
Through the kindness of the Roman Catholic orders I was invited to
attend the National Pastoral Congress in Liverpool in 1980, an event
which I am still convinced will eventually be seen as a landmark in the
renewal of the Catholic Church in this country.

Also during this period I came to learn more about the Quakers, not
least through the openness and generosity of the staff at Woodbrooke
College, Birmingham. I became increasingly certain that the Friends
possess a heritage which has given them very some important insights as
to what the church must become, insights which we all now need to share.

In 1977 I had built up such a collection of material about basic Christian
groups that our house was bursting at the seams. So in that year, in a less
crowded front-room kindly offered by good friends, these papers went to
make up the Community Resources Centre (the forerunner of the
present National Centre for Christian Communities and Networks). The
growing number of contacts established through my travels, the
'Community' magazine and the Resources Centre, led to the holding of
a first Community Congress in 1980 in Birmingham.

The 1980 Congress was a very significant happening. It was an exciting
and horizon-widening encounter of some 250 people who had been
actively involved in the life and work of Christian groups and
communities for many years, yet few of whom had met before. The
Congress demonstrated that a 'basic Christian community movement'
existed in the United Kingdom, even if its identity and future potential
were as yet hard to grasp.

The 1980 Community Congress supported the original establishment
of the Community Resources Centre — now with a part-time Resources
Officer — and welcomed its further development. So in 1981 the National
Centre for Christian Communities and Networks came into being as an
independent charity. It was situated on the campus and welcomed by the
Principal and Governors of Westhill College. Its management committee
appointed me as its Honorary Director. In this task I have been much
helped by the loyal support of its Chairman, Peter Houghton, the
Director of the Birmingham Settlement. Since its establishment, the
National Centre's main task has been to keep basic Christian groups and
networks well informed about what other basic groups and networks are
doing.

My first book was about basic Christian groups themselves. It was an
attempt to look at their contribution to a deeper and broader

understanding of community — how they could offer personal fulfilment, could enrich relationships, and how within them authority could be exercised in a way that fostered human growth rather than created dependence. This book is about the relation of basic Christian groups to church and world. It has come out of my wrestlings over the years since the 1980 Congress with the message and the meaning of the basic Christian community movement, a movement still taking shape.

I write as a person who has never lived in a residential Christian community (theological colleges apart). That does not disturb me as I have always believed community to be about a quality of life possible in *any* group (such as my family), and not synonymous with living in a community house. However, I still regard the residential Christian community as a vital contribution to our understanding of what community is all about and without which the church would be much the poorer.

I write very much as a sociologist. Since the church began it has been those mainly concerned with doctrine and theology who have attempted to point the way — it now seems clear with somewhat limited success. It is time that the experience of many more people was called upon. The debate about the shape of things to come needs the knowledge and insight of all Christians — we rely on the chosen few at our peril. Thus when I write about the need for a new 're-formation' I use the term primarily in a sociological sense — to mean the church's structures literally being 're-formed' (hence the hyphen) in a way that can liberate the whole people of God to fulfil their calling to build one world in Christ. Such a re-formation, of course, has major theological implications.

This new re-formation I see as re-shaping every denomination, Protestant as well as Catholic, Free Churches as well as Established Church, for all of us are at present held captive. When such a re-formation does come, and it can now only be delayed not prevented, it will I believe be as significant as any which has gone before it.

I write from within a western culture. The growth and development of 'basic ecclesial communities' in Latin America have provided extremely valuable insights into the nature of the basic Christian community movement as a whole. But an upsurge of basic Christian groups is occurring in many countries throughout the world. It is a mistake uncritically to transfer experiences from one milieu to another. We can only make sense of what is happening by drawing on the varied experiences of Christians living within a diversity of historic, social and political contexts, and pooling our discoveries. Thus my own definition of basic Christian groups (see Chapter VI) derives from the situation of church and society in the United Kingdom, and is the one I believe to be of most practical use in the circumstances in which we find ourselves.

I write often critically of the church — but I hope not glibly or cynically. I am profoundly grateful for the way it has nurtured, taught, cared for and guided me. I am far from forgetful of my Christian heritage. I am far from unaware of the sheer goodness of millions of Christians who day by day give more to the life of our world than can ever be calculated. I am far from unappreciative of clergy who shoulder the tiring responsibilities of domestic duty and public obligation on our behalf. But the church is an integral part of a world in crisis, and for which it is called to be a means of salvation. It has human assets beyond measure — yet if these remain unrealised then all of us will be the losers. It is a church which needs, as in times past, to be liberated and re-formed, if it is to be true to its own calling.

In this process of liberation and re-formation I believe the role of the basic Christian community movement to be crucial — in this country, and across the world. It is a prophetic movement heralding the means by which the church can take a quantum leap into the future — can begin to free itself from closed ideologies and old patterns of working which at present keep it jammed in tramlines from which it seems unable to break clear. The basic community movement exists to remind us once more that the church is the servant of the kingdom.

The basic community movement cannot be an end in itself. It is a model, but more important a catalyst, for wider change. Its function is not to go it alone. If it does so it will slowly fade from the scene, leaving it to another generation to read its purpose and potential aright. Its task is to bring all of us as the people of God to recognise the parlous state of our planet, to become aware of our captivity, to seek to free ourselves for service and mission, and to bring into being a church fit to be an instrument of the kingdom.

I know that liberation and re-formation will not come overnight and that they will be costly. I know that as yet the basic Christian community movement is itself only half aware of the possibilities inherent within it. I know that a new ecumenical missionary movement in which the laity play the key role is still only on the horizon. I know that the vision of free people living for one church and one world in Christ could look like a fool's paradise. But I also know that 'the foolishness of God is wiser than men' and 'the weakness of God is stronger than men' — and that gives me great hope!

8

I: CRISIS AND COMMUNITY

1. Crisis

'I see no possible end to the crisis at the moment — no way through at all. I find the whole situation pretty heartbreaking.' (City planning officer)

'We're moving through the biggest change since the beginning of the industrial revolution — whether we survive it of course is doubtful. We may just break up as a community.' (Businessman)

This book is about a church which has lost its way. It is about a great and glorious institution which has survived for more years than nations and empires, yet which now finds itself at the end of an evolutionary era. Like the dinosaur[1], the church now possesses a life-style and a form which prevent it making an effective response to the world of the present, let along that of the future. But this book is also about a church which God never abandons. It is about the hope of liberation and of a 'new re-formation' through which he is offering his people a new message, and showing them new ways of making the gospel real for our time.

For millions in our land today the fate of the church is of minimal concern. To some it appears an oppressive or patronising institution which condones, and thus helps to perpetuate, the dehumanising features of an unjust and materialistic society. To others it seems a typically British anachronism, kept going to grace national occasions, to give rites of passage a bit more decorum, or to provide the tourist industry with interesting architectural remains to show its customers. For these, whether the church lives or dies matters little.

But to a still significant minority it does matter, and matters very much. It matters because they know that of all institutions, each in its own way reflecting the plight of the dinosaur, the church has time and again throughout history shown that within it are contained the springs of new life and the hope of regeneration for the whole of society. Nothing could be more important than this when the world which God brought into being and for which Christ died is in a state of crisis; when men and women urgently need to discover the divine purpose for our planet: when they need to re-learn that faith, hope and love are properties without which mankind cannot survive.

9

a. Life or death?

Our human race has reached the most decisive stage since it emerged on the evolutionary ladder. David Attenborough in his book 'Life on Earth'[2] reminds us of the fact that the norm in evolution is for species to develop in response to a new environmental situation, to master it, and then to die away as circumstances alter and they find themselves unable to respond adequately. Richard Leakey, in his television series on the origins of man[3], concluded that here the human race is unique in two major respects. On the one hand, human beings alone have achieved the power to master their environment and thus perpetuate their kind into the far distant future. On the other, they alone now have the power totally to destroy themselves.

'It is a time of crisis for us all', states the 'Message' from the Sixth Assembly of the World Council of Churches meeting in Vancouver in 1983. The crisis we face is not simply that of the possible extinction of humanity through natural causes — the destruction of the least fit. It is one of our deliberately *choosing* our own annihilation. The greatest freedom given by God to any of his creatures can be used to wipe from the face of the earth everyone who enjoys that freedom[4]. This is a crisis quite different in kind from any known before in the life of our planet.

The crisis of potential human annihilation by human choice is intimately related to other life or death crises. We now have the power to blow our world to pieces; we also have the means to contaminate it in a way which will make human survival impossible. The shadow of the mushroom cloud could all too easily be overtaken by the darkness of a planet with its air, water and soil polluted beyond recovery. The earth currently has few friends.

The crisis of life or death has been escalated by man's rapidly and vastly increasing technological expertise. This has in turn brought daunting moral choices. At the end of 1982, the press reported on the first ever artificial heart fitted to a man in the United States, whilst an article in the same paper entitled 'Clones in a synthetic womb'[5] stated that 'nearly 150 test-tube babies have now been born. The new era is a fact.' Add to the major ethical questions these developments raise others about abortion and euthanasia, and the acute decisions facing each and every one of us already seem all but overwhelming.

b. Wealth or poverty? Justice or injustice?

'He who wants to ban war must also ban mass poverty'[6]. So bluntly states the Brandt Report. If the most obvious crisis facing many of us is that of life or death, just as pressing for millions is that of wealth or poverty. '30,000 children die on the average every day for lack of food. If present trends continue, that figure will rise substantially in the 1980s and could even reach 40,000 a day by the end of the decade. Yet that is only the tip of the iceberg. There are more people living in absolute poverty than ever before in the history of the world and, again, there are solid reasons for believing that their number will increase substantially in the 1980s. Super-imposed on these huge numbers of desperately poor people are even larger numbers of unemployed and underemployed on the one hand, and, fewer in number but nearly as tragic, the cruelly exploited working poor on the other.' Thus writes Charles Elliott, the Director of Christian Aid[7].

Once again the choice lies with each and every one of us. We now have the technology, the skill, and indeed the wealth, to perpetuate half a world mesmerised by 'the fetish of commodities'[8] whilst the other half starves, or to establish 'a new world economic order', as the Brandt Report urges[9]. At the Vancouver Assembly of the World Council of Churches delegates from the Third World saw this as a stark choice between justice or injustice. They argued eloquently that whilst the West is preoccupied with the issue of nuclear war in the future, their children die of hunger today. They reminded church and world, as the 'Message' from the Assembly puts it, that 'The tree of peace has justice for its roots'.

c. Meaning or despair?

Behind these crises of life or death, wealth or poverty and justice or injustice, lies perhaps the deepest crisis of all; that of lack of purpose. Where is the human race going? What point does life have in the context of the amorphous mass of humanity appearing daily on every television screen? Paul Tillich argues that the most profound question facing people today is not about fate and death, as with the Greek civilisation; nor about guilt and condemnation, which typified the Middle Ages; but about a lack of purpose and an uncertain destiny born out of a sense of meaninglessness and helplessness[10].

This last crisis has in part come about because the technological revolution, in particular the global explosion of the media, now exposes every one of us to a bewildering diversity of cultures, customs and creeds. 'Never before', writes Peter Berger, 'was the pluralisation of meaning and values experienced as massively by as many people'[11]. We are exposed to 'the vertigo of relativity'[12] which threatens to rock the assumed stability and superiority of our beliefs and traditions and send us spinning into limbo.

This age of crisis is already upon us. I use the word 'age' deliberately to mean 'a very long time'. The particular crises we face — of life or death, wealth or poverty, justice or injustice and meaning or despair — are no short-term affairs. None of us can sit back assured that our children, or even our children's children, will emerge again into calmer waters. Our planet is now at 'The Turning Point', as Fritjof Capra calls it[13]. We either draw on every resource God has given us to make it through the future years of terrifying freedom — or we will witness the end of the human race as we know it.

2. Community

'If our faith is not about community it is nothing.' (Housewife)
'The message of hope and purpose is not really here yet.' (City planning officer)

If an age of crisis brings the threat of unprecedented calamity, it also offers immense possibilities for good. The word 'crisis' (in its Greek usage) can mean not only an impending event with potentially disastrous consequences, but a time of great opportunity. In Chinese the characters for crisis are *wei ji*, meaning *both* danger *and* opportunity. An age of crisis is an age of wide open choices.

What as a world we face, what our age of crisis is ultimately all about, is the choice between chaos or community. It is a choice which God has been offering his people — be they individuals, groups or nations — since the beginning of time. It lies at the heart of the meaning of the Old and New Testaments; it has been pivotal for the story of human history since Christ died. Today we too face the same choice as our forefathers — only now the stakes are far higher because, for better or for worse, we now hold in our hands the destiny of the whole human race. In Bonhoeffer's words, we have 'come of age'[14].

Chaos or community? These are the options now before us. Chaos, which will be as grim and forbidding as that state which existed before God brought light out of darkness; or community, which will reveal a depth and breadth of human sharing and caring hitherto only glimpsed within previous civilisations. If we are to build a new world out of the crises which now face us, we will have to discover and put into practice a quality of communal living far richer and more demanding than has ever been known or experienced before.

What is the nature of this new community now required of us? What is is it for which we must search? What quality of life is it that has to come into being if we are to survive the crises of our age in a mature and lasting way?

The first difficulty here is that the word 'community' has already been much over-used. The concept gained prominence during the last century[15] because it then expressed a deep need of human beings passing through a period of great uncertainty, and challenged by their own particular crisis, that of the industrial revolution. In our time, however, we have labelled so many things 'community' that the concept seems to have been virtually emptied of useful meaning. Yet if the word appears to be growing old, it stubbornly refuses to lie down and die. I believe, therefore, that we must seek to reinstate rather than abandon 'community' so that chaos can be matched by an alternative concept of equal power and comprehensiveness.

a. The sociological dimension of community

To reach an understanding of community worthy of man come of age we must look briefly at its use as a sociological concept. To harness our resources to meet potential chaos means using to the full the analysis and reflection that has been going on in relation to this word for a century or more.

In the sociological context, it was Ferdinand Toennies who began the debate by using the term 'community' ('Gemeinschaft' in his language) to describe a way of life typical of the countryside and small towns of his homeland in the northern-most province of Germany, in the mid nineteenth century being fast overtaken by industrialisation[16]. Since Toennies' original work, sociologists have generally explored community from one of five vantage points. Each has yielded some insights, but all are complementary and must be held together if the most significant definition of community is to be found.

In the first instance, community has been used to indicate *a loose-knit collection of human beings.* Certain of the earliest references to community relate to 'the common people'[17], without any further distinguishing characteristics being given. The value of this approach is its taking the concept of community to be inclusive of those of differing sex, age and, to a certain extent, class. It places community in the category of terms which are generalist rather than particular. On the other hand, this definition is too vague and unqualified to be of more than initial use. So sociologists have been quick to explore other dimensions of the concept.

A second way of approaching the definition of community has been to attach it firmly to some *identifiable territory,* notably the rural village, though in the period just after the second world war it was increasingly applied to old inner city areas such as Bethnal Green and Bermondsey in London, or Barton Hill in Bristol. To associate community with such 'village-like' localities strikes a chord for many people — we often retain (as did Toennies) a nostalgic view of 'the good old days' when home, the neighbourhood in which we spent our formative years, and our experience of community seemed all of a piece. The place in which we were born and brought up, the area encompassing the friends we made (and the church we attended), for many of us became, symbolically[18], even if they were not always so in reality, what we believed 'community' was all about.

But there are problems in equating community with a particular place

13

or locality. The latter can easily disappear; physically, through such developments as slum clearance and rehousing schemes, or, socially, through our having to move away to be educated, find work or get married. Thus sociologists gradually came to realise that to tie their definition of community to one kind of locality (such as the village or even the old urban neighbourhood) still created difficulties. As rural villages became depopulated or inner city areas were razed to the ground, community would then have been destroyed with them. This was, therefore, a definition with little future.

A third way of understanding the concept of community was to see it as describing *shared activities, wherever* these were located. This approach brought with it a very important insight — the realisation that community was in evidence in a whole range of groups where people shared common interests and concerns, even if the participants lived many miles apart. Community could exist, and sometimes in greater degree, within the office, the college, the hospital ward or the choral society, than in the village or the neighbourhood as such. Sociologists thus began to look for evidence of community as much where people gathered as where they lived.

Fourthly, and closely related to community through shared activities, the concept became associated with *certain types of social relationship,* in particular with the 'primary' group, defined as one within which people encounter each other on a face-to-face basis. Such a group could be made up of those related by blood or marriage (as with extended families in the past, or with some immigrant families today). But it need not be. Just as communally important activities could take place away from the home, so too could communally important relationships be formed beyond the neighbourhood of residence and outside the family circle. Indeed some sociologists argued that community could be experienced even as a result of very temporary encounters, as when people met on holiday or at a conference.

There was, however, a major problem with defining community in terms of shared activities or close-knit relationships. It was the presumption that where these existed community would *inevitably* be present. This was obviously not the case. Every Monday evening I attend an art class and enjoy struggling with pencil, paint and paper. Yet though I have now met members of the same class on many occasions I still know few even by name, and I doubt many know mine. People come together to learn a skill not to engage in socialising. Thus the class is artistically worthwhile but communally of little consequence to me. Nor do even close relationships always indicate the existence of community. My pastoral work as a Methodist minister in Yorkshire brought me into contact with many extended families, yet some of the bitterest feuds I have experienced were evident therein (and often just because relationships *were* intense).

14

i. Significance and solidarity

Because it has not been found adequate to define community only as a collection of human beings, or as a certain kind of locality, or as shared activities, or even as close-knit relationships, some sociologists have gone a step further and argued that the most important indicator of community must lie with how participants *feel,* about themselves and others, in relation to the group of which they are members. I have elsewhere suggested that community is dependent on two such key feelings — *a sense of significance* or personal fulfilment, and *a sense of solidarity* or belonging[19]. It is only when people feel a sense of their own worth, on the one hand, and a sense of being intimately part of a group on the other, that we can be sure that community exists. What is more, such feelings give us at least some means of assessing the strength, and not merely the presence, of community. Be it as a family, a church, a trades union or even a nation, it is above all people's *feelings* that we must take into account to ascertain the strength of community.

That community is thus essentially a subjective phenomenon, that it is experienced and expressed in relation to what each and every person feels, is something we misunderstand or ignore at our peril. Community cannot be planned or engineered from 'the top down'. It cannot be engendered by forcing people to mix together — as certain local authorities have attempted to do by siting middle and working class housing cheek by jowl. It cannot be architecturally determined, however attractive the neighbourhood. Neither specially planned estates (such as that which the Bournville Village Trust has provided for my family, amongst others, to live on), nor modern churches (such as Coventry Cathedral or 'the brand new church down the road') can by themselves *make* community happen. Community cannot be created simply through courses or conferences to promote better relationships between people, be these encounter groups or meetings for reconciliation in places like Northern Ireland. These 'external' means of seeking to foster community may help. But in the end *community has to be discovered and expressed by the participants themselves, in their way and at their pace.*

This sociologically informed understanding of community is of great importance in an age of crisis. It can provide us with vital indicators of community. It can show us that community building is essentially a process of both personal and corporate experience and development. Nevertheless, such an empirical understanding of community is *still* not enough. There is no salvation through sociology alone. We need to go further.

b. The theological dimension of community

'Where can community be found? And where is the place of understanding?' (as Job might have put it[20]). It is certainly not found by

15

consulting only sociologists, or even those who are the objects of their studies. For if community is to be measured by what people feel, *whose* feelings are to be taken into account? To assess the strength of community in relation to the sense of significance and solidarity experienced by participants may make community a more meaningful reality. But such an approach also relativises it, and thus ignores the all-important ethical dimension. Community measured by the strength of people's feelings can appear a power for 'good', but it may in fact be a power for 'evil'.

It comes as a shock to many people (including some sociologists) to realise that community can be a demonic as well as creative force in human affairs, especially as Raymond Williams informs us that the word is constantly used in English as indicating something favourable[21]. But a genuinely sociological definition of community must be about *facts* not values. It is, for example, a fact that the mothers' and toddlers' group, the football club and the religious order can experience a strong sense of community. But so too can the Mafia, the Red Brigade and the I.R.A. Indeed horrific events often occur when two or more intensely communal groups (by sociological criteria) come into conflict, as we know only too well from regular news bulletins of atrocities across the world. The quality of community which we seek must, therefore, be about *altruistic values* as well as facts; about a richness of life, about a purpose for living, and about a power to make it all possible. Otherwise it is nothing.

I believe the values which we seek are Christian values. Without these as a foundation I would be writing with little optimism, or not at all. For me, as a Christian, they are values based on the conviction, as David Jenkins puts it, that:

'Man's nature is fundamentally good (created as good and created to be good), that the central practical key to the human situation is man's responsibility and man's choice, and that, while abuse of this responsibility is the prevailing feature of the human situation as we observe it and experience it, this "fallen" situation (of abuse) does not define or delimit the possibilities of being human.'[22]

I believe that through the grace of Christ, the love of God and the fellowship of the Holy Spirit, a new community can emerge to match the challenge of this age of potential death. It will be an immense human achievement; but it can be accomplished because this kind of community is also a divine gift.

What then does Christian faith add to our understanding of community? It does not deny or neglect sociology; but it infuses the dry bones with new vitality. It takes the insights of the social sciences and joins them to a different level of human experience, that of the divine presence and purpose.

16

i. Autonomy and ecumenicity

I have argued that community as a feeling is made up of two key components, a sense of significance and a sense of solidarity. A Christian understanding of community embraces these experiences, but goes much further.

For the Christian, community is not only about each person's sense of significance, but about the fulfilment (being made perfect or whole in biblical terms (Mt. 5 v. 48)) of an individual as 'a unique expression of the universe, incomparable, irreplaceable, and of infinite significance'[23]. Such fulfilment is the divinely intended destiny of everyone, it is 'the end of our exploring'[24]. It is attained by choice, following in the steps of Christ who calls, and by human endeavour (James 2 v. 26) in pursuit of that calling. It is also a gracious gift of God given to those who commit themselves to his service (Jn. 10 v 10).

For Christians a sense of significance is transformed into the experience of *autonomy*; each of us freely attaining our full potential as a person made in the image of God. Such growth is a demanding process of self-acceptance and self-affirmation, requiring, as Paul Tillich describes it, 'the courage to be as oneself'[25]. Community making requires autonomous individuals, each of whom 'chooses the rules he lives by, and feels free to modify them with increased experience'[26]. The autonomous Christian is not out to destroy the law but to fulfil and transcend it for the sake of a more fully human existence. He does so as a follower of one who first opened the way to complete human fulfilment (Mt. 5 v. 17).

The Christian knows that his own infinite worth as a person is also God's estimate of every other person. Thus his search for fulfilment can only bear fruit if he acknowledges that everyone else has the divine right to be involved in a similar search. The autonomy he seeks is not the opportunity to do just as he pleases. It derives from the establishment of open and altruistic relationships. The humanity of the part is intimately bound up with the humanity of the whole. Autonomy entails the wisdom to choose what will help him realise his own potential as a child of God, but in a way that enables others to do likewise. Whereas for the sociologist the experience of significance may provide adequate evidence of the existence of community, *for the Christian a sense of significance must be complemented by growth towards autonomy.*

In sociological terms, a second criterion of community is that people experience a sense of solidarity, that they feel they belong to one another. From a Christian perspective community is certainly about such a sense of belonging. But there is much more to it than that. What matters is how wide the doors are thrown open and how far the circle is extended. Tom Driver writes, 'What is holy is never an individual thing or person or even an individual God but rather the relation between one and another'[27]. Christian solidarity is about holy and whole relationships, it is 'ecumenical' in the sense of uniting in love (from the word's Greek

17

origins) 'the whole inhabited world'. *For the Christian, therefore, a sense of solidarity is transformed into the experience of ecumenicity*, an ecumenicity which means the unity of all humankind (not just of members of ecclesiastical institutions).

Ecumenicity is about a *depth* of belonging in which human love and friendship spring out of the love of God for men and women (1 Jn. 4 v. 19). For the Christian, human solidarity is always underpinned by God's solidarity with his creation.

Ecumenicity is about a *breadth* of belonging. It explodes the narrow loyalties of men and women in the name of a Lord who died for all (Gal. 3 vs. 27-28). It is about the wholeness of the human race, about a sense of solidarity which encompasses all people. In brief, it is about one world. Community for the Christian involves a dangerous and demanding kind of loving which the cynical see as impossible. Yet it is an experience in which Christians are called to be fully involved (Mk. 10 v 27), even if it requires what Paul Tillich describes as 'the courage to be as a part'[28].

As (in the sociological definition of community) significance and solidarity, though complementary elements, are sometimes in tension, so (in the Christian understanding of community) it can be with autonomy and ecumenicity. This tension arises from the age old struggle for the fulfilment of the individual over against the needs of the group, for the well-being of the member over against that of the body as a whole. It is potentially a life giving tension, but one which constantly threatens the rupturing of human relationships and fragmentation of human endeavour.

The Christian's response to this tension of individual against group, of the part against the whole, is of fundamental importance in an age of crisis. It is no exaggeration to say that on its creative resolution the future of our world rests. Facing this formidable dichotomy the Christian points first and foremost to the divine mystery 'of the Blessed Trinity, a holy community of Persons, in whom "none is afore, or after other; none is greater, or less than another"'[29]. Here is revealed the example of perfect community, wholeness without the loss of identity of any particular part.

The Trinity for the Christian represents that great communal synthesis on which his hopes are founded, and that power which brings into being the kingdom community. It reveals to him that his hope of free people living for one world is grounded in reality, and is not a product of vain fantasy. Loren Halvorson puts it thus:

> 'What can rescue the polarity of self and neighbour from narcissism or masochism is the alternative to dualistic thinking found in a trinitarian approach. The Trinity is the central truth around which the Christian faith and life is constituted . . . At the heart of human community lies the image of God. God, in Christian teaching, is not a polarity of opposites as typical of so many religions and philosophical efforts to

18

comprehend the deity. God is Trinity: a unity (could we say "community"?) of three Persons. Such imagery takes us into a completely different universe than the effort to balance out polar or dualistic formulations. The Trinity of Creator, Re-creator and Spirit lies so deeply in the fabric of creation itself that it emerges in diverse ways in creation. At the heart of community we find the trinity of self, neighbour and God.'[30]

In New Testament terms this understanding of community is encompassed by the word 'koinonia'. Of late this term has come increasingly to the fore, not least in the final report of the Anglican-Roman Catholic International Commission[31].

Koinonia describes, first, *the sharing relationship, or solidarity, of God with his people* — as Father (1 Jn. 1 v. 3), Son (1 Cor. 1 v. 9) and Holy Spirit (2 Cor. 13 v. 14). 'Union with God in Christ Jesus through the Spirit is the heart of Christian koinonia', states the Anglican-Roman Catholic report[32].

Secondly, the word indicates *the partnership between Christians in the faith* (Phil. 1 v 5), for, 'Koinonia with one another is entailed by our koinonia with God in Christ'[33].

Thirdly, the word emphasises the *identity and significance of those in fellowship as unique persons* (Gal. 2 v 9).

Fourthly, koinonia is used to describe the *mystery of the eucharist* (1 Cor. 10 vs. 14 ff.) *where God and his people are drawn together in intimate 'communion'*.

Finally, the word represents *community not only as a sharing of relationships but of material goods* (Acts 2 v. 42 and Rom. 15 v. 26), spelling out that the task of reconciliation and caring concerns the physical as well as the spiritual dimensions of human existence.

Koinonia thus transforms community into an experience of completeness, of each person and of society being made whole through their relationship to God, Father, Son and Holy Spirit; an experience of salvation. *Koinonia is about the unity of the Godhead, about one people of God, about one church and about one world.*

Halvorson sums up the implications for Christian faith in the late twentieth century — 'Humans can live in community because God is community'[34].

Christian community has to be lived out and not just preached about. The search for autonomy and ecumenicity is not ultimately a matter of sociological analysis or even theological exposition. It is a real life affair. Tom Driver writes, 'The danger religion poses to the status quo . . . is to enable people to experience, not only to hear about, communal equality'[35]. It is this lived experience of community that God is now asking his people to demonstrate in our age of crisis, and to set against the alternatives of death, poverty, injustice and despair. Men and women in

Christ are called to be the instruments of the salvation of the world, to enable all God's people to be made whole.

How is it then that we seem unable to respond to this high calling? What holds the people of God captive?

II: THE CAPTIVE CHURCH

'I can't stress how much I feel the church is in crisis and isn't aware of it.' (Director of a voluntary organisation)
'I believe we're living with the back-log of Christian tradition — we're living on the faith of our forefathers; and it's beginning to erode.' (City councillor)

Werner Stark, after his exhaustive historical investigation of the sociology of religion, concludes: 'Our whole investigation . . . has proved, if it has proved anything, that Christianity has sprung from and remains rooted in, community'[1]. Our own age of crisis is one in which the Christian experience and expression of community (koinonia) lived out in practical terms is now a necessity. 'The greatest need in our time is not simply for kerygma, the preaching of the gospel; nor for diakonia, service on behalf of justice; nor for charisma, the experience of the Spirit's gifts; nor even for propheteia, the challenging of the king. The greatest need of our time is for koinonia, the call simply to be the church, to love one another, and to offer our lives for the sake of the world'[2], writes Jim Wallis of the Sojourners community in Washington D.C.

Such a call for koinonia faces many obstacles. Perhaps the most formidable is that of the 'closed' social system, usually in institutional form, which prevents encounter and engagement with a wider world. Institutions which remain shut in on themselves become the victims of closed ideologies, closed structures and closed practices. They threaten community in two main ways.

In the first place, *closed institutions negate autonomy* because human choice, and the accountability and responsibility which go with it, is severely limited if not curtailed entirely. Growth towards maturity is impeded, and the freedom for individuals to choose to become fully human is not available. Secondly, *closed institutions block the development of ecumenicity.* They shut off the opportunity for men and women to share with and care for those beyond their own immediate circle. The possibility of a fully human society is no longer an option. Thus the closed social system is anathema to the Christian hope of free people for one world.

All institutions are liable to closure of this kind and to becoming destructive of community. Liberating them from restrictive ideologies, structures and practices is imperative if men and women are to be able to meet the challenges of the modern world. How much more important therefore, that a church which seeks to be a model of community, and which proclaims that such an experience is of vital importance for society as a whole, be able to practice what it preaches. What hope for secular institutions if the church itself is not able to blaze a communal trail of a kind which can help carry us through the crises of possible annihilation, poverty, injustice and meaninglessness?

Yet it is just at this point in our history, when the human race faces some of its gravest difficulties, that the church is found captive, itself at the mercy of closed ideologies, structures and practices which prevent it from getting on with its essential task of living out community. A steady decline in membership[3], financial problems and redundant plant are merely pointers to anachronistic traditions and forms which the church seems intent on taking with it into a quite different sort of world. But as John Kent warns, 'A passion for continuity might now be no more than a death-wish'[4]. *And what does Kent want to do?*

The captivity of the church as an institution is characterised by its being subject to two all-pervasive and closed *ideologies*; 'secularism' and 'sacralism'. Their restrictiveness is manifest through a number of 'heretical *structures*' (as Colin Williams described them some years ago)[5]. The latter are organisational forms and procedures which were once meant to maintain one or other aspect of church order, but which have over time become absolute, assumed to be properties without which the church cannot be the church. What were in fact useful *means* of building Christian community* and of furthering the kingdom have, through misunderstanding or misrepresentation, been raised to the status of *ends*. The 'heretical structures' which I believe to be most destructive at this point in time I term 'clericalism', 'parochialism', 'congregationalism' and 'denominationalism'. These closed ideologies and closed structures also lead to a closed theology.

If the church is to proclaim and live out the meaning of community for an age in crisis it must seek liberation from these restrictive ideologies and structures. In dealing with these constraints below, I shall attempt to specify the changes in our priorities that must occur if we as Christians are to regain credibility as community builders.

---

* I use the term 'Christian community' henceforth mainly in a *qualitative* sense, to indicate that depth and breadth of corporate experience, spiritual, social and material, described in section 2 of Chapter I. If I do use the term to describe actual groups of Christians it will normally appear in the plural — i.e. 'Christian communities' — and its meaning as a *collective noun* will be clear from the text.

1. Closed ideologies — secularism and sacralism

a. From secularism to faith

'One is living in a society which is basically *not* Christian in any really meaningful way.' (Director of a voluntary organisation)

'In the very desperate situation we're in, I get a lot of support personally from my own faith which sort of keeps me going in sometimes fairly impossible circumstances.' (City planning officer)

'Secular*ism*' is an ideology which denies the existence of a sacred order of any kind, or, in its less extreme form, an agnosticism which sees the sacred (even if it has meaning for a few) as irrelevant to the world as men and women actually experience it. Where secularism dominates, I define society as being 'secular*istic*'. *This is a very 1960's definition*

The open-ended process of 'secular*isation*' must be distinguished from the closed ideology of secularism. Secularisation encompasses 'differentiation', which refers to functions that the church once fulfilled but have now been taken over by other institutions; and 'disengagement'[6], which refers to responsibility for such functions being transferred from the church to the state, or its associated agencies. This process of secularisation I define as bringing into being a 'secular' society. Secularisation has meant institutions being given authority and status in relation to the functions they fulfil best, and the responsibilities they carry out most effectively on behalf of society as a whole. Secularisation means that the task of religious institutions becomes more clearly delineated; secularism means the eventual disappearance or demolition of religious institutions as redundant.

Secularism denies community and makes autonomy and ecumenicity a chimera. Often in the name of liberty and progress it imposes a world view closed to any possibility of divine love or mercy. The human race becomes the alpha and omega of all things, and the hoped for resolution of the crises of our time is built only on the shaky foundations of its past 'achievements'. There is no hope of a free people for one world in Christ.

Secularism's most potent allies have been *rationalism* and *materialism*. Rationalism has taken the liberating power of reason and paraded it as the gateway to salvation. Lesslie Newbigin sees the Enlightenment as establishing 'a new ideology (which) has replaced the Christian vision as the cultus publicus of western Christendom'[7]. But the 'bloodless intellect'[8] of rational man has proved no match for 'the organised communal power of the new paganism'[9], as the continuing rise of totalitarian and oppressive political regimes amply demonstrates.

23

Secularism's other ally has been materialism, an ideology which has permeated political ideologies of right and left alike. From materialism has stemmed a consumerism which has often perpetuated a rampant competitiveness, and helped to preserve a world divided between the powerful and the powerless, the affluent and the destitute.

In its encounter with a closed secularism some believe that the church has long since sold its soul. For example, Alan Gilbert in his study of 'Religion and Society in Industrial England'[10] sees all the main churches during that era increasingly compromising themselves under pressure from a pluralistic, urban and affluent society. An undermining of the churches' mission and 'a defensive shift to endogenous growth'[11] has been the result. The church has failed to realise that secularism has entered on the scene with a vengeance. In the name of 'progress', and despite vocal opposition by a few who recognise secularism to be parading in guises such as 'scientific objectivity' or 'professionalism', the church has allowed itself to be encapsulated by an ideology which threatens its very *raison d'être*.

The renewal of Christian community depends on breaking asunder the bonds of rationalism and materialism in the name of divine revelation and inspiration. It means saying 'Yes' to God, over against a man-centred secularism which would deny the existence of the love of the Father and the fellowship and unity of the Holy Spirit. *The fundamental change required of the church today is away from collusion with secularism to a living faith.*

This 'Yes to God', of which Alan Ecclestone has written with such profound insight[12], has to be a passionate 'Yes' or it is nothing. Without passion for God, our passion for evil will reign supreme. A heartfelt 'Yes' to God, which Karl Rahner speaks of as 'the evangelical joy of redeemed freedom'[13], is essential if the fetters of our compromise with a secularistic society are to be broken. Such an affirmation can only be made with the abandon of people in love. But when it is, it can let loose a power more than adequate to carry us through our age of crisis. Conversion from secularism to passionate faith frees men and women for a future of great hope and promise. This is because our 'Yes' to God is always met by God's 'Yes' to us. As Tillich puts it, 'Faith is the state of being grasped by the power of being itself'[14].

what is the church?

b. From sacralism to the secular

'The church's effortless paternalism based on the assumption of an authority which it no longer holds makes me wonder which century I'm living in.' (Housewife).

'The fervent militancy as well as brilliant business skills of the fundamentalist right scare me stiff.' (Councillor)

The Christian religion is about the sacred, that which is made holy by association with or consecration to God. But the sacred must be clearly distinguished from 'sacral*ism*', an ideology which legitimises or imposes, without let or hindrance, religious control over all aspects of human life. In a 'sacral*istic*' world the religious system reigns supreme. It is closed to the authority of the secular, which remains subservient or ignored.

Sacralism denies community and makes a mockery of the search for autonomy and ecumenicity. Yet because it appears to offer a safe and easy solution to man's apparent helplessness, it is an ideology constantly on offer and sought after — from the half-page advert promising an 'ideal civilisation on earth' through the medium of transcendental meditation, which appeared in the Guardian late in 1983[15], to the predictions of astrology believed in by millions. All the more reason, therefore, for the church to disassociate itself from such a paralysing heresy. Yet everywhere we find a deep resistance to surrendering a closed sacralistic hegemony which keeps men and women subservient or dependent, be it exercised by a national folk religion, a 'moral majority', an imperialistic evangelicalism, or 'the creationists'. *How does that fit the new ... point?*

If Christian community is to be seen as a meaningful option for late twentieth century men and women the church must change from sheltering behind the sacralistic to welcoming and engaging with the secular. Twenty years ago John Robinson wrote, 'At the moment we are simply trying to hold back the tide of secularisation at colossal and mounting expense'[16]. Such a Canute-like approach is not only doomed to failure but is the denial of an encounter to be welcomed and engaged in with eagerness and expectation. Christians should be in the van of those searching out the nature of human existence, be it through the social sciences, modern political and economic theory, current advances in medical research, the new physics, or in whatever fresh fields of knowledge and understanding open up.

The ending of the church's captivity to sacralism is necessary because without it there can be no 'Yes' to Christ and his incarnation, and thus no 'Yes' to men and women and their salvation. As Alan Ecclestone puts it, 'When we strive to know ourselves, we are seeking to know not a speck of dust nor the species man but the word that was spoken and took our flesh, the Yes that permitted us to be'[17]. Or as Lesslie Newbigin states, 'The Kingdom now (has) a name and a face, the name and face of Jesus'[18]. — *How do we know?*

Sacralism must give way to secularisation in order that in Christ men and women may become autonomous; in order that their reason, resourcefulness, spontaneity, creativity, imagination and spiritual discernment can be freed not only to glorify God but to serve their fellows and to build one world.

Such autonomy, such 'coming of age', can only occur where we ourselves have the courage to take responsibility for living out the implications of the truth revealed to us through 'the inner light', as Quakers describe it. Autonomy can only be realised when we freely choose Peter Berger's 'inductive option' — taking 'experience as the ground of all religious affirmations'[19]. (It is an option which stands over against 'the deductive option' — reasserting 'the authority of a religious tradition in the face of modern secularity'[20], as well as over against 'the reductive option' — re-interpreting 'the tradition in terms of modern secularity'[21].) The inductive option, argues Berger, 'Is the only one that promises both to face and to overcome the challenges of the modern situation'[22].

The overthrow of sacralism, and the acceptance of the inductive option, mean our treating *every* man and woman as a child of God and believing in their worth as unique persons. Such a choice leads to our holding as potentially valid for all, the intuitions, knowledge and skills of each. This goes in particular for the weak and the marginalised, as Christ showed by the attention and care he gave to them. But it also goes for the powerful and the recognised. 'Yes' to man, as Bonhoeffer reminds us, is 'to speak of God not on the boundaries but at the centre, not in weakness but in strength; and therefore not in death and guilt but in man's life and goodness'[23].

c. Secular faith

Christian community can only be forged out of passionate engagement with a secular world. Its achievement depends on a radical shift, from colluding with secularism and sacralism to 'secular faith'. 'There can be no reality without Christ and no Christ without reality', as Bonhoeffer knew only too well[24]. Lesslie Newbigin writes: 'What we have now to seek are forms of church and ministry which neither draw men and women out of the world into a private society, nor seek to dominate the world through controlling centres of power, but enable men and women to function within the secular life of the world in ways which reflect the reality of Christ's passion and thereby make the reality of Christ's resurrection credible to the victims of the world's wrong'[25].

Secular faith takes the world with the utmost seriousness and glories in man's potential for autonomy. At the same time, it refuses secularism the right to create God in man's image, to close the door to divine revelation. Secular faith opens itself to divine revelation with awe and humility, rejoices in the all-embracing love and power of the Trinity, whilst refusing sacralism the right to set aside the personal freedom and responsibility offered to each man and woman as a child of God.

Secular faith liberates men and women for koinonia. Community for our age means free people for one world in Christ. For many of us this is a terrifying possibility. 'Yes' to God *and* to our human experience takes us all deep into the unknown. It is a dangerous path to take because to move beyond secularism and sacralism is to leave behind familiar landmarks and embark on the real journey; it may even be to find oneself in a place 'without a name, a church, a cult, a theology,[26], as Tillich reminds us.

Secular faith is also costly. It challenges the vested interests of both secularistic and sacralistic principalities and powers. The passionate engagement of Christ with these showed just how costly a business it can be. It is no coincidence that a number of contexts in which koinonia is used in the New Testament indicate Christians sharing in the sufferings of Christ (Phil. 3 v. 10). As Bonhoeffer contended, there is no such thing as 'cheap grace'. 'Cheap grace is the deadly enemy of our church. We are fighting today for costly grace', he wrote[27]. The quest for community demands all that Christians can ask and offer.

At the same time secular faith is about hope — a deep conviction that through 'the dark night of the soul', and despite the costliness of grace, an inextinguishable light shines to guide and to encourage. Passionate engagement for the building of koinonia within church and world is the demanding yet exhilarating task to which God calls his people and for which he promises resources which are more than sufficient.

2. Closed structures — clericalism, parochialism, congregationalism and denominationalism

If closed institutions are the victims of closed ideologies, they are also at the mercy of closed structures. Secular faith, with its openness to rationality, has at its disposal numerous tools, not least provided by the social sciences, to examine such structures critically and constructively. This kind of analysis shows that closed structures — modes of organisation and management which circumscribe interaction and relationships — are far greater obstacles to our attaining a fully human world than we ever imagine.

This is in no case more true than that of the regeneration of community. Closed social systems in general, and closed structures in particular, shut off all routes to autonomy and ecumenicity. It is only by our freeing ourselves from the strangle-hold of such structures that the incentive, energy and skills needed to forge a new depth and breadth of community become available. Without this breakthrough chaos will have the last word.

If the church is to provide the assurance that koinonia is a realistic gift offered by a God who genuinely cares, and not a utopian fantasy, then it must be the first to recognise and to seek liberation from those structures that would cramp and distort the living out of its message of hope. Secular man believes not because of what he is told, but because of what he experiences for himself. Unless the church can end its own captivity to closed structures, and demonstrate in practice the reality of Christian community, the good news it proclaims will fall on deaf ears.

The church is currently imprisoned by structures affecting its understanding of authority, of its apostolic task, of Christian fellowship, and of unity, all of which in their turn circumscribe its theology. The result is communal attrition.

a. Clericalism and the move from priest to people

'So many fraternals operate as professional groups to decide what the churches are going to do. And I'm not interested, like many others. (Businessman)

'At the moment the lay response, particularly in Anglican churches, is, "We can't do that because we're not professionally qualified to do it", without asking what *that* is.' (Headmaster)

'They (the priests) hold the key to the finances — it's right down to the nitty gritty.' (Housewife)

I begin with the problem of clericalism because it relates to the vital matter of authority within the life of the church. Authority exists to ensure the internal good order of a social system. It also has the task of 'boundary keeping'. Authority has the power to bind or to free, to open or close doors to the wider world. Consequently, it is highly relevant to the issue of community.

The very term 'clericalism' points to the dilemma in which the church in the United Kingdom now finds itself. Clericalism indicates a situation where authority has become the property of the few when it should be exercised by the many, where power resides in the part when it should belong to the whole. It is the clergy who lead and control and the laity who follow and obey (or acquiesce). oh?

The life and work of the clergy is still of crucial importance. John Tiller, in his report on 'A Strategy for the Church's Ministry', lists eight roles[28] in which they are engaged, many of which are being undertaken with commitment, energy and enthusiasm. But simply because the clergy *are* such an important part of the church, and because where they lead many follow, attention has to be drawn to the continuing straight-jacket of *clergy is a legal term for deacons [?] & priest of the C of E.*

clericalism which, manifest or hidden, continues to hold the people of God captive to a limited view of Christian community.

That clericalism is still normative is underlined by the common use of the word 'laity' to designate those who are 'not ordained', the definition given by 'The Oxford Dictionary of the Christian Church'[29]. I shall retain this definition for the sake of simplicity, though fully aware that the New Testament employs 'laos' to mean 'the whole people of God' (I Peter 2 v 9) without distinction of person, function or status. To refer to those ordained, I use the word 'clergy' more than priest' or 'minister'. This is simply for convenience and not because I believe that clericalism is more a feature of one denomination than another ('clergy' being the word generally used of those ordained in the Church of England).

My contention is that only as authority is transferred from priest to people can the restrictive hold of clericalism be loosened and a new understanding and quality of Christian community come into existence.

To explain the origins of, historical development of, and ecclesiastical justification for clericalism cannot be done here. Others more competent than I are already engaged in that task[30]. For me the issue of clericalism is more immediate — how at present it blocks the development of autonomy and ecumenicity throughout the church.

Clericalism can be described as the existence of what John Robinson once called 'a clergy line'[31]. This line splits off those in 'holy orders' from the rest. It exists in *all* denominations. The clergy line, below which come (most) members of the religious orders, deaconesses, lay workers, and lay preachers, not to mention the laity as a whole, is the hallmark of clericalism. It inappropriately imports into the church the secular concept of 'professionalism'. This in effect relegates the laity to the ranks of the religiously unlettered and unqualified.

'The Clerical Profession' has already been examined thoroughly and perceptively by Anthony Russell[32]. In his book he has described the search by the clergy for a new professional status, from the late eighteenth century onwards, as many of their more diffuse and 'wordly' tasks were taken over by other institutions, a process which has continued unabated up to and beyond the establishment of the welfare state. During this period the clergy were increasingly obliged to focus their attention on more obviously ecclesiastical concerns — right of entry into and training for the ordained ministry, their liturgical, catechetical and pastoral functions, and institutional organisation and management — and less on a diversity of roles within society in general. As Russell points out, the problem with this attempted transition from an 'estate' of the realm to a definitive profession is that it has perpetuated clericalism in a new and increasingly untenable form. The result is that many clergy find themselves attempting to preserve a clergy line which fails to reflect an understanding of the church as the whole people of God, as well as of the more positive aspects of a modern profession.

29

For example, a number of churches (including some smaller evangelical groups) continue to insist on an all male entry to the clerical 'profession'. 'The best men's club in the world' is how a working party of the (then) Laity Commission of the Roman Catholic Church described its priesthood[33]. Whatever the theological arguments may be, the rejection of women as priests means that authority in many aspects of the church's life is denied to representatives of half the human race. This is not to assume that the ordination of women would solve the problem of clericalism. It could even make matters worse, for if women, once ordained, simply perpetuated the norms of male clericalism, the church's latter state could be more parlous than its former. 'It is not a matter of women finding a place in a male church, but of all of us finding each other in a more feminine church'[34] It means that authority has to be shared by women and men as equal partners in a common enterprise.

Despite the gradual opening up of clergy training in recent years, preparation for the ordained ministry has for at least two centuries been experiencing a steady narrowing of horizons and expectations. As denominations came increasingly to train their own priests and ministers in separated colleges or seminaries the strengthening of the clergy line was inevitable. For many 'the system has fitted men in structures whose force they came to realise only at a later stage'[35]. It is often not until clergy draw away from the conditioning that preparation for the priesthood involves that they begin to discover that even if they then wish to exercise their ministry in a different way, few will acknowledge it — or, put more pragmatically, few will pay for it. Some clergy, as they become aware of the constraints they face, look for a ministry less moulded by clericalism, some opt out of the church altogether, but many, as Leslie Paul found in his enquiry into the situation of Anglican clergy in the 'sixties[36], simply remain caught, feeling lonely and frustrated.

In order to retain their status in an increasingly pluralistic and professionalised society ordained ministers have not only sought to preserve their ancient functions, but been obliged to concentrate their attention ever more exclusively upon them. Their historical role as 'guardians of the tradition' has thus come to embrace the preservation of the past, not only for the sake of the tradition itself but in order to provide them with some form of continuing identity in a secular society. In most denominations clergy have kept a firm hold on liturgy, catechetics and pastoral work, in part because without these there is the possibility that their most distinctive functions would disappear, together with their 'professional' standing.

It is true that laity are increasingly involved in certain areas of ecclesiastical activity, but there still remains a tenacious clergy line which is extremely difficult for those not ordained to cross. Not only is clerical control maintained, behind the scenes if not on stage, but many laity themselves feel that without a minister at least present, few of the

30

traditional functions mentioned above can be 'properly' fulfilled.

Clericalism creates other stances which lead to closure. It is at best ambivalent to the existence of small Christian groups or cells which bring laity together in forms of fellowship and nurture not easily accessible to clerical control. Priests and ministers find the congregation per se an ecclesiastical unit much more conducive to the affirmation of their identity and the upholding of their traditional functions.

Clericalism also seeks to preserve boundaries not only of a 'professional' but of a territorial kind. This means that the parish (or neighbourhood) is given a prominence in ecclesiastical affairs above that which is needed or useful in a mobile society. (The associated problems of congregationalism and parochialism I deal with more fully below.)

Clericalism closes the way to community not only through its definition of ministerial functions, and through its being wedded to congregation and parish, but through its desire to be at the centre of institutional management. Four aspects of the latter reveal the clergy line to be still very much in evidence. First, forms of clerical leadership remain essentially hierarchical in all churches. Russell sees this as reflecting a 'military model'[37]. Hierarchy can in many situations provide an appropriate form of institutional administration. But whether it is suitable for a church seeking to move authority from priest to people, and looking for a new understanding of Christian community, is another question.

Just as problematic is the fact that an hierarchical form of authority often goes hand in hand with an individualistic, if not autocratic, one; the concept of team ministry, as we shall see, thus being difficult to sustain within most denominations. Here clericalism parts company with many modern professions which lay far more stress on continuing accountability not only to one's clients but to one's colleagues.

Second, clericalism closes the decision-making processes of the church to all but certain categories of lay people. There have been organisational changes in the direction of lay participation in church affairs in recent years in all denominations. But such developments, however well intentioned, often ignore the fact that the 'new deal' is still very much on clerical terms. The laity frequently have to alter or break into their normal work routines, time-tables and styles of life to be present and on duty when required. Even then the church finds itself lacking those people most needed to offer a new perspective on matters religious, and left with an over-representation of those not engaged in the mainstream of secular institutional life — the retired, wives not out at work, or paid 'lay' church officials. From the local congregation to the latest Assembly of the World Council of Churches in Vancouver, the dilemma of restricted lay participation in matters of Christian concern remains the same.

Third, clericalism holds sway within church management through its

31

control of resources. As one of the quotations at the beginning of this section indicates, the ordained ministry largely directs the use of manpower, plant and finance — 'it's right down to the nitty gritty', as our housewife states. This means that any movement to open local churches, dioceses or denominations as a whole to new initiatives which can signficantly shift the balance of power from priest to people, is unlikely to find the necessary support from within.

Clericalism encourages closure in a further all-embracing way. Because the clergy have remained 'central' and 'symbolic' figures in the life of the church, they have become the models by which matters 'Christian' (or at least 'ecclesiastical') are often judged. Both within the church and outside it, where as John Tiller believes the ordained minister 'is regarded by society as an official spokesman for the church'[38], the ordained minister is taken to be *the* representative of the people of God. 'Ministry' becomes measured by clerical concerns, behaviour, functions and life style. The clergy as symbolic figures thus exercise a subtle but profound influence on how the church is seen, a situation which leads to a distortion of what the ministry of the whole people of God (clergy included) is all about.

A number of important groupings within the church are held captive by clericalism. First and foremost are the laity themselves. There is certainly a good deal of collusion here, though for the most part unconscious. Few laity are hammering at the door (women wanting ordination apart) to take more control of church affairs. This is in part because it is more comfortable to let a paternalistic clericalism take responsibility for things spiritual, and in part because an alternative vision of the church and Christian leadership is hardly yet over the horizon. But content or frustrated, a laity captive to clericalism is still the order of the day.

Second are those, still part of the laity as I have defined them, who have committed themselves to a full-time vocation within the life of the church — notably the religious orders, deaconesses and paid lay workers. Their captivity lies not only in being subject to a good deal of clerical direction (see the history of the deaconess movement with Anglicanism[39]), but in being required to give priority to supporting traditional clerical functions and priorities. Their apostolate thus becomes shaped and moulded by the clerical model — with congregational and parish responsibilities dominating the scene.

Third come those, now within what is called the non-stipendiary ministry, ordained but earning a living outside the church. As Mark Hodges makes clear[40], there are some who had hoped that ordaining those in secular employment (now one in four of Anglican clergy) would have meant a new and more effective Christian presence within institutional life. The case has proved otherwise. Not only has there been a 'reluctance to encourage variation from the parochial model of ministry'[41], but the great majority of non-stipendiary clergy continue to see their vocation as local church not society based. Indeed, 'It is possible to predict that up to half of those selected for non-stipendiary ministry under 57 years of age will in due course transfer to stipendiary ministry'[42]. Yet the very last thing now needed is for articulate and able lay people to adopt a traditional clerical role.

A fourth group held captive consists of those who are ordained and exercising their ministry in institutions *other* than the church — in education, health, industry and so forth — as chaplains or sometimes as 'sector' ministers. These suffer from clericalism in two ways. First, their roles often seem inexplicable to many people (not least non-Christians) unless they are performing the traditional clerical functions listed earlier. They are thus under constant pressure to play an orthodox liturgical, catechetical or pastoral role, and given very limited opportunity to develop new forms or functions of ordained ministry. Secondly, the church generally regards many of them as peripheral to the 'real' work of the parish, shows little interest in their pioneering efforts in secular fields, and fails to offer them adequate material, organisational or spiritual support. *But why are they necessary at all?*

A final group held captive by clericalism is the main body of clergy themselves. Observers of the clerical scene here appear uniformly pessimistic. 'If ever the word "crisis" was appropriate in church affairs, it is in the matter of the ministry', wrote David Perman in the late 'seventies[43]. Speaking of the Anglican Church, Anthony Russell states that, 'The clergy have constantly indicated that they are unwilling to consider change in the area of the institutional context of their role'[44]. The same was found to hold true of Roman Catholic priests and Methodist ministers by Ranson, Bryman and Henings[45].

Despite such pessimism, there are of course many clergy and ministers increasingly aware of the need for a new understanding of the church as the whole people of God, and of the need to transfer more authority from priest to people. These are more than conscious of the fact that their role is far too tightly circumscribed by present constraints, and that the concept of Christian community they are having to live with is quite inadequate to meet the challenge of an age in crisis. Many would undoubtedly agree with Karl Rahner that, 'The church should be a declericalised church'[46]. The problem is that most cannot as yet see any alternative and, where they do glimpse a way through, are without the opportunity, colleagueship or resources to be able to break new ground.

If 'clericalism' in the deepest sense were simply an ecclesiastical problem it would hardly seem germane to the global crises outlined in the preceding chapter. In fact it is of immediate relevance to them because, in its wider secularistic form, 'clericalism' threatens to destroy community in *every* organisation and institution, sacred *and* secular, within society. The exercise of authority in a possessive or unilateral way — be it

33

all this Need to be much more specific.

paternalism within the helping professions, autocratic management in industry, or dictatorship in government — is 'clericalism' in a secularistic guise. *A new vision of community requires the opening up of all closed forms of authority.*

The misfortune is that a church captive to clericalism has little to offer to a world captive to the same sort of authority structures. Clericalism undermines the good news of the gospel because the message of Christian community embracing and offering significance and solidarity, autonomy and ecumenicity, in Christ is compromised or destroyed. The church cannot be a sign either of contradiction or hope because an experience of koinonia in its fulness is neither known nor sought after. The medium is no longer the message. As a result a form of authority and power antithetical to community becomes the undisputed norm in all sectors of society, and Christians find themselves unable to offer any way out of the impasse. Thus the church is unable to fulfil its calling to be a means of salvation to a world wherein many of the crises faced can only be resolved by a transfer of power from 'priests' of all kinds to 'the people' in every walk of life, not least to the poor, the suffering and the disadvantaged.

b. Parochialism and the move from community of place to community of concern

'The parish is outmoded in very many ways — in a building-based way. That organisational base for the structure of the church is wrong.' (Director of a voluntary organisation)

'The local church is about a Sunday Christianity.' (City planning officer)

'It would be a step in the right direction if the church thought of me first and foremost as a printer rather than a churchwarden or whatever.' (Businessman)

———————

Parochialism represents the imprisonment of the church within the parish (I use the word 'parish' to apply to any local neighbourhood, the problem of parochialism being as acute for those churches not formally operating this system as for those who do). Parochialism weakens community because it allows a particular territorial unit to determine and circumscribe the boundaries of Christian life and witness.

Parochialism sees community as an option mainly for those who reside in the same neighbourhood. In pursuit of community of *place*, it fails to recognise the importance of community of *concern* (in the sense of those drawn together by interests which command enthusiasm and energy). In particular, as I seek to show below, parochialism inhibits the search for significance and autonomy and fails to allow the development of fully

34

human persons. For Christians this means a domestication of their 'apostolate'*, a neglect of their calling to serve and witness within a wider world.

For a thousand years and more the communal importance of the parish has been a commonplace. Not only worship but the whole gamut of human affairs, including family life, work and leisure, were locally based and regulated. The church was simply reinforcing the status quo when, in the Middle Ages, residents were forbidden to worship anywhere other than in their own village[47], and when, at the Reformation, and for well over a century after, attendance at one's parish church was made compulsory. Though such legal constraints gradually diappeared, the assumption that community of place was all important has remained deeply embedded in our Christian consciousness.

But the United Kingdom is now far more 'cosmopolitan' than 'local'[48]. We are a mobile people, geographically, socially (where do we now draw the line between different classes?), and in cognitive terms (as the media ensures). This in turn has created a highly diversified culture requiring, as Trevor Beeson states in the conclusion to his book on 'Britain Today and Tomorrow', 'a pluralist message and a pluralist church for a pluralist society'[49]. Consequently, community is currently built as much around common concerns based on individual choice, as around shared territory and shared buildings. *Thus if the church is to be genuinely engaged with a secular world it must come to terms with the fact that the importance of community of place is now more than equalled by that of community of concern.*

Parochialism has been perpetuated by ordained ministers who have within the parish found their own greatest sense of significance, a situation exemplified by the difficulty of ending the parson's freehold. John Tiller in setting out his proposals for the next forty years sees the Anglican parish as continuing to be the fulcrum not only of Christian nurture but also of mission[50], and, as we shall see in the following chapter, the Roman hierarchy is ever reminding Catholics of just how central the parish should be in Christian life and work.

The parish remains, and undoubtedly should remain, an important focus of Christian worship and activity. It continues to offer a strong sense of significance to the less mobile: children, mothers not out at work, the elderly, the sick and the disabled. Life has to be lived out largely within

---

*I have found it difficult to find a term referring to the nature of the Christian's witness in the world which embraces vocation, service and mission. The term 'ministry' is still too closely associated with those ordained, and to employ only one of the other words mentioned is too limiting. Thus I settle for the term 'apostolate', familiar mainly to Roman Catholics, to describe the multi-faceted nature of the witness (not least through their work) of those who base daily living on a faith commitment.

a parish context by the poor, the disadvantaged and the unemployed. It is to the great credit of many of these that they are able to find ways of becoming fully human even when physical mobility is so restricted (though in many areas of deprivation the mainstream churches are found at their weakest and can claim to have made little contribution towards such an achievement). Nonetheless, parochialism which rests content with the local scene, which takes the parish to be all that life, and especially the Christian life, is about, weakens the meaning of, and sense of fulfilment gained through, a full-blooded lay apostolate.

Parochialism results in a number of damaging consequences. In the first place it encourages the laity to believe that their life and work beyond the parish is of little account, as the quotations at the beginning of this section indicate. Parochialism traps ministers and laity alike into assuming that the experience and skills which really matter to the church are those which can boost the takings at the summer fête, keep the flower rota going, or repair the heating system. Such expressions of Christian concern are not to be despised. But it does nothing to deepen and broaden our understanding of community when the church gives these talents pride of place, and virtually ignores the abilities of lay people occupied full-time as teachers, steelworkers, civil servants, students, typists, builders, nurses and businessmen (to list just a few of the occupations of the members of one of my own churches in the past).

Secondly, parochialism privatises the faith. Because a laity who are trained for, and spend their working lives serving, a cosmopolitan world find the church showing little interest in or concern to validate that part of their existence, religion comes to be seen primarily as a domestic affair which shows its public face only on Sundays. The fact that Christian community might be profoundly important for the salvation of institutions as well as of individuals, and that the mission of the laity beyond the parish might play a vital part in helping to resolve the crisis of our age, are ideas that rarely see the light of day.

Thirdly, parochialism leads to false illusions about the focus of power and naïvety about the nature of change within a secular society. The church continues to believe that through the parish system it can influence and change the social system, as witnessed by the recent efforts in several denominations to respond to the problems of institutionalised poverty and unemployment by attempting to move financial resources directly into deprived parishes. The motiviation cannot be faulted, but the end result is frequently to further emphasise the centrality of the role of the clergy (who usually administer the redirected resources), and to go on ignoring the apostolate of many lay people already working full-time for secular bodies in those very areas of acute need. It is the secular institutions of society which hold the key to social change (or inertia), and it is to help and support lay people exercising their apostolate within these

36

(I wish [that] book could be precisely defined). [handwritten annotation]

that the church should be directing far more of its energies.

Without the church taking seriously the shift from community of place to community of concern parochialism will continue to undervalue, domesticate and undermine the apostolate of the laity, prevent Christian men and women gaining a full understanding of, and giving full expression to, their autonomy in Christ. It will circumscribe community.

Secular bodies likewise find themselves held captive by their own forms of 'parochialism'. The latter often limits the horizons and development of many within teaching, the helping professions and local government, to name but a few fields of work. Here, too, secular institutions underplay and undervalue the potential of human beings — both of those employed by them and of those whom they seek to serve — for autonomy and a wider vision. But in the case of parochialism it is the church which, in large part because of its history, is the main victim, and which needs to break free if it is to enable the whole people of God to express their faith in a way that can give hope to a cosmopolitan world in crisis.

c. Congregationalism and the move from meeting to encounter

'I find Sunday worship of virtually no help to me. It is trivialised all the time. The meeting with people there isn't a *real* meeting with *real* people. It's a polite encounter at a superficial level.' (Headmaster)

Whose fault is that? [handwritten annotation]

'Congregationalism', as I define it here, applies to *every* denomination. By congregationalism I mean the assumption that the assembling of churchgoers each Sunday for worship (and for related purposes) represents Christian community in its definitive form. Other assemblies and groupings of Christians there may be, but for those wedded to congregationalism these are secondary. They assume that it is the faithful gathered weekly for worship within the sanctuary which is the normative expression of koinonia.

It may appear presumptuous, or at best naïve, even to question the communal importance of congregational participation for the Christian. Yet to prove an adequate means of fostering community, churchgoers have always had to supplement the Sabbath assembly by activities and events more able to promote interaction and exchange and, through these, a greater sense of solidarity.

In the Middle Ages, church services were not particularly attractive affairs, with the liturgy in Latin spoken (often inaudibly and at a distance) by the priest, a very occasional and formal sermon and no hymns[51], though, as Bettey writes, 'To some extent the ceremonial of procession and ritual accompanying the mass and other services supplied the place of congregational participation'[52]. What really gave communal zest to local congregational life were fund raising happenings such as the annual church-ale with its dancing and sports, food and drink, often held in the

37

churchyard or later in parish meeting houses. Christian community was fostered and sustained by far more than Sunday worship.

One of the unfortunate results of the Reformation was that the Sunday assembly gradually became almost the only regular public form of Christian gathering and, where Puritan influence was in the ascendant, a pretty spartan kind of gathering at that. The introduction not only of pews (from the mid-fifteenth century), but of a rigid pattern of seating and rents (which reflected the increasingly stratified system of parish life), simply increased the impersonality and formality of church worship. The nineteenth century saw a renewed attempt to open the church to communally important activities of a wide ranging kind, from Sunday schools to harvest festivals, from cultural societies to parish concerts. But the days when the church could claim to stand at the undisputed heart of community life were by then virtually over.

This century has seen the local church again stripped of many of those social functions which in Victorian times helped to engender a sense of solidarity. The continuing shift from community of territory to community of interest has given impetus to the extensive provision of leisure pursuits by secular bodies able to tempt even the most conscientious churchgoer[53]. New organisations have moved to the centre of the stage to offer a breathtaking array of educational, cultural and social activities to non-Christian and Christian alike, most now able to travel with ease to engage in them.

The congregational assembly as such is still of great importance. It is where Christians meet to celebrate and affirm their faith. For many it remains a reminder that they belong to the people of God. It is a gathering which can be a source of hope, inspiration and comfort. Yet, because it has become for many Christians the only occasion when they meet, its present inability to foster a high level of commitment and sustain a strong sense of solidarity are all too evident[54]. *Without new ways being found of moving from formal meeting to personal encounter, Christian community will become increasingly attenuated.*

In many churches the size of the worshipping assembly (especially for Roman Catholics), the physical arrangement of seating and the very decorum, help prevent the congregation being an effective means of enhancing a living experience of community. Indeed, it could be argued that some worshippers actually prefer congregationalism because it enables them to do their duty to God without having to bother with more than a passing acknowledgement of their fellow Christians. As Alan Ecclestone writes, 'Congregations . . . are all too often aggregations of people who never get any nearer to speaking a common language, growing in a common mind, acting with common purpose and praying in one spirit'[55].

Congregationalism fails to accept that 'we meet God most intimately where we meet each other most intimately, in primary community', as

38

Loren Halvorson puts it[56]. Unless regular Christian encounter within small sustainable groupings becomes much more commonplace, then Christian community for laity and clergy alike becomes dehumanised; and pastoral care, learning together about the faith, supporting one another's apostolate and indeed worship itself, grow increasingly impersonal. As a result the ability of Christians to nurture one another in the faith is lost.

This is evident in relation to the family. Congregationalism is in grave danger of draining the energy from Christian family life. In recent years many denominations have attempted to affirm and strengthen the concept of the Christian family[57]. But congregationalism, by placing so much emphasis on the gathered assembly as the major form and focus of Christian identity, neglects the home as a vital centre for the nurture of Christian community.

Rites of passage (for example baptism and marriage) are held predominantly in the local church building (often with the congregation absent) and rarely embrace the home as such in any significant way. By emphasising that Christian worship is virtually synonymous with the gathered assembly, congregationalism ignores the family as a potential power-house of spirituality for young and old alike. By over-stressing the importance of church-based catechetics and Sunday schools (and indeed church day schools), congregationalism undermines parental interest in and responsibility for Christian formation within the home. In short, by assuming the priority of 'the church in the church', congregationalism weakens the role of 'the church in the home'.

At the same time the church seems unable to respond to changing forms of family life, now as noteworthy among Christians[58] as non-Christians. In its many statements about 'the church as a family', it forgets the fact that, though three-quarters of households in Britain consist of 'families', only forty-four per cent of the latter are now made up of married couples with dependent children[59]. In this situation what the 'typical family', or even the 'ideal family', is, or should be, becomes very much an open question. By resting content with its own apparently unchanging and dominant situation, congregationalism fails to recognise that a domestic revolution is well underway. Thus the church is found wanting in its support of Christian parents, and indeed children, struggling to discover the meaning of being a Christian family amidst the social upheavals of the 'eighties.

For far too long congregationalism has neglected the importance of a dynamic experience of Christian solidarity as a means of building community. By claiming pride of place as the symbol of Christian fellowship, congregationalism ignores the need for lively and enduring face-to-face relationships. But congregationalism also loses out through the way that it prevents the growth of a sense of belonging to the church as a whole. It can thus check ecumenicity. It can impede any genuine appreciation of what it means to belong to the church universal.

There are some who still see the congregation as epitomising the wholeness of Christian community. John Tiller, for example, writes; 'It is here that we find the public, open door of the church through which any may enter . . . Within its walls all ages and types and intellects are challenged to work out their common membership in Christ'[60]. Nothing could be more desirable and in line with the concerns of this book. Yet in practice the story is rather different. Congregationalism fails to take into account that community of place is as likely to be the victim of a narrow conception of culture and class as any other form of community. Over twenty years ago Gibson Winter wrote a book entitled 'The Suburban Captivity of the Churches'[61] in which he argued that the Protestant church in the U.S.A. was 'imprisoned' within the white, affluent, middle class neighbourhood on the edge of the metropolis. The scene remains the same today, both within the U.S.A. and the U.K. By closely aligning itself with the culture of its immediate neighbourhood, congregationalism prevents what solidarity there is from opening out into a richer ecumenicity.

Many *secular* bodies also suffer from their own forms of 'congregationalism', in practice a recurrent weakness of all institutions. The advantages of the secondary group swamp and devalue the qualities of the primary group. Impersonal efficiency takes over from the need to share and care on a human scale, within social welfare, the health services, policing, industry and government itself. This is especially evident in the impact of modern organisations on family life, the prior requirements of institutions (in particular for a mobile work force) placing great strain on a sustainable form of community within the home.

'Congregationalism' within secular bodies can likewise lead to their 'suburban captivity' and consequent denial of ecumenicity, for example in education. A survey published in 1984 shows conclusively that the comprehensive school now reflects the social composition of its neighbourhood just as much as any church[62].

Because of all these problems, a church which claims to offer a new quality of community to a world in crisis cannot blandly ignore the limitations of congregationalism. New forms of community have to be found which can offer a deeper *as well as* more all-embracing experience of life together, a stronger sense of solidarity *and* of ecumenicity, so that the hope of one world in Christ can become more of a reality.

d. Denominationalism and the move from division to unity

'I look upon the churches as very much man made organisations — a lot depends which bedroom you were born in.' (City planning officer)

40

'A terrible fallacy pervades the Christian world — it is a belief that by talking to each other we are in fact arresting the evident decline of Christian faith. We are *not* doing that . . . The energy we put into ecumenism is not the task, but a step on the way.' (Director of a voluntary organisation)

Sociologists have spent a good deal of time and energy discussing the term 'denomination'[63] and giving it varying interpretations. However, for the purposes of this book I set aside a more sophisticated definition and use the term 'denomination', in the popular sense, to denote the main historic ecclesiastical bodies in the United Kingdom — the Church of England, the Roman Catholic Church and one or other of the Free Churches. I also see such bodies as the Quakers, the Salvation Army and the main Pentecostal churches qualifying as denominations although they would not always apply the term to themselves. 'Denominational*ism*' I take to mean the assumption that one's own denomination is 'the true church', that other ecclesiastical bodies are, at best, followers along the way and, at worst, misrepresenting the faith.

Where denominationalism rules Christian community suffers because the door is closed on communication and contact, and ecumenicity made impossible. *This situation can only be redeemed and salvation (wholeness) become a possibility by a decisive move from division to unity.*

On the positive side, the development of the historic denominations, above all since the Reformation, has demonstrated the potential of religious man and woman for autonomy, their ability to stand over against the powers that be, and their courage in openly proclaiming their personal experience of faith in Christ. With such a stand has come the privilege of and responsibility for choice in matters spiritual, and thus the opportunity to end immature dependence on parent or priest.

Denominations have also demonstrated the importance of different but complementary facets of Christian worship, with their varying emphases on ritual, silence, song or speech; and of Christian witness, through service, evangelism or social reform. Thus they have enabled the church as a whole to encompass diversities of human upbringing ('the bedroom you were born in'), temperament, ability and opinion. This heterogeneity has been their strength, opening up the way to a larger understanding and greater awareness of the variety possible within the Christian community.

But times have changed. Many would agree with Alan Gilbert that the effects of secularisation over the past two centuries have been to make one denomination appear very much like another[64]. The historic distinctiveness of denominations is now lost on most outside observers. Many thus argue that the obvious way forward is for denominations to come closer together in order to exercise a more effective ministry within an increasingly secular world.

Yet despite an encouraging start, the pace of the ecumenical movement does not seem to be quickening. John Kent, in his review of theological developments over the last two hundred years, believes that, 'The Protestant ecumenical movement had lost its momentum by the 1950s', and that, even after Pope John XXIII's initiatives, by the 1970s. 'It looked . . . as though ecumenicity had slipped back into "diplomatic" forms of encounter, in which concepts like the papal primacy, Mariology, and the possession of valid ministerial orders were discussed with very traditional seriousness'[65]. Jan Kerkhofs, a Dutch Roman Catholic, in reviewing the world scene from the vantage point of his own church, speaks of 'the silting up of ecumenism'[66]. Thus a church, which to many external observers appears to have little of major significance keeping it divided, still finds itself captive to denominationalism and unable to discover an acceptable path towards unity.

Some of denominationalism's most serious consequences are practical ones. Anachronistic divisions waste money and manpower. The church in Britain is not poor — even if it has 'liquidity' problems. It has simply tied its wealth up in structures which duplicate each other, as well as in the maintenance of unnecessary plant and property. Nor are we short of ordained ministers. If we pooled the resources of all our denominations, not to mention properly utilising those of the laity, we would have manpower and womanpower enough and to spare.

Parallel but separate church structures make quick and easy communication, and dialogue between denominations, difficult. Information is passed up and down respective communication systems, either national or diocesan, without regard to the need for a well established and effective channel of communication *between* those systems. A denominational press, denominational publications and bookshops perpetuate the problem. A poor flow of information leads to ignorance and misunderstanding and leaves traditional positions as entrenched as ever.

Captivity to denominationalism cannot be ended without a *decisive* move from division towards unity. However, the aim is not a dull uniformity but an ecumenicity which honours autonomy. 'There is but one road to real unity, and that lies through the land of diversity',[67] writes Stark. An ecumenicity of this kind validates differences, provided that these can be utilised in the service of the greater whole; it legimates pluralism, as long as this works for the building up of the entire body. It enables us to see that many of our denominational traditions can be resources for furthering, rather than stumbling blocks to creating, one church and one world.

The move from division to unity cannot be achieved by a vague and

How?

easy going 'spiritual unity', as espoused by some opponents of more realistic ecumenical endeavours. Unity has to be earthed; worked out in practice, and manifest to a secular society. Christian community has to be a *living* demonstration of free people committed to one world in Christ.

How such a new community might be created is the concern of the rest of this book. However, two points developed later are especially relevant here. First, *ecumenicity has to grow out of personal human relationships.* It cannot be imposed by institutions as such. As John Kent writes, this means 'That, instead of trying to deduce the structure of the church from some form of the doctrines of the church, one must allow the doctrine of the church to reflect that life of the actual Christian community as it finds itself moving from one new historical situation to another'[68].

Second, *the fundamental purpose of unity is the salvation of mankind and the coming of the kingdom; not the rationalisation of ecclesiastical structures, the sharing of church plant, nor even the 'integration' of ordained ministries,* however laudable those things may be. A mainly church-centred 'ecumenism' would become another form of 'denominationalism' writ large. Genuine ecumenicity is founded on the divine imperative that Christians share their heritage, their abilities and their resources first and foremost to bring reconciliation and hope to a divided world.

The human race is in conflict because 'denominationalism', in the widest sense, holds not only religious but also *secular* man captive. Cultural, social and organisational identity and pride are important, and the solidarity they engender has great communal potential. But 'denominationalism' closes the door too soon and prevents solidarity developing into ecumenicity. Thus division not unity has the last word.

There is a 'denominationalism' of sex, culture, race and class. There is an institutional 'denominationalism', which creates inter-organisational and inter-professional competition and conflict of a communally destructive kind. There is a 'denominationalism' which divides village, city, nation and continent.

There can be no resolution of our crises, no way forward towards the salvation of our world, unless such fundamental divisions are overcome. 'Denominationalism' of any kind is a denial of ecumenicity. The world is now our parish, as John Wesley once put it; or, as Willy Brandt has written rather more recently, 'Solidarity among men must go beyond national boundaries'[69].

There is all the more urgency, therefore, for the church to proclaim through its life as well as by its words the meaning of unity and community. The church is called to stand as a symbol of judgment and of hope within a secular world. Lesslie Newbigin describes the position thus:

c/look upon the whole
World as my parish '

43

'(The church) must be a sign and foretaste of God's universal kingdom, in the way and only in the way that Jesus was the sign. It must make clear always and everywhere its claim upon the total life of the world, and yet not make that claim in the Constantinian manner. It must therefore find a style of living and speaking which holds together in tension the accepting, blessing and fostering of the whole life of the world with the challenging and exposing of it in the light of the cross. Such a style of living and speaking can only mean that the church itself bears the marks of the cross in its own life. The risen body of Christ is recognisable by the scars of the passion . . . Only so is it also the place where the Spirit is present to release men and women from the grip of evil.'[70]

3. A theology of community

'We get so little opportunity to hammer things out as Christians.' (Doctor)   *Whose fault is that?*
'What I'm after is an obligation on laity to explain how they're operating as Christians. There ought to be a requirement laid on me so that I'm *forced* to say what I'm up to.' (Headmaster)
    by whom?

A captive church means a captive theology. If the quest for community is to be taken seriously, then theology too must be liberated from the same ideologies as those which cripple the church. The content and process of theological reflection have to be set free from secularism and sacralism, from clericalism, parochialism, congregationalism and denominationalism. To move forward with a sense of purpose and direction, a new theology of community is urgently required. This means a theology of community's essential elements: of autonomy (the nature of individuals) and of ecumenicity (the nature of society). Both are also vital components of a theology of church and of kingdom.

Theology has to be liberated from *secularism*. It cannot discern and interpret the meaning of Christian community if it remains captive to a secularistic rationalism. Theology will be still born if it is nurtured in the womb of secularistic scholarship, a situation not now unknown within certain university faculties and departments actually involved in theological studies. Nor dare theology collude with a secularistic materialism. The responsibility of theologians is to point to the consequences of a man-centred consumerism, even if that be to criticise the very institutions which support them. The vitality of a theology of community depends not only on academic scholarship but on a living faith, as well as on prayer and reflection in the company of Christian men and women actively engaged in a secular world.

Theology has to be freed from a *sacralism* which would keep it in a state of experiential remoteness and intellectual naïvety. Ecclesiastical dogmatism and biblical fundamentalism simply perpetuate the church's captivity, offering false security and fostering an immature and dangerous religious imperialism. The whole of man's experience, not least his powers of mind and reason, is required if we are to fashion a theology able to give purpose and hope to an age facing the crisis of meaninglessness.

To find a dynamic theology of community means choosing Berger's 'inductive option'. We have to begin with the light which is in each and every person and, by sharing our knowledge and skills, build our understanding of God on his revelation to ordinary people living in a real world. As Bonhoeffer noted, 'It is only in the midst of the world that Christ is Christ'[71].

A theology of community is the work of the whole people of God; not just of theologians and ministers of religion. Theology has to be freed from *clericalism*. Without a theology born of lay faith and experience a secular world will quite properly pass us by. Feminist theology which has of late made an impressive appearance on the Christian scene is underlining just this point. A theology of community needs to reflect the mobile and pluralistic world of the 'eighties. Therefore it has to be freed from the narrow horizons of *parochialism*. Lay people's diverse interests in the modern world, through which the search for autonomy can be pursued, must be treated as matters of fundamental importance. Theology has to relate to the apostolate of the laity wherever located, be that in industry, commerce, local government, health, education or any other sphere of secular life, if it is to be meaningful today.

A theology of community must reflect the need for deeper human encounter. It cannot be born of an impersonal *congregationalism*. Rex Ambler writes: 'Theology has to be a *social* activity, rather than simply an individual or professional affair. Theology is people talking and listening to one another about their most basic human experiences, including of course their continuing experience of one another. For obviously, the best way to understand the reality of God is to find how to reflect on the ways it impinges upon us — in ourselves, others and in the world'[72].

A theology of community has to be liberated from *denominationalism* — it exists not for the church but for the kingdom, not to show people how to be 'Christian' but how to be human. Theology's task is to demonstrate ways in which ecumenicity can be better understood as the means of making church and world whole. A theology of community is about how Christians can learn from and share with one another in the service of humanity. A theology of community is also about the nature of the church's concern for those who suffer injustice and deprivation. Here

meaning   45

new types of theology — political theology, black theology, as well as liberation theology itself — have blazed a trail. Though each on its own has limitations, together they are a major contribution to a theology of community for our generation.

A theology of community will require not only an experience of secular faith, a new partnership and a new perspective on church and world, but a new vocabulary. What this will be is as yet unclear. But the words of Bonhoeffer, writing from prison in the midst of his own uncertainties, perhaps point the way:

'It is not for us to prophesy the day (though the day will come) when men will once more be called so to utter the word of God that the world will be changed and renewed by it. It will be a new language, perhaps quite non-religious, but liberating and redeeming — as was Jesus' language; it will shock people and yet overcome them by its power; it will be the language of a new righteousness and truth, proclaiming God's peace with men and the coming of his kingdom.'[73]

4. A whole new beginning

If a new quality of community is to be found Christians must be liberated from *every* ideology and structure which threaten to hold them prisoner. No breakthrough can be decisive unless it occurs across the whole board. To break clear of one restrictive ideology, or of one closed structure, whilst remaining at the mercy of the rest offers no hope of liberation.

The grip of secularism and sacralism has to be broken. Some observers see the former as the key problem. Alan Gilbert, for example, in his book on 'The Making of a Post-Christian Society' concludes that, '(Secularism) is a much deadlier foe than any previous counter-religious force in human experience'[74]. He sees the church in England as being largely under the influence of 'left-liberal Protestantism' and accepting 'an accommodation (to a secularistic society) so extreme as to amount to a kind of dechristianisation from within'[75].

The situation is seen differently by Robin Gill who puts forward 'a radical alternative to the secularisation model'[76]. For him it is values (rather than beliefs per se) which are the hall-mark of a Christian society. Gill suggests that there has been a 'transposition', not destruction, of Christian values; that 'Western society is embedded in Christian values and concepts to such an extent that it can scarcely even detect these values'. This implies that 'Christianity has been astonishingly successful in converting Western society, so successful, in fact, that it is extremely difficult to tell Christians from non-Christians within it'[77]. Though Gill is unsure as to how far the churches can decline before Christian values are undermined, he would undoubtedly view any move towards a new form of sacralism as a retrograde step.

Nonetheless, for the regeneration of Christian community to take place *both* secularism *and* sacralism have to be abandoned. There has to be the recovery of a passionate faith which, at the same time, accepts the achievements of and seeks to engage fully with a secular world. Secular faith expressed through passionate engagement is the only way out of our impasse.

However, to end captivity to such ideologies cannot bring liberation unless closed structures are also broken open; and not just this one or that one, but *all* those holding Christians prisoner. If even one of the four structures described above retains its hold, the growth towards autonomy and ecumenicity will be checked. To break clear of the rest but remain captive to clericalism would undermine the authority of the whole people of God. To remain captive only to parochialism would still deny the autonomy of the laity. To be held fast only by congregationalism would still seriously weaken Christian solidarity. To be free of all but denominationalism would still leave the way to ecumenicity blocked.

For the church to remain bound by any of these ideologies or structures also has serious repercussions for a *secular* society. If the latter is to find a new depth and breadth of community then it too has to be liberated from its own related forms of captivity. A church that is unable to heal itself has no right to claim to act as physician to others. A church that does not know the meaning of salvation, of itself being made whole, is in no position to be a sign of contradiction or hope for others.

Over the past decade or two the church has made a number of genuine attempts to shake off such encumbrances and to find a quality of Christian community able to match the needs of the time. In the chapter which follows I examine the success or otherwise of certain of these attempts to break new communal ground.

III: BREAKTHROUGH?

'The church sees hope in things in which there isn't hope.' (Director of a voluntary organisation)
'What the church views as appropriate is actually the opposite of what I would think of as Christian.' (Headmaster)

The past two decades have seen the church catching at least a glimpse of its parlous situation, though the tide of awareness has ebbed and flowed. Whatever they did or did not achieve, the 'sixties at least sowed the seeds of many movements of renewal and the influence of that decade of 'ferment in the church'[1] still lingers on.

Thus the last fifteen years have witnessed the emergence of a number of noteworthy attempts by the church in this country to equip itself to face the crises of our time. These initiatives have sprung from different sections of the church, emphasising different aspects of renewal, but all have borne witness to at least some effort to respond to those closed ideologies and restrictive structures discussed in the last chapter. That none has as yet enabled Christians to find a way through the impasse is an indication of the formidable undertaking facing the church in the late twentieth century.

I have argued that the priority for the church today is to be involved in witnessing to the urgent need for a new quality of community. It is against this task that the initiatives described briefly below must be measured. Their ability to liberate the church from its subservience to secularism and sacralism, to clericalism, parochialism, congregationalism and denominationalism, in order to build Christian community, is our overriding concern. I shall also look in passing at the extent to which these initiatives have been able to produce a theology of community for the 'eighties.

Five major initiatives will be dealt with in this chapter (roughly in chronological order) — the charismatic movement, team ministries, ecumenical initiatives, the Nationwide Initiative in Evangelism and the National Pastoral Congress. *These ventures are seen as of note far beyond the immediate moment.* All contain important features that have characterised attempts at Christian renewal in the United Kingdom (and elsewhere) over many previous decades. Thus their success or failure in liberating the church from the closed ideologies and structures which beset it are of lasting consequence. To fail to learn from the results of such initiatives is to ensure that even more energy, time and money will in future be invested in ventures of limited value.

1. The charismatic movement

a. Background

The so-called 'charismatic' or 'neo-pentecostal' movement first appeared on the scene on the West Coast of the United States in the late 'fifties, spreading rapidly eastward during the early 'sixties[2]. In the United Kingdom it became manifest in 1962 in a number of Anglican parishes. Two years later Michael Harper (till then on the staff of All Souls, Langham Place) moved to found the Fountain Trust[3]. The latter became an important centre through which the charismatic movement (especially within the Anglican Church) was serviced, by means of publications (such as the magazine 'Renewal'[4]), tapes, conferences and assemblies. In the words of 'Renewal', the Trust stood for 'Christ-centred, charismatic, corporate, compassionate renewal'.

Besides the Anglican Church, the other mainstream Christian body notably involved in the charismatic movement was the Roman Catholic Church. Catholics first became prominent in charismatic renewal in the United States in 1967, a year later a small but important conference of Roman charismatics being held at Notre Dame, Indiana. The first Catholic-sponsored charismatic prayer groups started in Britain in 1970. From then on the movement grew rapidly on this side of the Atlantic[5].

The first major Anglican-sponsored charismatic assembly in Britain was held at Guildford in 1971, followed by very large gatherings at Nottingham and Westminster in ensuing years. Conferences sponsored by Roman Catholic charismatics were held at Roehampton in 1972 and Guildford in 1973[6]. In 1974 a Roman Catholic conference at Notre Dame (U.S.A.) attracted some 27,000 people. In 1975 nearly 4,000 people gathered in Dublin for an ecumenical charismatic assembly. The same year a congress was held in Rome attended by nearly 10,000 Catholics, 'from Bogata and Birmingham, Belfast and Brussels, Brisbane and Bombay'[7], during which the Pope addressed the crowds, giving the movement his blessing and encouragement, a gesture hailed by at least one section of the mass media as of epoch-making significance.

In the United Kingdom the charismatic movement maintained its popular momentum until the late 'seventies when questions about its future (including queries about its offspring, 'the house church movement' with which I deal later) began to increase. In 1980 the Fountain Trust disbanded, in part because its members felt that renewal should now become more the concern of local (Anglican) parishes than the 'specialist task of an agency'[8], but also because the movement had ceased to grow at its early prolific rate.

The 'eighties have witnessed differing views as to the state of the charismatic movement in the United Kingdom. Some talk of it as 'a movement which is now essentially over'[9], whilst others speak of it as becoming increasingly 'mature'[10], or of 'a blurring of the boundaries between the charismatic movement and wider church life'[11]. The movement certainly no longer hits the headlines as in earlier years. Nor is the number of charismatic congregations or parishes growing at anything like the pace of the 'seventies.

At the same time there are still signs that the charismatic movement is very much with us. Overseas this is clearly true, Michael Harper speaking of 'another tremendous growth phase'[12] in the United States, especially amongst Episcopalians and Lutherans. A similar boom in interest is occurring amongst white episcopal and even Dutch Reformed Churches in South Africa, as I can personally testify from a visit there in the summer of 1982. However, it should be noted that in New Zealand the director of a national charismatic organisation stated in 1982 that 'the first wave of renewal had passed'[13].

Michael Harper also believes that interest is rising again on the British scene. He cites[14] a consultation for Anglican ministers in 1981 attracting some 400 clergy, a good number of 'very successful' non-residential charismatic conferences, an increase in the circulation of the magazine 'Renewal' (still continuing after the demise of the Fountain Trust) and, though here he is more circumspect, the growth of the house church movement.

Overall, it would seem that, in the United Kingdom at least, the influence of the charismatic movement is still fairly strong and that its impact on the Anglican and Roman Catholic Churches in particular has been significant. It seems probable, however, that it has 'plateaued', if not begun to decline. Whether one can describe what is now happening as a 'second phase'[15] depends on the meaning of that somewhat ambiguous term.

b. Breakthrough?

Has the charismatic movement in the United Kingdom been able to bring about, or to offer the hope of achieving, the liberation of the church from ideologies and 'heretical structures' hampering · its task of community making in the modern world? In several respects the movement appears to have made an important contribution to Christian life.

It has undoubtedly enabled many to experience 'an overwhelming sense of the presence and power of God not previously known in such a combination of otherness and immediacy'[16] (called by some 'the central feature of the movement'). The charismatic movement has offered the possibility of passionate faith in a secularistic age. Secondly, it has given impetus to the move from meeting to encounter, of vital importance if Christian community is to become a meaningful reality. The witness of numerous (especially Anglican) parishes[17], as well as of a multitude of smaller groups in most denominations, to a genuine 'renewal in the Spirit' is impressive.

These two major contributions of the charismatic movement have been complemented by others of note. The need of a transfer of authority from priest to people has been recognised by the emphasis placed on what is called 'every-member ministry'[18], which has increased the involvement of lay people in pastoral work and evangelism. The move from division to unity has been assisted by charismatic gatherings wherein denominational differences have been treated as irrelevant to the cause of true renewal.

No more compelling example of the latter is found than in Northern Ireland. Some time ago, at the Christian Renewal Centre at Rostrevor in County Down, I was present at a Monday evening prayer meeting where more than fifty people (sometimes as many as a hundred attend), including Roman Catholic sisters and Presbyterian ministers, were crowded into a small front room. One of the ministers reported that his congregation would condemn his participation outright if they knew he had been there. A number of people attending had travelled for several hours from Belfast, risking the hazards of dark roads in a country where cars are regularly stopped and drivers molested. In this context, the charismatic movement is endowed with a 'bridge-building'[19] potential of considerable communal importance to the ecumenical future of the church.

Yet if the charismatic movement promises something of a new vision in these areas, it still offers little evidence of a breakthrough into a new and lasting dimension of koinonia, either at present or in the foreseeable future. One of the changes essential for community building in the modern world, given little attention by most charismatics, is that from sacralism to the secular. Nothing as yet within charismatic renewal shows that it is as serious about 'engagement' with a secular society as it is about 'passionate faith'. Charismatics may enable us to say 'Yes' to God with new spontaneity and zeal, but there can be no communal breakthrough without an equally powerful 'Yes' to man. The 'romanticism' of the charismatic 'sub culture'[20] may be helpful to some, but without the movement's ability to address itself with mind as well as heart to the secular condition of our world in an age of crisis, we are left with only half a loaf. To mount an effective and positive response to issues of life or death, wealth or poverty, justice or injustice, purpose or despair,

Christians have today to bring into play all their powers of thought and reason — those fruits of the Spirit espoused by charismatics are very significant, but not enough. As the authors of the Anglican report on the charismatic movement state, 'The critic is still free to say that charismatics duck the harder intellectual tasks of Christian discipleship'[21].

'Every-member ministry' also promises more than it delivers. The charismatic movement has been very much clergy inspired and clergy led. It is true that charismatic renewal has mobilised lay resources, especially in the direction of evangelism and pastoral care. At the same time, the emergence of new ministries, such as so-called 'eldership', has often perpetuated clericalism in a different form and caused disquiet in certain parishes[22]. Men continue to dominate the scene. Indeed, a number of more 'fundamentalist' charismatic groups look with considerable disapproval on women occupying any significant position of leadership within the church.

The charismatics have made a major contribution to personalising and enriching the life of the local congregation and have facilitated a shift from meeting to encounter. But they have failed to complement it with real commitment to the laity's apostolate in a secular world. Parochialism is still dominant. The laity is conceived of more as an army of church-based troops than as the people of God pursuing their diverse ministries out in the world in order to forge a deeper quality of community within a secular and pluralistic society.

Nor has all been well with the charismatic movement on the ecumenical front. It is true that charismatic assemblies have often brought those of different denominations to worship together. But there have been and remain many problems. Though much less acute now than over previous years, charismatics and evangelicals have often failed to see eye to eye. The movement also ran into serious trouble with the Catholic hierarchy because, as Harper commented in 1979, 'The prevailing mood of charismatic Christians, both Roman Catholic and Protestant, is that to take communion together and to receive each other at such services is right in God's sight even if it is prohibited by the official church'[23].

In more recent years in the United Kingdom there has been evidence of a growing trend within the charismatic movement 'towards denominational fellowships and renewal within those denominations'[24]. Most denominations now have their own 'renewal' associations. Thus it is not likely that the kind of full-blooded ecumenism needed to bring a new Christian community into being will be achieved.

The apparent denominational retrenchment of charismatics is perhaps another result of the movement's inability to grasp that genuine ecumenism must relate to one world as well as one church. This is nowhere more in evidence than South Africa where the surge in charismatic renewal is almost totally 'vertical' and has little to say about the 'horizontal' issues of apartheid and black poverty. Tom Smail writes, for many charismatics there has been 'a failure to reckon with the *via crucis*'[25].

In the United Kingdom there is a little evidence that the 'second phase' of which some charismatics speak will herald a more wholistic form of renewal. There are reports of a charismatic parish setting up a shop to help disadvantaged families, of the purchase of a home of healing and of a growing concern with Third World issues[26]. But examples of a ministry strongly addressing the cause of justice and reconciliation (outside of Northern Ireland), and concern for ecumenicity in the fullest sense, are not yet abundant.

The charismatic movement in Britain has offered some significant signs of hope, above all in its rediscovery of passionate faith and the fostering of intimate Christian fellowship. But it has missed out on other changes vital to the building of community. It has failed, according to Tom Smail, 'to get down into the structures and take them on'[27], in particular the structures of a secular, pluralistic world.

For all these reasons the movement's attempts to work out a theology of community, evident for example in a number of publications of the Fountain Trust, have been limited in scope. In content and process its theology remains as subject to closed ideologies and structures as the charismatic movement itself.

2. Team ministries

a. Background

The modern concept of team ministry is believed by some to have first appeared on the church scene in this country in connection with an experiment in South Ormsby, Lincolnshire, which began in 1949, though this venture was in fact little more than the Anglican Church utilising a form of Methodist circuit system to deal with an acute shortage of clergy in a rural area. In reality, the first real change of style in clerical leadership did not emerge until from 1960, for a decade or more, a team of three Methodist ministers and their wives living in Notting Hill, London, worked as a close-knit core group with a clear division of labour (in relation to worship, pastoral matters, welfare concerns and racial issues)[28].

By the mid-'sixties the Methodist Church led the field, having established a national team ministries committee with considerable expertise to promote teams in many areas. The Anglicans held their first group ministries conference at Lincoln in 1967. By the end of the decade the establishment of a number of ecumenical teams (though despite

Vatican Two with no significant Roman Catholic participation) was well advanced[29], one of the better known being that led by Nicholas Stacey in Woolwich, until its disbandment in 1968[30]. The Anglican Pastoral Measure (1968) and the Sharing of Church Buildings Act (1969) gave further impetus to both team ministry and to ecumenical co-operation in this context.

In 1973, a Directory entitled 'State of the Teams' was produced by Peter Croft listing some 124 teams; when the 1977 edition was published the number had risen to 312[31]. In 1982 a broadsheet on teams[32] put the number at some 450, though an accurate count is virtually impossible. In 1976 the first major team ministries conference was held at Swanwick with 170 (predominantly Anglican) participants, an event repeated successfully in 1979 and 1983. By that time the term 'team ministry' was being supplemented by that of 'collaborative ministry'[33], the latter attempting to broaden and deepen the meaning of the concept. Two workshops were held on this theme in early 1984, one sponsored by the British Council of Churches' Working Party on Collaborative Ministry, the other by the Methodist Team Ministries Committee and the Urban Theology Unit (Sheffield).

b. Breakthrough?

As an ideal, team ministry has been an important step forward, above all in changing clerical attitudes and practice. Its major contribution to a new dimension of Christian community lies, without doubt, in the emphasis placed on the sharing of thinking, planning and resources by ordained ministers (and sometimes lay people).

Team ministry has introduced many clergy to the novel (to many of them) and demanding experience of working as a close-knit group. As well as giving support and companionship in what has often been isolated work, this has allowed for some experimentation with corporate management, shared decision making and new modes of exchange and communication. The organisational patterns vary enormously, but the principles of mutual help and more democratic forms of leadership are generally evident throughout. This has certainly helped to facilitate a shift from meeting to encounter as a first-hand experience for the clergy.

At the same time teams have helped to give ordained ministers a greater sense of autonomy by fostering a division of labour related to the skills of team members. Even though the united Presbyterian-Methodist church in West Greenwich where I worked for four years only supported a team of two ministers, my Presbyterian colleague was able to concentrate on new forms of worship, chaplaincy and administration, whilst I gave much of my attention to Christian education and contacts with the secular bodies in the surrounding neighbourhood.

The emergence of team ministries has also influenced the relationship of minister and people, the conduct of church affairs and Christian witness in the locality. Of note here was the Notting Hill team ministry in the 'sixties and early 'seventies, which blazed a trail for many. Its spirit of exuberant involvement in the everyday affairs of that part of inner-city London was well summed up in 1972 by one of its members, Norwyn Denny;

> 'What we *have* learned in Notting Hill is joyful celebration. All is not weakness; God is not without witnesses; there is so much to make you glad within even the sordid areas of life. Sufficient indeed to bring back joy to community life and to facilitate the establishment of a new order of joyous mendicants. The palm processions, the street parties, the wedding feasts, the community organisation pageants, the free participation of the congregation, the spontaneity within liturgy, the baptismal jamborees, all show that gladness is as much a preoccupation of Christian community as is human need. Celebration is the note of discovered community that we would want to strike above all others'[34].

Other teams have since espoused and implemented the spirit of Notting Hill.

Team ministry, however, now seems to have reached the peak of, or at least a levelling off in, its growth and development. There are numerous reasons for this. One is the widespread existence of patronage, and the freehold, within the Anglican Church, which continues to hamper moves towards more collaborative forms of ministry, as John Tiller underlines in his own attempt to formulate a strategy for the future[35]. Another difficulty is that team ministry has by and large remained a form of *clerical* re-organisation. Even here, however, the gains have been less than world shattering. Whilst many Anglicans have found team ministry an exciting innovation, the form of these to Methodists often seems to go little further than their own everyday experience of circuit ministry.

Nor has much of a shift from community of place to community of concern taken place. Few teams have been able or ready to extend their work beyond the local neighbourhood. If those employed outside the parish (chaplains or non-stipendiary ministers) have been attached to teams, it has been the needs of the local congregation which have continued to dominate the agenda. The hope, affirmed by the Methodist Team Ministries Committee in the 'sixties, that teams might be a means of enabling clergy *and* laity to engage more effectively with extra-parochial secular institutions, has rarely been realised.

Movement from priest to people has been very limited, despite a number of notable exceptions. Teams have remained dominantly clerical, the only lay people usually incorporated being those on the payroll of the local church (for example as youth leaders or community workers). In 1978 in the Anglican diocese of Derby it was stated that, 'Official team and group ministries were not the place to find most "sharing of the ministry" with the laity'[36]. The times of meeting, the nature of the business, the 'style' of conversation, have all remained clerical in orientation. There has been no real liberation of the laity; only the facilitating of clergy to work more closely together. From time to time clerical teams have reported back to and consulted lay management committees, but the last word has inevitably been with the team.

Denominationalism as well as clericalism has prevented any major breakthrough on the ecumenical front. The (Anglican) Pastoral Measure of 1968 did a good deal to facilitate the formation of teams within the Church of England, but a supposedly legal guarantee of their continuity, a key matter if the work of the initial group was to be built on, was in practice often set aside[37]. If lack of continuity has proved a hazard within any one denomination, it has often been disastrous as far as ecumenical teams have gone, the latter remaining extremely vulnerable to staff changes.

My own experience in West Greenwich, London, bears witness to this dilemma. Over some years we had managed to create a loose-knit but effective team of ministers drawn from all the main churches in the area. For a time a spate of innovative ventures involving many lay people resulted. Then the energetic curate of the parish church left and, not long after, the vicar was taken seriously ill, neither being replaced for a considerable period. The final blow was the departure of the Roman Catholic priest who had been outstanding in the way he had brought a reluctant congregation into the post-Vatican Two era. By his graciousness, sense of humour and considerable organisational ability he had made the local Roman church a full-blooded partner on the ecumenical scene, as well as greatly encouraging and stimulating our clergy meetings. His leaving was seen as of vital significance for the future of the whole team; so much so that the West Greenwich Group of Churches sent an urgent written appeal that he be replaced by someone sympathetic to further ecumenical co-operation. The unhappy result was the eventual appointment of a priest conservative in theology, inexperienced in parish work and less than lukewarm about matters ecumenical. *allowns like clericalism!*

The breakdown of the West Greenwich team was symptomatic of the fact that active Roman Catholic participation in such forms of ministry is still uncommon. Team ministry has been mainly a Methodist, Anglican and (more recently) United Reformed Church initiative, with only very committed individuals from other denominations playing an active part.

Team ministry has provided a genuine source of encouragement and inspiration for many clergy, predominantly Anglican and Methodist. It has resulted in a great deal more clerical openness and sharing than hitherto existed. But it has given little impetus as yet to those moves urgently needed to free the church to face up with confidence to an age in crisis.

In 1979 Peter Croft wrote, 'Team ministry isn't one pearl on the necklace, it's the thread that holds the necklace together. It's a style of ministry that should characterise the whole church. It's what ministry is all about'[38]. That same year, after the second major team ministries conference at Swanwick, Hugh Cross commented: 'Sitting through the final plenary session . . . one might have come to the conclusion that nothing had changed except the numbers attending and a few more non-Anglicans participating'[39]. It seems that team ministry, at least for the present, has had to settle for the place permitted it within the confines of the ecclesiastical system.

3. Ecumenical initiatives

a. Background

It is not possible here to review in any detail the many ecumenical initiatives which have been going on within the British churches over the past decades. I take, therefore, the two most widely recognised areas of ecumenical endeavour, simply as examples of the opportunities and difficulties faced by a church in search of renewal — the talks between major denominations to promote unity, and a number of initiatives sponsored by the British Council of Churches.

The 'sixties saw a veritable fever of activity on the boundary between the Anglican and Methodist Churches in this country. In 1963, 'Conversations between the Church of England and the Methodist Church: a Report'[40] was published. As a young Methodist minister in circuit, I was one amongst many who spent a great deal of time engaged with their church members debating it. In 1969 the Methodist Conference passed the proposed scheme for unity only to find that the Anglican Convocations had rejected it. The pot, however, was kept simmering, until a second adverse vote by the General Synod of the Church of England finally extinguished the light. It is interesting to note that whereas in 1969 the Daily Mirror splashed the results of the voting across its front page, three years later the news received a mere one inch insert at the foot of an inside column.

Meanwhile the Presbyterian Church of England and Congregational Union were doing rather better. In 1971 they agreed to unite, and in 1972 the United Reformed Church was formally brought into being with only a few dissenting congregations deciding to go their own way. In 1981 the

United Reformed Church was itself joined by the Churches of Christ.

By 1974 another initiative for church unity was underway with the setting up of the Churches' Unity Commission, which two years later issued the 'Ten Propositions' for discussion by the major denominations. The propositions launched the English churches into a heart-searching debate about 'convenanting for unity' and, though the Roman Catholic Church, Baptist Union and Congregational Federation withdrew from the fray in 1978, the active involvement of the Methodists, United Reformed Church and Anglicans kept the issue of unity very much alive. All to little avail. In the summer of 1982, the United Reformed and Methodist Church opted for covenanting (the latter by a substantial majority) only to learn that once again the Church of England had failed at the last hurdle, with the House of Clergy of the General Synod unable to attain the required majority. Thus, as was soon noted in the press, 'For the first time in almost 30 years no inter-church talks are taking place about unity'[41].

This was because fourteen years of 'international' discussions between Anglicans and Roman Catholics had also come to an end (in 1981)[42]. The meetings had been useful and, in the latter years in particular, forward-looking. But by their terms of reference they were only 'advisory' in nature and in no way binding on either church. However, a second joint international commission was set up in 1983, given impetus by the common declaration signed by the Pope and the Archbishop of Canterbury during the former's visit to Britain a year earlier.

Despite this latest resumption of talks, it has been the British Council of Churches (BCC) which has found itself back in the driving seat. First launched in 1942, the BCC took some time to get itself fully accepted as any more than an optional extra. But the increasing influence of the World Council of Churches, especially from its assembly in 1961 in New Delhi, was complemented by the growing standing of its counterpart on the British scene. In 1966 the Roman Catholic Church, responding to the spirit of the Second Vatican Council, joined the BCC with 'observer' status.

In 1964, an extremely successful conference on 'Faith and Order' was held at Nottingham and put out a call for the establishment of 'areas of ecumenical experiment'[43], as well as an invitation to member churches 'to covenant together to work and pray for the inauguration of union' no later than 'Easter Day 1980'[44]. Desborough in Northamptonshire became the first designated 'area of ecumenical experiment' in 1965.

In 1966-67 the BCC embarked on a major educational attempt at consciousness raising with regard to the economic and social needs of the modern world. Called 'The People Next Door', it involved upwards of 80,000 people across the whole country in small group study[45]. Throughout the 'sixties the number of local councils of churches rose from 300 to 650[46], Roman Catholics participating in three-quarters of these[47]. During the 'seventies the BCC continued to spur on its member (and observer) churches. In 1972 it promoted a major Church Leaders' Conference in Birmingham, and in 1976 it launched a full-scale enquiry, called 'Britain Today and Tomorrow', into the state of the nation and the churches' response. Meanwhile it continued to promote the designation of areas of ecumenical experiment, now called local ecumenical projects[48], which amongst other things required formal and overt commitment to local co-operation, by the end of the decade well over 300 such projects having been established[49].

Since the mid 'seventies the BCC has taken fewer major ecumenical initiatives, preferring to await the results of the debate on covenanting for unity. In the early 'eighties the Council faced financial problems but renewed commitment by several major churches, in particular the Church of England, the Methodist Church and the United Reformed Church, saw it through a difficult period.

A visit by a BCC delegation to Rome in April 1983, at the Pope's invitation, opened up new ecumenical possibilities, though the pace of future developments now appears to lie very largely with the Roman Catholic hierarchy of England and Wales[50]. The latter made a positive move in this connection in January and April 1984 when they met in residential conference with the leaders of the other main English churches, though communiques emphasised that the gatherings were meant to express a common concern for unity and not in any way determine the future. However, as a result of these meetings the Roman Catholic bishops of England and Wales and the BCC have agreed to work together to prepare for a major conference of the churches in 1987. The purpose of this event will be to consider the nature of the church in the light of the Lima document on 'Baptism, Eucharist and Ministry', the papers of the Anglican-Roman Catholic International Commission and the documents of the Second Vatican Council.

b. Breakthrough?

Ecumenical initiatives in community building have to be evaluated first and foremost against their success in freeing the church from the constraints of a constrictive denominationalism. Despite a great deal of dedicated endeavour by many enlightened church leaders the reality is that within the United Kingdom no decisive breakthrough has yet occurred.

The conversations between the major denominations have foundered most obviously on the rock of clericalism, though one must not underestimate the conservatism of a not always well informed or enthusiastic laity. The failure of the covenanting proposals in 1982 brought some forthright comments in this regard. For example, Kenneth

Greet, Secretary of the Methodist Conference, stated that, 'It must be particularly frustrating to Anglicans, who once again see the will of the majority frustrated by clerical domination'[51]. The post-mortem report of the Churches' Council for Covenanting frankly acknowledged that it had remained silent on important matters of common concern (such as lay ministries) because, 'We were apparently pre-occupied with the ordained ministry'[52]. And not just with the ordained ministry, but the *male* ordained ministry. The Council accepted that, 'The division over the ordination of women' has been 'a major factor'[53] in the failure of the proposals.

Likewise, though the talks between Anglicans and Roman Catholics have made a good deal of progress, the mutual acceptance of ministries (including the issue of there being ordained women ministers in some parts of the Anglican Church) remains a major stumbling-block.

All these prolonged negotiations have failed to bring about a decisive move from division to unity, in part at least because certain denominations have been unable to countenance any significant transfer of authority from priest to people. As a consequence there has been little hope of the churches *together* addressing themselves to the problems of parochialism and congregationalism, let alone secularism. It also remains a matter of conjecture how much even an affirmative vote for unity in 1969, 1972 or 1982 would have really liberated the church for community building and mission in a new age. There is little evidence, from the formation of the United Reformed Church for example, that business would have been very much different from before.

Pre-occupation with 'lateral growth' (expansion by amalgamation) as opposed to 'frontal growth' (expansion through acquiring new members) has led to an 'ecumenism of decline', as Alan Gilbert describes it[54]. Our endeavours so far seem to underline yet again that an ecumenicity which fails to put the needs of the world *before* those of the church is standing the debate about unity on its head.

Immediately after the rejection of the unity scheme in July 1982, the Churches' Council for Covenanting issued a statement which included the following sentences: 'The search for unity will continue but it will inevitably take a different path from that which the churches have followed since the Lambeth appeal in 1920 and Archbishop Fisher's Cambridge sermon of 1946. Attention will now be focused on local ecumenical projects, the British Council of Churches and the Pope's invitation to the British churches (to meet him in Rome)'[55]. Does the hope of a breakthrough, therefore, now lie mainly with initiatives sponsored by the British Council of Churches?

The Council's nature and function make this doubtful. This is in no way to undervalue the stimulus to and encouragement of ecumenicity given by the BCC over past decades. The BCC has proved of considerable significance as a cross-denominational forum in relation to concerns ranging from race relations to unemployment, from 'the community of women and men in the church' to inter-faith dialogue, from Northern Ireland to the threat of nuclear war. For example, in 1977 a Committee for Relations with People of Other Faiths was established to help build bridges between those from different cultural backgrounds, whilst early in 1984 a 'Peace Forum' to promote links between Christian groups involved in various forms of peacemaking[56] was set up. Through its Youth Unit the BCC has sponsored workcamps, exchanges and a number of major youth festivals to give many young people a first-hand taste of ecumenism in action.

The BCC, too, has played an important part over the years in raising its member churches' awareness of some of the key issues of the day at home and overseas. Christian Aid, a division of the BCC, has here made an outstanding contribution and is currently engaged in expanding its programme of development education throughout the United Kingdom.

The BCC has been instrumental in fostering a great deal of ecumenical co-operation at local level through both councils of churches and local ecumenical projects, in many places, such as Swindon and Oxford, impressive progress having been made in this connection[57]. After the failure of covenanting, it is at the local level that the BCC is hoping that the ecumenical movement will again come to life, though 'there has not been a vast increase in (the number of councils of churches) in the last ten years'[58].

Nonetheless, it must be remembered that the BCC is essentially a council of *churches*. It has to travel very much at the pace of its constituent members, or problems ensue. Although it has the freedom to take certain initiatives — as with resolutions passed at its 1983 Assembly condemning the manufacture and possession of nuclear weapons 'as an offence against God'[59], or in the setting up of its Peace Forum, there are limits as to how far it can go. For example, its modest donations to the World Council of Churches' Programme to Combat Racism, and to those in Toxteth trying to pick up the pieces after the race riots in 1981, brought immediate and outspoken criticism from a number of quarters.

The root problem is that as a council of churches the BCC is in the end the servant of a captive church. The ideologies which restrict the latter also encompass and constrain the effectiveness of the Council. For example, failure of the church to engage adequately with a secular society was reflected in the inability of the BCC's 'Britain Today and Tomorrow Project' to enable its member bodies to translate high level deliberations (on such issues as 'Law, Freedom, Justice and Equality', 'Power and Powerlessness' and 'Leadership') into effective and continuing action. The church's captivity to clericalism is reflected in the dependence of most local councils of churches and local ecumenical projects on the ordained ministry, and in the generally limited level of lay interest. The

61

failure of many local councils of churches to get much beyond celebrating the week of prayer for Christian unity or collecting during Christian Aid week[60] is in part a result of congregationalism, as well as of the church's parochial view of the scope of the lay apostolate.

Above all the church's captivity to denominationalism restricts the work of the BCC in a host of ways, not least in preventing effective corporate decision making and in hindering the sharing of resources, a dilemma which the failure of covenanting has again brought to the fore. Furthermore, and despite papal overtures, the Roman Catholic Church still retains its observer status, thereby making any real breakthrough extremely difficult to achieve. The major conference of the mainstream churches now scheduled for 1987 could well prove to be ecumenically significant. However, if it is planned by clergy for clergy it is unlikely that any decisive breakthrough will be made.

The initiatives mentioned above, in relation both to the search for organic unity and to the endeavours of the BCC, have brought the British churches into closer and more regular contact than ever before in their history. It is no mean achievement. Yet it seems that a gradual 'silting up' of the ecumenical movement has been occurring for some time and that, at least in the United Kingdom, we have now reached an impasse, still held fast by those ideologies and structures which keep the whole church captive. The feelings of those increasingly frustrated by this situation might be summed up in the *cri de coeur* of one member of the Anglican Synod immediately after its rejection of covenanting: 'We have got to go on being Christians, despite the church'[61].

4. The Nationwide Initiative in Evangelism

a. Background

The Nationwide Initiative in Evangelism (NIE) originated in the mid-'seventies when the Evangelical Alliance, the Church of England Evangelical Council and the Billy Graham Evangelistic Association met to consider whether or not to invite Billy Graham in 1978 to conduct a final Earl's Court campaign. There was, however, a strong reaction to 'yet another' national evangelical mission from some of those present. The result, after further consultations, was that the so-called Lambeth Group, under the chairmanship of the then Archbishop of Canterbury, Dr. Donald Coggan, issued in April 1977 a statement calling on all churches and other Christian bodies: '(i) To share immediately in reporting and evaluating evangelistic efforts of many kinds now being undertaken by the churches. (ii) To plan new local initiatives in evangelism arising out of local reconciliation. (iii) To explore the convergence in understanding of both the message and the methods.'

Despite a somewhat lukewarm response from the mainstream British churches (the old suspicions of an evangelical 'takeover' of the field of mission lurking in the wings), an Initiative Committee was set up early in 1978. The NIE was formally launched in January 1979 at a dedication service in the chapel of Lambeth Palace attended by most of the top church leaders including the Archbishop of Canterbury and the Cardinal Archbishop of Westminster. The NIE was commissioned 'to encourage and stimulate intelligent and effective evangelism throughout England, Ireland, Scotland and Wales'.

The Initiative Committee adopted 'a five-phase strategy'. The first two phases were to help local churches, both the better and less well motivated, towards more effective evangelism. Phases three and four were to make contact with selected groups of 'unreached persons', to gain experience of how to carry out evangelistic work amongst them and to share these experiences and insights with the denominations to assist in the latter's missionary activities. Phase five, to be completed 'sometime in the 1990s', was to see all that the NIE had achieved fully integrated into the ongoing life of the mainsteam churches — and thus the natural end of the NIE[62].

During 1979 the Initiative Committee undertook a major survey of church life in England entitled 'Prospects for the 80s', giving a profile of church membership and comments on each denomination[62]. In January 1980 the NIE estimated that some 5,000 churches used their special service sheets which called 'every local church to prayer for evangelism and to rededicate itself to Christ's service in the country'[64]. By the summer of that year, regional 'support groups' for the Initiative existed in 23 counties and three London boroughs (the number was to rise to its maximum of 35 support groups in early 1982). In September 1980, the NIE held a major week's assembly at Nottingham University, though reports on the success of this varied.

The first signs of decline in the fortunes of the Initiative came in mid-1981 with the re-organisation of its central structures. The initial core bodies, the Initiative Committee and a Council of Reference, were 'integrated' into a new Initiative Council of seventeen members from the major denominations (though only one was a Catholic). Comments published by the NIE relating to this 'streamlining' portray optimism but also growing uncertainties — 'I have been involved with the NIE from the beginning and I have more hope for it today than I have had at any time in the last three years' (Harry Morton); 'This is not the end of the NIE, there is very real work to be done' (David Russell); 'It is unfair to say that we have shut down the NIE . . . We have affirmed a continuing task for it' (Charles Henderson)[65].

In fact the writing was on the wall and, despite an attempt to set up numerous working parties on evangelism amongst such groups as 'the urban poor', 'young people in the pop culture' and 'solitary senior citizens', to name but a few, 1982 saw a steady withdrawal of support, not least financial. By October of that year 'the Methodist Church was a lone voice in maintaining that NIE should continue as a separate concern', and the Initiative Council was soon formally to ask 'the British Council of Churches to take up the work of promoting local evangelism'[66]. By this time certain evangelical bodies were already independently organising 'Mission England', to culminate in a visit of Billy Graham to England in mid 1984 and with an estimated overall 'budget of around £3 million'[67].

b. Breakthough?

Though the NIE has formally terminated its life it would be wrong to ignore its ambitious attempt to bring into being a church working together for a more effective mission to Britain in the 'eighties. The NIE had two main concerns; first to further 'intelligent and effective evangelism' and, secondly, to bring every major denomination in the country into a form of partnership toward that end.

Its attempt to pioneer a new and more relevant form of evangelism certainly took the Nationwide Initiative some way towards achieving a move from the sacred to the secular and from community of place to community of concern. In 1980, for example, its published material was already expressing a genuine wish to engage with the world of industry, to set up 'special interest groups' and to focus on key issues such as unemployment, law and order, and power and powerlessness[68]. Its proposed working parties on evangelism (most never set up as it happened) were imaginative in conception and took the secular world seriously.

At the same time the NIE sought to use the secular tools of sociological analysis and business management to further its work. It engaged in a major survey of the state of church membership prior to its 1980 assembly, encouraged local churches to evaluate their evangelistic work objectively (with the careful use of statistics) and set out in flow-chart form the stages by which the NIE hoped to achieve its purpose throughout the 'eighties[69].

The NIE also showed its awareness of the need for an enabling approach in its leadership style, constantly asserting that it was 'an opportunity rather than an organisation'. Its five phase programme was meant to facilitate more effective evangelism by local congregations and not to do it for them. In all this there was an emphasis on a 'popular' rather than 'priestly' style of leadership.

However, any decisive communal breakthrough was blocked by the lack of receptiveness by many churches, at national and local level, to the NIE's aims and objectives. For some it was not evangelical enough, and the independent launching of 'Mission England' underlined that the influence of those who wished to return to traditional evangelistic approaches (Billy Graham first came to England in 1954) was a powerful separatist force. For others the NIE was too evangelical, as in its use of the militant language of mission — 'We now have a different kind of spearhead (the new Initiative Council) but the same thrust because we are still engaged in the same warfare' (David Russell)[70]. The attempt by the NIE to play the role of an enabling body also ran into difficulties, many churches at national and local level looking with some suspicion on an organisation which implied that they were lacking in missionary concern or skills. Local organisations did not readily respond to what, despite all protestations, was inevitably a 'top down' approach to promoting evangelism.

These problems carried over into the NIE's attempts to bring all the mainstream churches into partnership around 'intelligent and effective evangelism'. The setting up of the ecumenical Initiative Committee and the service of dedication early in 1979 were ambitious endeavours — but who could really be against 'evangelism'? What it proved was that a decisive move from division to unity could not be given adequate impetus simply by constant use of such an ambiguous word. Though ecumenical concern for human need and one world also surfaced from time to time it was in practice a relatively minor theme.

Although the NIE demonstrated 'the possibility of an evangelistic shape to ecumenical relationships', it failed to build 'firm bridges across some of the traditional chasms in the denominational landscape', as Donald English puts it[71]. This was 'particularly true of the British Council of Churches / Evangelical Alliance relationship and the Roman Catholic / Protestant scene'[72]. In the former situation, the tenacious and separatist strength of independent evangelical bodies was clearly demonstrated. In the latter, the Roman Catholic hierarchy was 'extremely careful all along not to be seen to give official commitment to NIE'[73].

Thus the NIE was in the end a victim of what it hoped to remedy — lack of ecumenical co-operation in Christian mission. It somewhat naïvely asserted early in its life: 'That the main streams of Christian theological thought about evangelism are closer together now than for a long time is established beyond doubt'[74]. But this did not prove to be the case and, as with the failure of the covenanting proposals, so with a common approach to evangelism, no breakthrough was achieved. The lack of an agreed theology of mission only underlined the churches' lack of a shared theology of community.

5. The National Pastoral Congress

a. Background

On the 6th May 1980, I found myself sitting in the Metropolitan Cathedral of Liverpool participating in the final mass of one of the most memorable religious occasions of my life. As an observer (invited by the Roman Catholic religious orders), I was deeply impressed by virtually every aspect of what many believed to be a genuinely historic event.

The Congress had its origins in a search by Roman Catholics for a national pastoral strategy relevant to the modern world. The process began with the document 'Church 2000'[75], published in 1973 by a joint working party set up by the (Catholic) Bishops' Conference and the National Conference of Priests. The working party's final report, 'A Time for Building' suggested a 'National Pastoral Conference'[76] to be held in 1978. In the event, this was a far more significant occasion than initially envisaged and, with the backing of the Roman bishops, took place over a long weekend in May 1980 in Liverpool.

The National Pastoral Congress was attended by 'over 2000 delegates from all the dioceses and Catholic national organisations, including 42 bishops, 255 clergy and 150 religious, and 36 ecumenical observers'[77]. A real attempt was made to ensure that the Congress agenda grew out of the concerns of ordinary Catholics, expressed in their responses to 'Church 2000' and 'A Time for Building'[78]. Delegates were enabled to prepare for the Congress by consideration locally of eight papers circulated for group discussion, as well as of a digest of reports from the dioceses sent out three months before the assembly.

The National Pastoral Congress itself was not only an event but a 'happening'. It brought together the personnel, administrative skills, liturgical imagination, spiritual vitality, pastoral concerns and social awareness of the Roman Church in England and Wales in a way never witnessed before. It was an occasion of impressive worship, deep discussion, sharing in many forms, and warm hospitality never to be forgotten by those privileged to be present.

The participants were divided into seven main 'sectors' to explore the themes of 'The People of God — Co-responsibility and Co-operation', 'The People of God — Ministry, Vocation and Apostolate', 'Family and Society', 'Evangelisation', 'Christian Education and Formation', 'Christian Witness' and 'Justice'. The four days of deliberation led to reports from each sector covering almost every aspect of church life[79], these being publicly read out in a final plenary session in the Liverpool Philharmonic Hall. After the Congress the bishops spent some months considering the sector reports and recommendations and, in August 1980, published their own response entitled 'The Easter People'[80]. This was widely read and discussed in the dioceses, especially by those who had attended the Congress.

b. Breakthough?

The National Pastoral Congress was a comprehensive event in all senses of the term. Nonetheless its aim was dominantly twofold — first, to seek to develop a means by which the Catholic Church could discover a relevant 'pastoral strategy' for the 'eighties; secondly, to involve the whole 'people of God', and above all the laity, in this endeavour. At the same time, there was constant reference to the search for a quality of Christian community which could match a time of crisis. 'The Church is community', stated Cardinal Hume in his homily at the closing Congress mass, a theme continually referred to in a diversity of contexts in 'The Easter People'.

The sector debates came to grips in a lively and realistic way with the task facing the church in a secular society. There was informed and articulate discussion of major and complex issues, from unemployment to race, from Northern Ireland to justice at home, from disarmament to the poverty of the Third World. The delegates were fully alert to the needs of the moment and quite prepared to put forward new and imaginative ways of engagement. There was also a deep concern to bring the parish back to life, to enrich it as 'a worshipping community' and to strengthen its ability to care for the sick and disadvantaged. There seemed, however, less awareness of the limitations of parochial structures, and over-optimism regarding the ability of the local church to provide the means of meeting the needs of a cosmopolitan and pluralistic society.

There was a deep desire for greater unity between churches, local and national, and a strong recommendation that the bishops 'reconsider the question of the entry of the Catholic Church in England and Wales into the British Council of Churches'[81]. This was allied to a powerful voice urging that Christians be as involved in the search for one world as for one church — 'Our efforts to live as sisters and brothers are our efforts to say with integrity "Our Father"'[82].

These were all hopeful signs of a move towards a church able to fulfil the exhortation of one sector that, 'Bishop, priest and people must set out together to implement the teaching and spirit of Vatican II'[83]. Nonetheless this was a Congress, not a church as such in action. Thus the key issue was whether debate and recommendations could lead to real change and a new model of Christian koinonia. At the heart of the latter, for a substantial majority at the Congress, was the matter of increasing lay participation in and through the life of the church, of a change from the centrality of the priesthood to that of the people.

The pre-Congress 'Contact', summarising comments sent in from the dioceses, stated: 'Running right through the diocesan reports on this theme (the People of God) is a strong desire for more consultation and participation by the laity in the life of the church. This is not an attempt at a take-over, but a wish for the laity, as part of the baptised, part of the "royal priesthood" of God's people, to share more fully and responsibly in the life of the church'[84]. The same appeal was echoed time and time again in many Catholic magazines and papers giving their views on matters to which the congress should give priority. In just one I picked up at random, a member of the Young Christian Workers wrote: 'Many of my hopes for the Congress focus on how well it does the job of finding ways to explore and tap the potential of lay people within the church . . . This participation will, I hope, extend beyond consultation to sharing in decision making in matters affecting the life of the local church and its missionary involvement'[85].

The final sector report on 'The People of God' contained similar sentiments: 'We hope that nationally and at diocesan level women and men will be involved together in planning and decision-making . . . Ordained ministers should see themselves as servants of the lay-service of the world. It was felt that too many clergy use authority not as service but to contain lay initiative . . . Bishops and priests are asked to place more trust in lay initiatives'[86].

The Congress is now an event of the past. There has been ample time for a change of attitude and indeed practice to demonstrate that the plea of the lay participants has been heard. Three months after the Congress when the Bishops' Conference of England and Wales met to give their verdict on the sector reports in 'The Easter People' there were signs of progress. The bishops noted that: 'Perhaps the most striking expression of Christian love which emerged from the National Pastoral Congress was that we trusted each other, and listened to one another, as each having something valuable to contribute, each with a unique witness to give . . . For all it was a recognition of true status and mature responsibility in the Church of Christ'[87].

In the section on 'Different Ministries but Shared Responsibility', the bishops made some hopeful comments: 'In many ways the lay contribution to the Congress was its most striking feature . . . In the Congress in Liverpool the maturity, strength and apostolic courage of the lay delegates were clearly to be recognised, together with their desire for a more responsible role in the future . . . For they are not simply delegates of the bishops and clergy, they are gospel-inspired lay-people, members of the *laos* (or people) of God, and in their own right missionaries of Christ to the world'[88].

Yet despite what for many at Liverpool, bishops included, was a deeply moving experience of the meaning of 'church' for our day, no communal breakthrough seems to be in evidence. 'The Easter People' remains in general a conservative document. The clerical 'order of merit' — bishops, priests, religious and laity — is retained throughout (though the religious are here and there placed in fourth position)[89]. The parish, though also in reponse to *lay* wishes it must be added, is reaffirmed as the natural centre and dominant focus of ecclesiastical activity. Only 'further consideration' of the delegates' ecumenical requests (for example that the Catholic Church become a full member of the British Council of Churches) is promised. Indeed, the fact that the outcome of deliberations by experienced, articulate and deeply committed lay delegates should have to wait on the independent judgement of a council of bishops, however sympathetic or enlightened, highlights the continuing dilemma faced by the Roman Catholic Church. Coming through the cautious pages of 'The Easter People' is more a sense of uncertainty and ambiguity than a joyous shout of Easter triumph that *all* men and women have been set free from the principalities and powers of this world to share fully in the life of Christ.

Indeed the bishops appear to have managed to defuse a potentially explosive sentence from an Apostolic Exhortation of Pope Paul VI which they themselves risked quoting: "'The primary and immediate task of lay people is to put to use every Christian and evangelical possibility latent but already present and active in the affairs of the world. The more gospel-inspired lay-people there are engaged in these realities, clearly involved in them, competent to promote them and conscious that they must exercise to the full their Christian powers which are often buried and suffocated, the more these realities will be at the service of the kingdom of God and therefore of salvation in Jesus Christ" (Evangelii Nuntiandi, n. 70)'[90].

Some of those deeply involved in Catholic affairs appear more hopeful. Michael Hornsby-Smith, who carried out a comprehensive post-Congress survey of participants' views, believes that, in 'The Easter People', the bishops 'have legitimated quite unambiguously the search for a fully participating and active lay involvement at every level in the life of the church'[91]. In the present historical context (especially of 'a strong, traditionalist and centralist Pope'), he doubts 'if more could have been expected of the bishops'[92]". Indeed, he even thinks that the Congress 'represents, at least potentially, the *rite de passage* from a childlike passive deference and conformity to a mature and responsible adult Christianity'. The sting lies here in the word 'potentially' — to be or not to be, that is the question.

Follow-up enquiries and comments appear to bear out the problems faced by the Roman Catholic Church in seeking to put the principles so enthusiastically espoused by the laity at Liverpool into practice. The National Conference of Priests' mid-term report, published early in 1982[93], showed a few dioceses seeking greater lay involvement in church affairs (notably Westminster and Liverpool), and a number of pastoral councils at diocesan or deanery levels in existence or proposed. But the comments of the priests themselves were more revealing: 'Sadly things are only happening in limited ways' (East Anglia); 'As far as the general body of priests in this diocese is concerned, it is questionable if the Liverpool Congress has affected their ministry at all' (Hexham and Newcastle); 'The early days of preparation for the Congress impinged upon few of the priests — after the event this number has not increased greatly' (Middlesbrough); 'The Congress came and went and for many priests might never have been' (Southwark). A final word from one priest is typical of a good deal of the frustration manifest: 'If the Liverpool Congress takes as long to influence us as the Second Vatican Council, God help us!'

Michael Hornsby-Smith's own survey of the views of lay delegates to the Congress by and large bears out these comments. Only about a quarter considered the response of the clergy to have been satisfactory[94]. 'The evidence suggests', writes Michael Hornsby-Smith, 'that large numbers of priests continue to exercise a veto-power at the local level and so manage to prevent the consideration even of matters on which the bishops have invited all Catholics to reflect and respond'[95].

In November 1982, the Roman bishops strengthened the fears of those believing that a retreat from the progressive principles of the National Pastoral Congress was underway with their publication 'In the House of the Living God'[96], which dealt with a restructuring of the processes of consultation and decision making within the Catholic Church in England and Wales. The proposals were circulated for general discussion and comment, but the final document published in June 1983[97] showed few signs of advance.

The bishops seem to have taken the exhortations of Vatican Two for greater 'collegiality' to mean that representation on the six new departments, which have replaced the 'permanent commissions' (the latter having included a rather unwieldy though definite lay constituency), should now be exclusively episcopal[98]. Though the new committees serving these departments are to have lay members, the latters' main role is that of 'consultants' or 'experts'[99]; the committees themselves remain advisory.

The hierarchy no doubt believes with sincerity that such restructuring will place the bishops' conference and its departments more fully at the service of 'the mission of the diocese as the local and particular church'[100], and wishes to encourage, despite obvious lack of progress so far, the development of diocesan and (deanery) pastoral councils[101]. Yet the latter are also restricted to 'a consultative status'[102] under the authority of the local bishop, and it is difficult to see how lay enthusiasm will be engendered as a result. It is thus likely that the direction of Catholic policy will become more not less dependent on the bishops' conference.

The disappointing conclusion must be that, despite the National

Pastoral Congress, the Roman Church still seems unable to involve its laity in any authentic form of decision making at national or local level. Despite the bishops' obvious desire for 'genuine partnership'[103] and 'shared responsibility'[104], they appear to be held captive by the constraints of clericalism, not to mention those of parochialism. There seems an inability to appreciate that 'participation', as understood by most laity today, cannot be achieved unless there is a decisive and manifest shift of authority and responsibility from priest to people. The vision of the church as the whole people of God, on which the National Pastoral Congress was built, looks like taking a long time to become a reality.

IV: BASIC CHRISTIAN GROUPS

1. The human scale

The several attempts outlined in the last chapter to renew the life and witness of the church have one thing in common: they continue to take for granted the present form of ecclesiastical institutions. There is little obvious awareness that unless secularism and sacralism, together with clericalism, parochialism, congregationalism and denominationalism, are *fundamentally* challenged, the changes required to enable a new community to come into being are impossible to make. To shake the old foundations is not enough; *new* foundations and *new* structures are called for to meet the needs of a world in crisis.

This should come as no surprise. Ever since man built the tower of Babel, God has been cutting our pretentious structures down to size. We still fail to acknowledge the constantly reiterated biblical message that no city or institution can give men and women a permanent home. Community is a living experience, both divine gift and human achievement, which each generation has to rediscover and express in ways and forms which are meaningful for its time. What has been of value in the past can be a rich resource, but can never suffice for the present and the future.

Throughout history there have been occasions when institutions, both secular and sacred, have become intolerably anachronistic or oppressive. Time and again the divine response to these situations has been to take the apparently small, weak and foolish efforts of men and women in order to begin once more the process of rebuilding community. At the heart of many of the most creative communal changes in Christian history has lain the small group, gathered, inspired and guided by the light and power of the Spirit. 'Is this the mystery of creation?' asks Loren Halvorson. 'Are the problems that overwhelm us by their size, complexity, and remoteness actually as accessible to us as understanding and responding to our closest neighbour? Has God's strategy all along been the small scale? The leaven? The "least of these"? The "two or three"? The mustard seed?'[1].

As the point of departure for beginning again, for liberation and for the rebuilding of community, the answer must be an unequivocal 'Yes'. The small group holds within it the essence of those qualities of community life needed to meet the crises of our age. The human group (I shall henceforth take its small scale for granted) is that form of association in which individuals can most readily experience what it is to be, and to be known, as whole persons. The human group, above all other human aggregates, holds together people's deep need for significance and for solidarity. Herein each one of us has a name, each is valued for what he or she is, each has *significance* as a person. Herein each can find a deep sense of companionship and belonging; it is where *solidarity* is often at its strongest. The group can strengthen *autonomy* by providing diverse situations in which we learn the meaning of mature and altruistic choice. It can encourage *ecumenicity* by providing a whole range of opportunities for widening first-hand experience and broadening solidarity. *The human group is a God-given means of experiencing, discovering and learning about the essence of community.*

The group can be a sign of contradiction and a means of radical change. Its potential adaptability means that it can move from an old world into a new, as many frontier families have done. Groups on the move, the symbol as well as the reality of 'the journey', have frequently been pointers to a change of gear in human history.

The group, too, is 'powerful' despite its apparent vulnerability and insignificance. Within it, as within the atom, lies the potential 'to move mountains'. In its ability to nurture the seeds of community and foster the growth of strong communal roots lies a strength out of all proportion to its size.

Nonetheless, we have to remind ourselves that the group can be a force for evil as well as good. This is why autonomy and ecumenicity must take pride of place over significance and solidarity. The group can be the microcosm of that quality of koinonia our world so urgently needs. But where its energies turn inwards and its pre-occupations become narcissistic it can be the very antithesis of community.

The group has immense potential to nurture and free men and women to be fully human, in all the relationships of life, yet only insofar as nurture and freedom spring from the love of God. It is no wonder, therefore, that the emergence of small communities of faith at times of crisis in human history have so often brought light out of darkness and hope out of despair. It is such 'basic Christian groups' (as I shall call them*) which today offer the means of liberating a church in captivity and of achieving a communal breakthrough for church and world alike.

---

*I use the word 'group' because I wish to emphasise the breadth and diversity of present day gatherings of Christians and not pre-suppose their form, life style or ecclesiology, as is sometimes the case when 'community' is used as a collective noun. Where I use the term 'communities of faith' this refers to the Christian beliefs and commitment of basic groups and not to any particular ecclesiological or sociological form. A fuller definition of basic Christian groups appears in Chapter VI.

2. A glimpse at past re-formations

The history of 're-formations' (a term I use primarily in a sociological sense, though it has far-reaching theological implications) has frequently been of major changes in church and society initiated by basic groups, communities of faith, blazing a trail through the unknown until others have caught the vision and taken up the challenge.

The Old Testament is the story of a small tribe being brought out of captivity to an oppressive and alien culture in order to find and follow God in the desert, eventually enter into a promised land and create a new society. It is about the disobedience of a tribe which themselves succumbed to false gods and corrupt institutions, and about their reduction in exile to a suffering yet 'righteous remnant' which was again to take up the commission to be God's chosen people.

When Christ was born into that same nation it was once more at the mercy of constricting institutions, and of religious leaders who could perceive the hand of the Lord only in closed traditions and forms past. With his small band of followers Christ challenged their perception of God and their code of values, proclaiming the kingdom to be at hand. The group of twelve were the forerunners of momentous change. The church they established was for many years composed of small communities of faith, meeting wherever secrecy and safety permitted, linked by itinerant preachers and pastors sufficiently mobile to keep hope dynamically alive[2].

New groups of Christians again appeared when the Desert Fathers, and the monastic 'tribes' which gathered around them, took their own journey into the wilderness. Benedict of Nursia gave clarity and realism to this search with his wise and practical rule of life a couple of centuries later.

About the same time it was the small monastic communities of the Celtic Church which were keeping the flame of Christian faith alight on the north-western edge of the empire as the Pax Romana fell apart and pagan invaders landed in Britain from across the North Sea. From their base in Ireland, via Iona, came bands of missionary monks to convert the Picts of Scotland and the Angles of northern England, as well as bringing the riches of learning and art which they had guarded over long years of isolation.

Many times thereafter the church had to be reminded of what the corporate quality of Christian discipleship should be like, be that through the reforms of Cluny after a century of monastic decay[3], or through the foundation of Citeaux, followed closely by Clairvaux, for the pursuit of a more devout and simple life.

In the early thirteenth century small bands of friars introduced a different concept of community, not as a life of holiness and prayer to be lived in seclusion, but as a corporate apostolate to be exercised through humble service out in the world, as well as through the preaching and teaching of the gospel. The Franciscans and Dominicans formed communities of faith that were constantly on the move, both demonstrating and declaring the meaning of being Christian for their day.

The Reformation saw an explosion of small Christian groups, this time affirming people's right to find, worship and serve God in their own way, and above all challenging an inhibiting clericalism. Despite many aberrations and eccentricities[4], new dimensions of autonomy, if not so immediately of ecumenicity, were explored, and ecclesiastical structures brought under searching scrutiny. In the Jesuits the Roman Church itself gave birth to a post-reformation community which, despite ardent opposition, began to forge new models of mission across the world[5].

Seventeenth century England witnessed the emergence of many small communities of faith, Baptists, Independents and Quakers amongst others, giving rise to 'Non-conformity', in itself a re-formation of the life of the church of lasting consequence. When the Church of England lost its zeal and impetus, the Methodist revival drew on the energy of the small Christian group, or 'class meeting' as Methodists called it, as the foundation-stone for its work of evangelism and nurture.

The nineteenth century brought fresh life to apostolic religious communities, with Roman Catholics active on the continent, and the new Anglican orders being founded in England for service and mission amongst non-believers at home and overseas. At the end of the century, first the Salvation Army and then the Pentecostal Movement promoted revival through small Spirit-filled bands of Christians, many taking their inspiration from the Acts of the Apostles.

3. The re-formation process

These re-formations in the history of the church had different communal emphases. Some were more about autonomy, the individual's search for fulfilment and significance. Others were more about ecumenicity, a desire to widen people's understanding of solidarity, so that they saw their neighbour as brother or sister not enemy. All these re-formations were creatures of their time; they addressed themselves to the crises of their own age. But all made some major communal breakthrough and all relied for that purpose on the basic Christian group.

These re-formations shared similar features relating to their origins and development, important to note if we are later to assess the significance of similar movements of renewal in modern times. First and foremost, they were born out of *protest* and often rebellion against a church which appeared to be distorting or subverting the fulness of the

Christian message. Those involved sought to challenge what they saw as ecclesiastical captivity, and attempted to set out an alternative way of salvation. This occurred almost as soon as the Constantinian Settlement seemed to have decided the religious issue in favour of the Christian faith. As Lesslie Newbigin puts it: 'When the whole of society . . . is baptised and the Church is the spiritual arm of the establishment, the critical role of the Church devolves upon separate bodies — the monks, the radical sectarian groups, the million and one movements on the fringes of the Church'[6].

The reaction of church, and often state, to protest and rebellion was inevitably hostile. Protesters were either ostracised, or accused of heresy and persecuted. Thus the second stage of the re-formation process was usually one of *withdrawal* and *dispersal* — into the ghetto, the desert or the wilderness. At this stage the drive towards autonomy dominated the scene. Re-formers were forced into what Harvey Cox has called 'the fertile interstices'[7] between the ruling institutions of the day, or else onto their margins. Here for a time the protesters were compelled to become a people homeless and on the move. Many were still unsure whether they or the system were under judgement, and thus sought reassurance that they were not alone in their dissatisfaction with church and society.

The third stage of the re-formation process was one of *'networking'*, the establishment of links and continuing communication between dispersed groups facilitating the sharing of experiences, ideas and resources. Prominent at this stage were itinerant leaders who moved from group to group supporting, guiding and passing on news of what was happening across the whole network. The main problem for re-formation movements was networking in a way which enabled each group to retain its own distinctive identity, whilst remaining open to wider contacts and sharing. Networking meant that the pendulum was swinging away from the search for autonomy towards the need for a greater degree of ecumenicity.

Networking was closely associated with a fourth stage of the process, an attempt by re-formers to *clarify the message* they were seeking to communicate to church or society. It was a time of self-examination and reflection which helped them to perceive their calling with greater lucidity and to formulate their concerns with greater precision. Groups and networks at this point sometimes entered into a form of covenanting in order to give expression to and strengthen the bonds between them.

The nature of networking and clarifying the message determined whether protesters were going to opt to remain on the margins of church and society and accept the status of a sectarian fringe, or whether they were committed to challenge the ecclesiastical system in an active and direct way. If the latter option were chosen, and with it the possibility of a genuine re-formation, then the task of *re-entry* and *re-engagement* became the crucial fifth stage of the process. At this juncture protesters were often seen to be fulfilling a prophetic role, proclaiming as a body[8] a new understanding of salvation for their own historical and cultural situation. This prophetic role was given expression in various ways. Some groups looked to individual leaders or founders to speak on their behalf. But many more sought to declare their message through corporate example, as a living sign of the kingdom[9], offering new communal models of spirituality and prayer, of witness and mission, of compassion and caring, of making peace, and of justice for the poor[10].

The effectiveness of re-entry and re-engagement has depended on historical and cultural contingencies. But certain features have been prominent. The relevance of the protesters' message to the church and society of their time, their ability to further not only the cause of autonomy by withdrawal, but that of ecumenicity by networking, and a prophetic message which has been linked to a realistic alternative, have been particularly important. The results of effective re-entry and re-engagement have also depended a great deal on time and place. They have varied from a modest renewal of church life to a major re-ordering of church and society, as at the Reformation itself.

In time, however, a stage of *assimilation* is reached. The contribution of re-forming groups is gradually taken into the system, the former lose their originality and vigour, and institutional rigidity again becomes normative. The re-formation process must then begin all over again, only this time it is to be hoped a little further along the way towards the kingdom then where it began before.

4. Basic Christian groups in the post-war world

'The renewal of the Church will certainly come from a new type of monasticism, which has in common with the old only the uncompromising nature of a life lived according to the Sermon on the Mount as a disciple of Christ. I believe it is high time for men to band together to do this',[11] wrote Dietrich Bonhoeffer. Over recent decades, and in many countries around the world, that process has begun. The emergence of basic Christian groups is already regarded as of outstanding importance by a number of informed writers. Loren Halvorson comments: 'Both subjective and objective data have led me to the conclusion that the critical matrix for faith and form, piety and politics, church and society, is the basic human community'[12]. Johann Baptist Metz writes: 'The second Reformation is the true "Reformation from below", what we might call the "grass-roots Reformation"'[13]. Karl Rahner states: 'The church of the future will be one built from below by

basic communities as a result of free initiative and association'[14].
Rosemary Haughton believes that: 'The "new" little churches and "pre-churches" are the spiritual future of the world'[15].

The emergence of a modern basic Christian group movement first became evident in the 'fifties in Latin America. The reasons were historical and political as well as ecclesiastical. Chief amongst these were (secular) the increase in population and its concentration in urban areas, the growth of secularisation itself, endemic poverty and deprivation, and the rise of a militant nationalism; and (ecclesiastical) the decline in the number of Roman Catholic priests, the slow growth of a more educated Catholic lower class, and a new desire to relate faith to the whole of daily life. These features of Latin American society produced the birth and proliferation of thousands of basic Christian groups (in 1975 it was estimated that 40,000 existed in Brazil alone[16]) to a considerable extent characterised by the changes I have outlined in Chapter II as necessary for a communal breakthrough. In the 'Pro Mundi Vita' Bulletin of 1976, their key characteristics are described as follows:

'In the communities there is evident growth in the capacity for autonomy . . . an aversion to any sort of dualism between life and faith, a feeling for the church's universality. With their anxiety to keep structures to a minimum goes a firm trust in the Spirit . . . a conviction that liberation comes through community . . . They are noted for their pluralism in matters of self-expression, their sense of responsibility and participation . . . an insistence on having leaders who have emerged from the community itself . . . the recognition given to the equality of women, shared financial responsibility, and diversification of groups depending on the type of local community . . .'[17].

In Latin America these groups took the title of 'basic ecclesial communities'[18], and were very much defined in terms of Roman Catholic ecclesiology and theology because that was their pedigree. Though this model of basic Christian group has been much written about and has at times been assumed to be normative, it should be remembered that it is by no means the only, or necessarily the most relevant, model for western society.*

In the years during and immediately following Vatican Two, basic ecclesial communities spread like wildfire, not only throughout Brazil, but in Bolivia, Chile, Colombia, the Dominican Republic, Equador, El Salvador, Honduras, Nicaragua, Panama and Paraguay. Indeed, the growth of these new communities made it necessary for the Latin American Roman hierarchy radically to re-think its relationship to them.

---

*A chart setting out features distinguishing basic ecclesial communities in Latin America from basic Christian groups in the United Kingdom is included in the Appendix at the end of this book.

In 1968 the bishops of the entire continent met at Medellin, in part to respond to what was happening[19]. The Medellin Conference gave recognition and support to basic groups in twenty-three different paragraphs of its published documents. From then on this new form of koinonia was given further impetus through training programmes across the whole of Latin America. In 1975 a first congress of representatives of basic communities in Brazil was held at Vitoria.

There have been several attempts already to define the raison d'être of basic groups, not only in Latin America, but in other countries around the world. A useful typology is provided by Kate Pravera who distinguishes three forces which can bring them into being: '(a) Efforts towards parish revitalisation (organised from above); (b) Efforts based on discontent with the institutional church (organised from below, or from outside the institution); (c) Efforts centred on a collective experience of oppression'[20].

In the Latin American situation the first and third of these types of basic group converged. Rosemary Ruether believes that by and large the Roman bishops viewed the communities as sub-groups of the parish. However, in the popular mind they were also seen as cells critical of too hierarchical a conception of church, as well as of political oppression[21]. In the 'seventies the South American situation began to reveal what became typical elsewhere, a conflict between local leaders with a socio-political left-wing stance and conservative bishops (evident at the American Bishops' Conference at Puebla, Mexico, in 1979) wishing to stress the church-centred character of basic groups and their allegiance to their "legitimate pastors"[22].

Nonetheless, the growth of basic ecclesial communities in Latin America has continued apace, often stimulated and given impetus by priests, nuns and theologians as well as numerous bishops. Out of their experience has been born the so-called theology of liberation, and the use of the action/reflection/action method of relating faith and life based on open use of the bible. This method of 'doing theology' in a situation of oppression has been seminal for many other parts of the world. It is an important example of the renewal of community producing its own theology.

Basic ecclesial communities in Latin America are a Catholic phenomenon and much influenced by the life and structure of that church and its relation to South American society. Basic groups have developed in that continent in particular because there is a strong religious sub-culture in which they can take root. Add to this the size of parishes, the shortage of priests and the desperate need for community in a situation of economic crisis and political oppression, and their appearance becomes not only understandable but almost inevitable.

One achievement of the Roman Church in Latin America is that it has possessed the wisdom and the ability to keep basic groups earthed. Though the latter have often been actively engaged in ecclesiastical or political renewal, unlike some Protestant (Pentecostal) congregations on that continent, they have not become encapsulated by an other-wordly theology or taken off into a one-sided eschatological spirituality.

Basic groups have appeared in other countries where a strong Catholic Church exists. Most akin to Latin America is perhaps the Philippines where, in the face of harsh political persecution, basic groups have begun to proliferate, especially since the mid-'seventies[23].

The continent of Africa presents a different picture with the pastoral revitalisation of the parish being the major concern. The African Catholic bishops at their synod in 1974 resolutely opted for 'implanting the church not by adaption but by incarnation or localisation'[24]. This meant in effect an attempt to create basic groups 'from above', as an instrument of ecclesiastical policy, in such places as Malawi, Tanzania, Burundi, Zaire, the Congo, the Cameroons and Mozambique[25]. The emphasis was on the Christian nurture of a population facing steady communal disintegration, much more than on political protest. Once again, however, the tension between autonomy and control emerged. In Tanzania, for example, the Roman hierarchy had considerable difficulty in relating to President Nyerere's policy of creating ujamaa villages, and the corresponding ecclesiological re-formation that implied.

The growth of basic Christian communities characterised by the changes described in Chapter II has been much less in evidence in Asia where the church, as a small minority, has little reason to challenge traditional ecclesiastical structures. The same is true for Eastern Europe where anything other than assemblies for worship are rapidly nipped in the bud (though the Christian peace movement is presenting both secular and church authorities, Orthodox and Protestant, with a challenge to normative Christian gatherings).

In the United States an immense diversity of basic groups exists, characterised not only by their variety of interests and concerns but by the number of different denominations with which they are associated. The small group phenomenon has always been a feature of American life, but it was given further momentum by popular movements in the 'sixties. One of the latter was the human potential movement which sought to offer participants the opportunity for personal growth and development over against the limitations of the nuclear family, on the one hand, and the impersonal structures of a cosmopolitan society, on the other. Impetus also came from movements of political protest focusing, at home, on the issue of civil rights and, abroad, on that of the Vietnam war. These were fuelled by the 'youthquake'[26] of San Francisco's 'summer of love' in 1967 and of the student riots of 1968. Out of these and other forces for change, personal and political, emerged a whole spate of groups, from growth centres to communes, from house churches to pressure groups, in all of which Christians were actively involved. The appearance of a plethora of small Christian groups and communities continued throughout the 'seventies presenting a much more diverse and complex phenomenon from that evident in Latin America or Africa.

In Canada the basic group movement has been influenced by factors comparable to those operative in the United States. Great variety also exists there. Tony Clarke, a Canadian, distinguishes (within the Catholic Church) between what he calls 'popular Christian communities' (similar to Kate Pravera's third category and the so-called Latin American 'iglesia popular', or church of the poor), and 'progressive Christian communities' (which are included within Pravera's second category, but are also engaged in activities to support the disadvantaged and oppressed)[27]. Popular Christian communities in Canada include factory workers, 'the welfare poor' and 'poor immigrants'; progressive Christian communities are exemplified by those concerned with industrial exploitation, 'regional disparities' and the repression of human rights.

In western Europe, the Latin American type of basic Christian group (in Europe often known as 'grassroots' communities) appears to be most evident in Italy, again a dominantly Catholic country. Here the influence of Vatican Two and the protests of 1968-1969 were important catalysts. Their effect was to produce a movement of protest during the 'seventies, at times strongly influenced by left-wing politics. However, Ed Grace maintains that basic Christian communities are 'a loyal (if radical) opposition . . . (rather than) . . . the harbingers of a breakaway or sectarian movement'[28]. They have been designated by Ed Grace as 'working class, middle class or third world groups', the last kind being found in the poorer southern parts of the country[29]. Most are Catholic, a few Protestant. Basic Italian groups held their first national congress in 1971; 2500 participants were involved representing 279 basic groups. But 'despite the refusal of the communities to cut themselves off from the institutional church and despite their growth and vigour, there are only a few dioceses in Italy in which they operate with the blessing or even the tolerance of their bishops.'[30] The Italian Ecumenical Centre was set up in Rome in March 1982 to gather and disseminate information about, and to act as an advocate for basic groups and, amongst other things, publishes 'The Bridge' newsletter (available in English[31]).

One other west European country (other than the United Kingdom) wherein basic groups have made a significant impact has been Holland. Here, though Catholic influence is strong, a more varied denominational picture has emerged. Following the upheavals of the late 'sixties, a number of basic groups arose combining a desire for church renewal with

81

a critical attitude towards society[32]. Documentation and a newsletter circulated between these groups, and in 1975 a 'working group' was formed to help service this 'grassroots movement'. In 1978, a congress was convened in Amsterdam, 41 groups being represented on the new 'council' which resulted. The Dutch groups acknowledge their middle class nature (in the Canadian sense they are mainly 'progressive'), but are very committed to the radical re-formation of church and society — though they have no 'wish to be a new church institution'[33]. Their focus is a biblically based critique of western capitalist society and a concern to identify with the poor and the marginalised world wide.

Basic Christian groups and communities have also appeared in France (notably Taizé), Spain, Switzerland and West Germany, but in these countries are not such a prominent feature of church life. Nonetheless, an informal network of basic groups from many Western European countries is developing, kept in touch through such initiatives as the 'All-European Basic Christian Community Bulletin', edited by the Italian Isolatto Community[34], and through the first 'European Grassroots Congress' held in the Netherlands in May 1983 and convened by the Dutch movement. This was attended by over 1,500 people, 350 being guests from thirteen other countries, namely Belgium, the G.D.R., West Germany, Britain, France, Italy, Switzerland, Austria, Portugal, Spain, Poland, Hungary and a tiny invited contingent from Nicaragua[35]. It was an event which gave expression to great hope as well as some confusion, sentiments not uncharacteristic of any movement of re-formation seeking to discover a corporate identity and common purpose in the name of koinonia.

V: HOUSE GROUPS AND HOUSE CHURCHES

If basic Christian groups in the past, and increasingly around the world today, have been pioneers of renewal and re-formation, what of the United Kingdom? Is there anything here which can encourage us to believe that the creation of a new quality of Christian community so much needed in an age of crisis is occurring? If the attempts to achieve a communal breakthrough outlined in Chapter III have proved limited or abortive, is there evidence of the emergence of basic Christian groups in our country which can offer real hope to a captive church?

There is in fact no shortage of Christian groups on the British scene. The situation in terms of multiplicity and diversity is far more akin to that of the U.S.A. than Latin America. Britain, as a nation of many denominations and with a tradition of energetic voluntary endeavour, has always provided the opportunity for a plethora of groups of all kinds to contribute to the life of society. Is there, therefore, anything of *particular* significance happening here?

In examining this question it is essential to keep in mind the earlier comments made on the quality of a new community (and the related changes) required if the church is effectively to address itself to the crises of our time. The existence of just any, or just many, Christian groups proves little. What matters is not quantity, but quality; not those who claim to be prophetic, but those who are, in deed as well as word, actually being so.

To examine the situation in the United Kingdom it is useful to recall the three categories suggested by Kate Pravera[1]: first, groups concerned mainly with the revitalisation of the parish; secondly, groups arising as a result of discontent with the institutional church; and thirdly, groups arising in response to oppression and marginalisation. It will be helpful to divide her second category into two: those groups I shall call 'reactionary' and which adopt a more inward and backward looking form of protest, and those I shall call 'progressive' and which look outward and forward as a result of their discontent. *It is progressive basic Christian groups (and networks) which I believe hold the key to the liberation of the church and to a new re-formation in the United Kingdom.* It is, therefore, with these that most of the rest of this book is concerned.

However, in this chapter I deal with two other kinds of group, the house group and the house church, which despite their many limitations have hitherto stolen much of the limelight.

This involves
a value judgement
before argument.

83

1. Parish house groups

a. Background

Concern for parish (here the word is taken to include the neighbourhood ministry of *all* denominations) renewal in Britain in recent years became evident almost immediately after the last war. One of its earliest manifestations was the launching of 'Parish and People', a movement within the Anglican Church, in 1949[2]. This was committed to liturgical reform focused around a family-centred and lively morning communion, with a parish breakfast to follow. The original aim 'was to establish the people's Eucharist as the central act of Anglican worship, in which the congregation would play an active part in the ritual, the singing and even the prayers'[3]. This desire to move towards a more participatory style of parish life was given further impetus in the 'fifties by the establishing of diocesan conference (as opposed to simply retreat) centres, particularly concerned with promoting parish life conferences. At the same time there was a rapid growth of interest in 'Christian Stewardship' campaigns (by 1961, 36 out of 43 Anglican dioceses had stewardship advisers[4]). All these intitiatives sprang from an era when people believed that the parish still held the key to the revival of English church life.

It was this hope which gave the title ('The Parish Comes Alive') to the first post-war book to appear about house groups, published in 1957 and written by a Leeds parish priest, Ernest Southcott[5]. Though Southcott laid a good deal of emphasis on the eucharist taking place within the home, and spoke about 'house churches', there was never the slightest intention that the latter should separate themselves from the church as such — I shall thus reserve the term 'house church' for a more recent breakaway movement to be described later in this chapter.

The participation of the Free Churches in stewardship campaigns and their desire to get to grips with the post-war world led them also to look at the home based cell with great interest. Thus by the early 'sixties the house group was in vogue in many denominations as seemingly *the* answer to enliven moribund congregations.

In 1967, the British Council of Churches managed to involve nearly 80,000 people in its house group course on 'The People Next Door'[6]. It is less well known that two years before that the Anglicans' Lent house group programme entitled 'No Small Change' was estimated to have involved some 200,000 participants[7]. As a young Methodist minister in Sheffield at that time I remember putting a good deal of effort into establishing and maintaining a number of house groups for my regular churchgoers, as well as for those who rarely called themselves Christians.

Meanwhile the Roman Catholic Church witnessed some steps towards parish renewal, such as the establishment (in Italy) in 1952 of 'Movement for a Better World'[8], an organisation which appeared on the British scene a few years later committed to the re-creation of community as an experience earthed in the parish. Likewise Focolare (1943)* and the British section of the Christian Life Movement (1962) were concerned with the establishment of vital Christian cells at the parish level. But these few swallows did not make a summer and, by and large, interest in the house group as a means of parish renewal remained low on the Catholic scene.

The end of the 'sixties saw a pronounced change of gear in approaches to parish revitalisation. The neighbourhood house group, with which I am here concerned, faded somewhat into the background, its role as a regenerator of koinonia being taken over by three other movements. One was the charismatic movement which I have already discussed. Another, and in part derived from the charismatic movement, was the 'house church movement'. The third was the basic (and progressive) Christian group movement itself. Nonetheless, the parish house group has lived on throughout the 'seventies and early 'eighties. Its main value has been as a means of Christian fellowship and informal education, often with a strongly biblical focus, though here and there groups have been more directly involved in Christian action or caring.

Not until the National Pastoral Congress in 1980 did Roman Catholics advocate publicly and forcefully the development of small groups to facilitate parish renewal. One sector report stated: 'We overwhelmingly recommend that parishes should become a communion of Christian communities incorporating small, neighbourhood, area and special interest groups . . . Such small groups, house groups and neighbourhood groups, for prayer, study of scripture, and celebration of the eucharist . . must be seen as necessary for the building up of the parish community'[9].

In fact most Roman Catholics who seek to apply the Latin American model of 'basic ecclesial communities' to the West do so mainly in terms of the house group with a predominantly pastoral function[10] rooted in the parish. This is as true of Edward Schillebeeckx looking at the future of Christian renewal in general[11], as of Adrian Smith (of the Movement for a Better World) talking of the United Kingdom in particular. Though the 'basic ecclesial communities' proposed by the latter would be 'made up of some 40 or 50 adults', it is still 'in homes like its model in the Early Church' that their members would usually meet[12].

b. Breakthrough?

The parish house group's major achievement has undoubtedly been in a significant move from meeting to encounter. Though this has varied in

*The date in brackets refers to the year in which the group was founded.

extent according to local circumstances, the house group has demonstrated that it is possible for Christians to strengthen their fellowship and gain support and enlightenment in a way impossible through congregational gatherings as such. It has enabled Christians and, as in my own circuit in Sheffield, those on the edge of the church, to meet in a personal and intimate manner to share their concerns and ideas. The parish house group has been a pioneer in calling attention to the nurturing community needed as an essential 'base camp' if Christians are to be able to grow in the faith and address themselves to the demands of a world in crisis.

Nevertheless, the parish house group has major limitations. Any attempted move to genuine encounter has been restricted by most members of house groups taking the ecclesiastical status quo for granted and thus remaining captive to its defects. Congregationalism has still loomed large, and meant that local church meetings are always assumed to take precedence over house groups, the latter being regarded as optional extras for the faithful few. Few groups meet very frequently, and many are restricted to certain periods of the Christian calendar, such as Advent or Lent. Denominationalism, too, has contained membership and resulted in few house groups being ecumenical in composition, those that are usually being promoted by local councils of churches mainly for study purposes, and often lasting only for a short time.

But it is clericalism which has been the main impediment. It is just possible that there might have been a major breakthrough in the renewal of Christian faith and practice in the United Kingdom if the church had a clerical profession committed to house groups as a tool for communal re-formation, as well as skilled enough to service and sustain them through the ups and downs of their growth and development. Neither is the case. Though in principle house groups are often advertised as being organised and led by the people and for the people, the ordained minister rarely takes a back seat. Most groups (from those in Leeds in the 'fifties onwards) have been initiated, arranged and monitored by clergy. Some of the latter are prepared to play the role of enablers. But many more are either dominant and directive, or simply unco-operative, because they fear that such groups might become too independent and removed from the local congregation.

At the same time bishops, chairmen and moderators rarely regard house groups with much enthusiasm, either because they seem so much a parish concern, or, in some cases, because they relate uneasily to the normal pattern of clerical control. For example, the Roman bishops, in 'The Easter People' acknowledge that small groups 'are a source of strength to the parish as a whole', but immediately follow this statement with the proviso that they 'must not be exclusive in themselves nor be seen as an alternative to parish commitment'[13], adding that, 'small groups . . . *properly established* (my italics) in parish or deanery, can meet

The role of lay initiative here seems to be acknowledged 86

a variety of needs'[14]. The long arm of the clerical law is not far away.

Even where clergy are keen to revitalise the parish, many lack the skills to help sustain such groups. Few appreciate the principles of group dynamics, many are unaware of both the strengths and weaknesses of small groups, and most are unable to act as facilitators in the group process. As many lay people are likewise inexperienced, skilled leadership for house groups is thus at a premium and disappointments and failures frequent.

The parish house group has one other important limitation. It is tied to community of place, often to the exclusion of community of concern. Because the group remains so closely associated with the neighbourhood, it fails to encompass the more specific needs of laity whose daily life is lived out on a larger stage. This is not to deny that the parish remains central for some. It is simply to reiterate that we live in a cosmopolitan, pluralistic and highly mobile society, and thus the agenda of groups which rely heavily on the proximity of residence of their members as the vital link is inevitably limited by that fact.

For these reasons the parish house group has usually found the changes required to pioneer a radically new dimension and expression of community beyond its horizon or its means.

2. The house church movement

Kate Pravera's second category of Christian groups includes those which have arisen as a result of discontent with the institutional church. It is this attitude of 'over againstness', ranging from dissatisfaction to complete disillusionment, which separates off a large number of new groups from the parish house groups just discussed. One such stream of disaffected Christians to emerge in recent years in Britain has come to be known as the 'house church movement'.

a. Background

The origins of the house church movement can be traced back as far as the 'fifties when the South Chard church was built[15], though the movement did not really begin to gain momentum until the mid-'seventies. It was estimated in 1980 by Walter Hollenweger (using material supplied by Joyce Thurman) that the movement then had well over 50,000 members and several hundred churches. In the 'Methodist Recorder' in February 1984, David Pawson went much further claiming that the house church movement now encompasses up to 100,000 fellowship groups.

The house church movement is so named because it began within a variety of house groups meeting independently in different parts of

England. These house churches (for they were seen as much more than parish house groups or sub-groups of local congregations) 'grew out of the conviction that the existing church system, be it Anglican or Free Church, is unlikely to be renewed . . . The traditional liturgies are a hindrance for a proper teaching ministry and the evangelical sermon does not fulfil its function as a missionary tool. Therefore, other tools have to be shaped'[16].

Though the house church movement has numerous sections or strands (those involved would probably reject the term 'movement'), many of its leaders were originally linked with Pentecostal, Baptist or Brethren churches, and later with the burgeoning charismatic movement. The latter in particular has inspired and influenced the house church movement, which sets a great deal of store by the exercise of 'the spiritual gifts' of speaking with tongues, prophecy and healing. All the branches of the house church movement began when lay leaders broke away from what they saw as moribund local congregations (Pentecostal and Free Church, as well as Anglican) and set up their own small group of dedicated followers which in time spawned more groups.

As the house church movement has grown and proliferated, its distinctive home base has shifted and gatherings have had to be transferred to larger premises, such as halls and churches hired or bought from the mainstream denominations. The movement maintains its life 'through common conferences and a common stock of hymns and choruses, through a chain of highly successful shops, common behaviour patterns, and visits between churches . . . This hardly visible subterranean network explains why suddenly and apparently spontaneously house churches are mushrooming in different parts of the country and following the same pattern'[17].

Nonethless, the house church movement can be divided into three or four main 'streams', all operating more or less independently. Most prolific are the Harvestime Churches based in Bradford and with fellowships as far away as Brighton, 'its annual Dales Bible Week attracting 10,000 people . . . and the Downs Bible Week in the south now attracting about 3,000'[18]. It is perhaps of at least symbolic significance that the Harvestime Churches have purchased the former Anglican diocesan headquarters in Bradford as the centre for their administration. Two other streams are the Chard group, based on the earliest house church in Somerset, and Pastor North's groups which originally took hold in Liverpool. A fourth stream known as the 'Fullness group' is based mainly in the Surrey area.

The house church movement gains a good deal of its energy from the intimate relationships between its members. The latter have come mainly from the mainstream denominations, young married couples being especially prominent, though of late there is some evidence of non-churchgoers also being attracted. Services are usually charismatic in nature, though there is resistance to the traditional gospel type evangelical sermon (their own sermons are seen as more of a teaching tool and often very long). Pastoral care of the members is highly organised and very thorough. Ministry beyond the local church is extending steadily, not least through publications (each section of the movement has its own magazine) and extensive sales of tapes of music and sermons. The Harvestime Churches support 'missionaries abroad, travelling ministers, and the poor at home and abroad'[19].

Here and there entire congregations have adopted the house church model. Derek Williams writes:

'In Basingstoke, for example, a former Baptist church, again under the influence of charismatic renewal, radically altered its structures from the mid-1960s onwards. It replaced democratic committee leadership with the exercise of authority by elders, coupled with a development in "body ministry" with each member contributing his talents to the church. In 15 years it has grown sixfold, and now has 25 house groups, with the emphasis on building relationships, six congregations (the whole church meets only monthly for worship), four salaried staff and a leadership team of 15 men'[20].

By and large, however, the house church movement has expanded through small groups withdrawing from traditional congregations, and then dividing and proliferating before again coming together into larger associations to pursue their own distinctive forms of worship and ministry.

b. Breakthrough?

Does the house church movement provide evidence that a real communal breakthrough has been achieved and that a quality of Christian life able to bring hope and purpose to an age in crisis is beginning to reveal itself on the British scene?

There is no doubt that the movement is meeting a deep need amongst Christians extremely dissatisfied with the captivity of the institutional church. Nor is it surprising that such a need focuses on the search for the establishment of forms of Christian fellowship able to facilitate a strong sense of significance and solidarity in place of an often lifeless congregationalism. Of the changes necessary to promote a new experience of Christian community the house church movement, like the parish house group, has concentrated on that from meeting to encounter. The small, personal, intense house church gathering has been its corner stone.

However, there is some evidence that this phase of the life of the movement is nearly over and regrouping in larger congregations is rapidly taking place. Though, as in the Basingstoke church described, there is still

89

retention of house groups, this change of character will have many repercussions. One is undoubtedly a slow move towards a more traditional form of Christian fellowship, for larger congregations are more about meeting than encounter. It thus seems likely that the movement, as Derek Williams predicts, could gradually 'become as institutionalised as everyone else'[21].

Nor does the house church movement seem to offer much scope for the growth of personal autonomy, though a kind of new found 'spiritual' significance there certainly may be. The house churches and their congregations tend to be homogeneous in character, giving limited scope for the open-ended exploration and development of diverse views and ministries. The apostolate of the laity is defined in traditional church based terms, albeit with more emphasis on personal evangelism.

Strong pressure towards conformity of belief (relatively orthodox) and practice (charismatic) is evident in the house church movement, probably essential if the various streams are to retain their identity. Complementing this is an emphasis on discipline and the authority of church leaders. Here it seems that the movement is in danger of substituting an autocracy of lay (often officially male only) control for that of clerical leadership. Tom Smail comments: 'The majority (of house churches), especially the Bradford-Harvestime Circuit, are as sectarian, leader-dominated and legalistic as any denomination, but refuse to admit it'[22]. The founders of the various sections of the movement certainly seem to have become something akin to 'cult heroes', if only amongst their own followers, and the influence of associated American personalities is already marked.

The pastoral organisation of the house churches also gives some cause for concern. What at times is a genuine need for a caring fellowship can give way to 'a desire for a dependent-relationship, for directive forms of spiritual oversight'[23]. So-called 'pastoring' in the house church movement is 'arguably tighter and closer in its extension than any form of oversight in the church of God ought to be'[24]. As such the thirst for a deep experience of Christian community can become inward looking and even narcissistic.

The house church movement is, with its charismatic parent, certainly a passionate movement. The move from secularism to faith is perhaps its greatest attraction in an age of doubt. There is often an enthusiastic and joyous 'Yes' to God, with music, singing and dancing to celebrate his living reality. 'Many of us have been salvaged from the scrap heap of dry, legalistic evangelicalism, in which we would have surely perished', writes Dave Tomlinson[25]. The movement has been 'born of the Spirit' and as such reflects the vivaciousness of that stream of Christian spirituality. But faith in our time must also lead to a positive affirmation of secularisation (though not secularism) and to an incarnational expression of belief. The house church movement seems more adept in engaging with a secular society in order to sell its own model of the church, and maintain its funds, than to help build a new community alongside those of all convictions.

The movement is not ecumenical. It has frequently split local churches asunder and turned its back on the major denominations as a source of truth and wisdom[26]. Though there are signs that 'the leaders of many streams' are themselves seeking closer relationships, two joint gatherings having taken place in 1983[27], the sections of the movement remain distinct. Despite the fact that its leaders refute the suggestion, in practice small new 'denominations' are coming into being with their own independent and self-supporting organisations.

The movement is here and there engaged in a genuine caring ministry for those not of its immediate circle, and service and funds are offered to the poor at home and overseas. But there is little evidence that the house church movement, either within its own life or in its orientation to mission, pays much attention to the economic, social or political divisions which hinder the emergence of one world.

'I think we must express some doubts about the authenticity of the house church movement', writes a leading figure in the mainstream of charismatic renewal[28]. This would seem to be true as far as the search for the *fulness* of Christian community is concerned. At heart the movement is not reformatory so much as reactionary. It is more inward and backward than outward and forward looking. As far as offering real hope to a *world* in crisis it appears something of a diversion. That many sincere Christian people are eager to invest so much energy, time and money in the house church movement is, however, but another sign of the captivity of the church at large.

VI: THE BASIC CHRISTIAN COMMUNITY MOVEMENT — BACKGROUND

It is interesting how in matters religious the sensational and the sectarian attract more attention than ordinary Christians unpretentiously doing extraordinary things. Thus the charismatic movement and the house church movement have hit the headlines, whilst behind the scenes the beginnings of a quiet revolution of a very different kind have gone almost unnoticed.

'The basic Christian community movement' is the name I give to a vital catalyst in the process of re-formation occurring within the United Kingdom, quite distinct from anything mentioned in the last chapter. It is *basic** in the sense that it is composed of small, face-to-face (primary), and usually informal, groups which offer intimate, supportive and dynamic forms of human relationships. Basic groups can be 'local' or 'cosmopolitan' in membership. They are diverse and ubiquitous. They are found around the fringe, within and *at all levels* of institutional life. But they lie at the heart of community; without their continuing, birth, growth and multiplication, society would eventually collapse. Basic groups affirm the fundamental importance of the human scale for a world in crisis.

The movement is *Christian*. Those engaged in it believe that, though there will be many fellow travellers, the quality of koinonia needed to save humanity can only be adequately received, known and made manifest through communities of faith openly acknowledging the Lordship of Christ.

The movement is a *community* movement: community here referring as before to a quality of life, and not to a form of human collective as such.

---

*It will be clear that my definition of 'basic' does not refer only to groups made up of the poor or disadvantaged, as in some other contexts. *In this book I define 'basic' in essentially sociological not economic terms.* This definition of basic Christian groups may not seem to accord sufficiently with the nature of 'basic ecclesial communities' as witnessed in Latin America. My contention is that working definitions must be fashioned out of the historical, economic, and political situation in which each culture finds itself. Definitions are neither 'right' nor 'wrong', but either 'more' or 'less' useful. However, to help highlight some of the actual differences between Latin American and British communities/ groups a chart of distinguishing features is included in the Appendix at the end of this book.

This quality of life is, for example, manifest amongst those who live together and hold their possessions in common, like the religious orders. But it is also demonstrated by many other groups which meet regularly to share experiences, ideas and resources. The movement is about Christians searching for autonomy and ecumenicity, dedicated to the cause of free people for one world. It is a quest for personal maturity in Christ, and for fulfilment through purposeful engagement in a variety of apostolic work to further his kingdom. The search is also an ecumenical one, expressed pre-eminently through the solidarity of basic Christian groups working in partnership in order that koinonia may be given a new depth and breadth, and an appropriate form for our age.

Finally, the emergence of basic Christian groups in the United Kingdom is a *movement* because it is a corporate process of liberation and re-formation involving protest against, withdrawal from and re-entry into a society and world in crisis. It is a progressive movement which looks outwards and forwards, not inwards and backwards.

1. Origins

The basic Christian community movement in the United Kingdom, like a number of other similar movements around the world, was born out of the ferment of the 'sixties. Its origins were both sacred and secular.

Throughout the late 'forties and 'fifties there had been some indication of the upheavals and changes to come, but getting the British economy moving again, launching the welfare state and a massive housing programme in old cities and new towns, absorbed nearly all the energy available.

For the church, too, the task of reconstruction dominated the scene. Most effort and finance went into renovating bomb-damaged buildings or putting up new ones. The aim was 'business as before', though there were a few experiments in new forms of mission (such as the so-called 'commando campaigns') and signs that greater interest in the role of the laity was gathering momentum (for example, the establishment of the William Temple College as a kind of English lay academy in 1949). The growth of house groups, as noted above, was an attempt to revitalise, though not to revolutionise, traditional ecclesiastical structures.

The 'sixties hit British society like an earthquake. Two developments since the war were of major importance in enabling such an upheaval to occur. One was rapidly growing affluence which, though not as impressive in this country as elsewhere, created hitherto undreamt of wealth, and thus choice, in all spheres of life. The other was the expansion of rapid and highly efficient communications, by road and air, or through the media, above all by means of radio and television.

The catalyst in this new and volatile situation was the post-war

93

generation. Kenneth Leech states that the 'sixties saw Britain rocked by a veritable 'Youthquake'[1]. Not only were young people better off and better educated than ever before, but they pioneered the first youth culture this country has known. Aided and abetted, and often exploited, by the media, they were able to mount a challenge to the values and norms of their parents and grandparents on a scale never previously experienced. New styles in music and dress, and brash forms of anti-establishment behaviour, were the forerunners of a more serious and sustained revolt to come towards the end of the decade.

Slowly an awareness grew that things were not only being changed, but changed radically. A new spirit of expectation and excitement was in the air, making the immediate post-war scheme of things seem dull and unadventurous. The 'secular city' of the 'sixties, as Harvey Cox described it[2], came to be seen as a place of immense possibilities. Outgrowing a sense of dependence on 'the powers that be', the 'sixties' generation became convinced that the world could and should be redesigned, and rebuilt from its very foundations. The institutions of society were placed under searching scrutiny, and judged to be dehumanising and destructive. *How Very English!*

Within the church this wind of change was felt in numerous ways. It permeated the world of ideas, symbolised by the publication of John Robinson's best-seller 'Honest to God' in 1963[3], followed two years later by his sequel, 'The New Reformation?'[4]. Other theologians became deeply engrossed with 'the secular meaning of the Gospel' and went so far as to consider 'the death of God' as a legitimate Christian affirmation. That all this was having a disturbing effect on some of the hitherto most trusted Christian thinkers was demonstrated by the sudden departure of Father Charles Davis from the Roman Catholic Church on 'A Question of Conscience'[5].

Of far-reaching significance was the new mood within a number of major ecclesiastical assemblies. The Second Vatican Council, meeting from 1962 to 1965, heralded a change of orientation in Roman Catholic thinking, the major repercussions of which are still to be realised. The World Council of Churches meeting at New Delhi in 1961, but particularly at Uppsala in 1968, reflected the spirit of a church now disquietingly aware of the crises of the modern world. At the same time, on the British scene, plans for unity were going on apace and a mood of considerable optimism existed, typified by the call of the first British Conference on Faith and Order in 1964 for the main Protestant denominations to covenant for union, to take place no later than Easter Day 1980. The conversations going on between the Anglican and Methodist Churches, and other ecumenical initiatives, have already been mentioned in Chapter III.

The importance of lay life and witness was also a matter moving rapidly up the agenda of most churches. Decrees of the Second Vatican Council called for 'The People of God' to be made a central concept in understanding the church[6], and took the phrase 'active participation'[7] as 'the watchword of the revised liturgy'[8]. In 1967 the Roman Catholic Church in England and Wales established its first ever Laity Commission. In 1969 the Church of England set up synodical government with a House of Laity, giving lay people more of a voice in church affairs. In 1966 the Methodist Church had created a Board of Lay Training with a full-time director.

The 'sixties was also a decade of liturgical change and experiment. The innovations given impetus by the 'Parish and People' movement were followed in 1966 by the publication of Series 2, a first step in revising the Book of Common Prayer. For Roman Catholics the mass moved into the vernacular, the altar moved into the centre of the church (as in the new Metropolitan Cathedral of Liverpool), and giving communion in both kinds became commonplace. All denominations were influenced by a spate of modern hymns and music, with Sydney Carter's work much in vogue. Methodism's 'Hymns and Songs', including contributions from many modern writers, was published in 1969.

All these factors created a climate of high expectations and considerable excitement. Visions had been seen and hopes raised. Commitment to a new world and a new church was not only evident in aspiration but in practice. Yet what brought the basic Christian community movement into being was not just a vision of a liberated and re-formed church. It was a painful encounter of the forces of radical change with those of continuing institutional impersonality and rigidity.

In the late 'sixties the euphoria of the idealistic young experienced the chill winds of human violence and oppressive vested interest head on. This was most dramatically witnessed in the United States as protest groups took up the cause of civil rights and sought an end to war in Vietnam. In Europe, the French students' revolts of 1968 set the scene for similar, though more restrained, sit-ins and marches on British soil. But the tenacity and practicality of the ideals of the young were soon put to the test. The outcome was not long in doubt as by force or attrition their world of freedom, fraternity, fun and flowers was demolished. The 'sixties, as Bernard Levin described them, proved to be 'The Pendulum Years'[9].

Progressive Christians in the United Kingdom had run into similar resistance from the church. The plans to train 'a lively laity'[10] were proving far more difficult to implement than predicted. The grouping of clergy in teams had created some initial interest but was already running into the problems mentioned in an earlier chapter. Renewal of the liturgy was well underway, but did not seem to be accompanied by any major re-formation of church life and order. There were signs, with 'Humanae Vitae', that the more conservative forces in the Vatican were again

95

surfacing. And by the end of the decade the scheme for union between the Anglican and Methodist Churches had all but foundered on the rock of clerical intransigence. *Was it only that?*

Those striving for change, both secular and sacred, responded in two main ways. The majority settled for an uninspiring compromise and were gradually absorbed back into mainstream institutional affairs, a situation which in part at least accounts for the sense of disillusionment and even fatalism permeating many facets of life in the 'seventies in Britain. However, a notable minority launched out on their own, pioneering new communal initiatives within the only space left to them, the institutional margins. Here a multitude of small groups committed to a more truly human society attempted to perpetuate the spirit of the 'sixties: 'small is beautiful' became the catch-phrase summing up the mood of the moment. *or is it elitism?*

These groups were extremely diverse. Prominent were communes which grew rapidly in number after 1970 (though a steep decline set in during the mid-'seventies)[11]. Other groups attempted to humanise institutional life by establishing small scale initiatives in the fields of work (e.g. co-operatives), education (e.g. free schools), welfare provision (e.g. self-support groups for bereaved parents) and health (e.g. self-help groups for those suffering from depression, hypertension, etc.). At the same time, a large number of groups committed to justice and social reform arose, expressing the needs of such as the single parent and the mentally handicapped, the rights of women, or of homosexuals[12].

2. Protest, withdrawal and dispersal

The response by progressive Christians to the closing of ecclesiastical ranks was similar to that of the radical minority on the secular scene. Some basic Christian groups had been set up in the early and mid-'sixties but, towards the end of the decade, the number of new ventures rose dramatically and remained so throughout the 'seventies.

This upsurge was indicative of the first stage of the re-formation process outlined in Chapter IV, that of *protest*. Keith Kimber writing about this time believed that, '(These groups are) communities of protest (whose) spirit cannot be destroyed by oppression, but rather is that which will give life to all new movements which emerge in the hope of transforming our future'[13]. The protest was initially ill-defined but one theme was central, the urgent need, as Parker Palmer writes, 'To assert and act upon the hope, however naïve, that community can be found, because only by acting "as if" can we create a future fit for human habitation'[14].

Basic Christian groups came into being to bear witness to the dehumanisation of life in every sphere, sacred and secular alike. Their protest was sometimes outspoken and vigorous, though more often quiet and tenacious. In all cases it was characterised by a determination not to compromise their vision of free people for one world.

The alternative way to a new depth and breadth of community offered by basic Christian groups met ignorance and apathy, rather than hostility and rejection as such. But the consequences were the same. With very limited resources and lack of support most groups had to *withdraw* from the mainstream of church life and find a place and means of pioneering their understanding of Christian community wherever they could, in the interstices or on the margins. True to their calling they cut loose 'to do their own thing', in the jargon of the early 'seventies.

Initially it was the emergence of groups of Christians living together and sharing a common life style which was most in evidence. But the establishment of basic groups as signs of contradiction and hope developed in an increasingly pluralistic way throughout the 'seventies and early 'eighties.

I have already written at length about these groups in my book 'Basic Communities' published in 1977, but to meet the need for some kind of overview I mention below a *selection* of ventures typical of the time[15]. I list these under headings relating to their particular spheres of interest and activity in order to give some framework to the great diversity of new initiatives taking place throughout this period.*

a. Basic Christian groups in action

i. Living together

One of the first Christian initiatives of this period concerned with communal living was the **Blackheath Commune** set up in 1969 on an ecumenical basis in a large house in south-east London. Its aim was to be a centre for political activity seen in terms of community development at neighbourhood level. There were eight more or less permanent residents. This commune lasted some two years. By 1970 the first of the **Ashram community houses** had opened in Rochdale. The Ashram houses were originally Methodist, consisting of some half dozen residents living together 'to discover new implications of the way of Jesus for today's world, especially through contemporary Christian life-style'. Later Ashram houses were opened in Sheffield, Middlesborough, Kennington (London) and Sparkbrook (Birmingham) and became more ecumenical. Next on the scene was another community house established in **Copenhagen Street** (1970), London (near Kings Cross), with a Catholic membership. Its purpose was to work out 'the meaning of being Christian in the local community, including political activity as well as community involvement'.

* The name of each basic Christian group, religious order and network appears in **bold type** the *first* time it is mentioned in any section of this chapter. Dates in brackets refer to the year in which the group or network was established.

These residential or 'intentional' community houses were the forerunners of many more to come during the 'seventies — for example, in south Birmingham (**Shenley House** — 1972), in the East End of London (**Some Friends**, a Quaker group — 1974), in County Down, Northern Ireland (the **Christian Renewal Centre,** Rostrevor — 1974), in Nottingham (the **Beeston Community House** — 1975), and in Manchester (the **Firs Christian Community** — 1979). By the early 'eighties well over fifty Christian community houses existed across the country[16].

The community house (the term 'commune' soon faded from the scene) embraced a varied pattern of corporate life. At the one end of the spectrum was the small family-oriented venture where those involved were married couples with children, largely intent on a closer sharing of domestic responsibilities and giving one another mutual support. Such was the case with the **Albert Road Community** (Aston, Birmingham — 1974) and with **Victoria Road**, Barnsley (1980), in both of which two families (including children) formed the core group. More open-ended ventures were projects like that in **West Pilton** (Edinburgh — 1978), where a number of families occupied six adjacent flats in one council house block. This form of communal living involved a high proportion of clergy families, not least in the inner city areas where they linked up for mutual support, as well as to be able to exercise a more effective ministry.

At the other end of the spectrum was a more ambitious form of communal living, sometimes on a much larger scale and situated in more rural settings. There had been similar endeavours in pre-war decades, but in our period the pioneers were the communities at **Post Green** and **Little Gidding.** The former began in 1968, and grew out of a healing and teaching ministry based on the estate of Sir Thomas and Lady Faith Lees in Dorset. From 1973, shared family households were established in various properties on the estate drawing members not only from this country but from the United States, overall numbers soon reaching about seventy. In 1976 a close link was established between Post Green and another similar venture, the **Community of Celebration**, which had arrived from the States in 1972 and, after stays in Coventry and Berkshire, had eventually settled at Millport on the Isle of Cumbrae. Both Post Green and the Community of Celebration were based on shared households committed to a teaching ministry for the renewal of parish life. Of late their work has increasingly related to justice and peace concerns, typified by the radical content of Post Green's magazine 'Grass-roots'.

Little Gidding began as a venture in community living in 1972. It aimed 'to hold in balance the need to be with God in prayer, and man's struggle to survive without exploitation of the earth or his fellows'. The community has over the years consisted of married couples and single people, with some fifteen people in residence. The community lives on a Huntingdonshire farm, the home of the renowned Nicholas Ferrar and his extended family community in the mid-seventeenth century. A simple life style, corporate prayer and worship, work on the farm and beyond, and hospitality, have been the main features of life at Little Gidding. In 1981 it took the name of the 'The Community of Christ the Sower' and became increasingly involved in local church and parish life.

The attempt to establish large residential communities in the United Kingdom has not been a prominent feature of the basic Christian community movement here. The **New Creation Community** (of over 300 people) began at Bugbrooke, Northamptonshire, in 1973, and acquired numerous community houses, a farm, and shops in local towns, but its ethos and structure have more in common with that of the house church movement than most of the basic Christian groups described in this section. In 1978 a project was launched to establish a series of linked Christian family households on a new development at **Bowthorpe** in Norfolk. This is slowly gaining ground after some initial sebacks. All in all, however, the availability of land, the cost, and perhaps lack of inclination amongst British people to resurrect the old village form of community life, has meant the predominance of small rather than large scale residential ventures.

The move to communal living was initially the most conspicuous way in which the basic Christian community movement gained momentum. Since then the emphasis has shifted from living together as a valid end in itself, to living together in order to exercise a more effective apostolate in areas of often deep need. Such was the case with **Cornerstone** (1982), a small community of Catholics and Protestants situated between the Falls and Shankill in Belfast and acting as an open house to all who wish to use it irrespective of religious or political affiliation. Likewise **Columban Houses** (1982) — now over twenty in number — are being established by the Iona Community in deprived urban areas of Scotland (as well as one or two in England) not only to develop new forms of corporate life style, but to serve their neighbourhood and the cause of justice and peace in any way possible.

ii. Family and friends

Many frustrated by the lack of support and stimulation offered by the local church to those struggling to deepen and express their Christian faith in a secularistic society had neither the resources nor the opportunity to live together. Nonetheless, their need of kindred spirits and their determination to live as Christians meant that a way of meeting, sharing and praying together had to be found. The result was the emergence of progressive Christian groups seeking an experience of koinonia rarely available within the neighbourhood congregation as such.

These groups were very different from those associated with the house church movement in that they were open, extremely outward looking and often ecumenical in composition. Leadership was shared. Their aim was not so much renewal of 'the church', but how to enable one another to grow up as mature and socially concerned Christians in a secular, pluralistic and cosmopolitan world.

The groups that formed were of two main types. First, were those whose members were drawn together by a shared experience of family life. Typical of this kind of group were the **Grail Family Circles** (1950s)[17], each circle consisting of some half dozen, usually Roman Catholic, couples who came together in one anothers' homes about once a month. These circles exist across the country and vary greatly in their nature and style of meeting. Some have remained merely an opportunity for casual meeting and discussion, others have become 'a "community of families"'[18]. (They have now dropped the word 'circle' and speak of themselves as part of the Grail Family Network.) Akin to the latter are more ecumenical and less well defined '**family clusters**'[19] (from the mid-1970s) consisting of a number of families (including children) who 'play together, eat together, laugh together and argue together'[20], but still live in separate households. Other groups have sprung up to support Christian one-parent families, such as **Noah's Ark** (1979)[21] in the Roman Catholic diocese of Arundel and Brighton.

Secondly, groups for nurture and discussion have emerged which are not based explicitly on the family as a unit. For a decade or more, my wife and I were members of two such ecumenical Christian groups, first in London and then in Birmingham, meeting monthly for a meal and conversation about Christian faith and practice. Of a similar kind have been groups organised on a national scale such as the 'companies' of the **Servants of Christ the King**, local groups associated with the **Life Style** movement (1972), and the **Christian Life Communities** (revived as a world wide Roman Catholic movement in 1963). These last are now especially active on the Irish scene where 'by prayerful pondering of the gospel, the sharing of insights and a growing closeness to Jesus Christ' members seek to 'see the needs of the world in the light of their increased understanding of God's will'. There are, too, groups which form for a much shorter time, such as the **Shalom** meetings (1980) which last only for a weekend, and have been pioneered by the Ammerdown Study Centre near Bath. Shalom gatherings offer, amongst other things, 'a small community . . . a point of deep peace . . . a sharing . . . a celebration . . . and a chance to pursue your own personal pilgrimage with a group engaged in that task'.

iii. Spirituality and prayer

High on the agenda of many basic Christian groups has been the search for a new depth of spirituality and prayer able to meet the needs of a world in crisis. A large majority of basic groups has in one way or another engaged in this search; a number, however, have been explicitly set up for this purpose.

100

Although it occurred well before this period, the appearance of the **Servants of Christ the King** (1943) must be mentioned here as they were in many ways the forerunners of what was to come. The Servants of Christ the King aimed 'to offer to God small communities bound together in a common fellowship'; to wait in quietness on his guidance, and then to carry his leading into practice. By the 'seventies there were some sixty 'companies' (local cells) in Britain and twenty-five overseas. The founding of the **Farncombe Community** (1964) in Godalming, Surrey, was another significant development. This consisted of five women, previously involved in missionary work in South India, living together according to a simple rule in order to pray regularly for Christian unity.

By the 'seventies, the search for a new dimension of spirituality (as opposed to liturgical renewal, which had been going on within the mainstream churches for some years) was taking many different forms, with basic Christian groups playing a prominent part. One expression of this concern, already dealt with, was that of charismatic renewal. This was not only evident on the parish scene and in mass rallies, but to some extent within basic Christian groups too. Both **Post Green** and the **Community of Celebration** sprang out of this tradition. The **Barnabas Fellowship** (1971), which staffed a conference centre in Dorset, the **Centre for Christian Renewal** (1974) in Rostrevor, Northern Ireland, and the Roman Catholic **Katimavik movement** (which commenced in England in 1973) were also charismatic in ethos.

The search for a spirituality more linked with its classical exponents was pursued by the **Julian Meetings** (named after Julian of Norwich), established in 1973. These groups sought to discover a richer spirituality for modern man and woman (within the great mystical traditions), and themselves practised contemplative prayer. The **Jubilee Group** (1974), more of a network of individuals, gave a different emphasis to a similar quest by encouraging its members to explore the integration of the Anglo-Catholic tradition of contemplative prayer with a radical political stance on current issues.

Meanwhile a number of initiatives were taken to offer those interested the time to experience and explore the spiritual life through short residential gatherings. Amongst these was **H.O.P.E.** (Houses of Prayer Ecumenical), a residential experience, ranging from a weekend to several weeks in length, enabling Christians to look afresh at spirituality within a communal setting. Another was **Centre Space** (1976) which ran courses 'to open up the creative interaction between spirituality on the one hand and psychology, arts and crafts, ecology, politics, worship and culture on the other'. A further innovation (which originated in the United States) has been '**at home retreats**', which provide mutual spiritual help for small groups, mainly of Roman Catholics, meeting weekly in their own homes over a six month period[22].

Basic Christian groups, perhaps rather later in the day than might have been expected, also began to enter the field of inter-faith dialogue. In 1971, the Presbyterian Church of Ireland and the (now) United Reformed Church helped to establish **Seva Sadan**, a community house in Sparkhill, Birmingham, staffed by two or three workers (one from India), to offer pastoral support, language teaching and general advice to neighbouring Gujerati families. In 1974 **Wolverhampton** became one of the first places to form an **inter-faith group** 'to promote understanding, meaningful dialogue, and personal friendship between people of different faiths'. Since then other Christian groups and communities have become involved in this field, if only as part of a broader apostolate[23].

iv. The arts

A number of basic Christian groups laid great store by an apostolate specifically related to new developments in music, song, dance and drama. In 1971 the **Arts Centre Group** was established in London to act as a meeting point and forum for those professionally involved in that field, as well as 'to develop an intelligent understanding of the validity of art as an expression of a Christian's enjoyment of God'. Two years later, in Edinburgh, the **Netherbow** was set up as an arts centre for Christians seeking to utilise their artistic skills to enrich the life and witness of the church in Scotland.

Other ventures have continued to spring up all around the country, locally based but often with an itinerant ministry. A number of groups influenced by the charismatic movement have here been prominent, not least the **Fisherfolk** (associated with the Community of Celebration and Post Green) and the **Riding Lights Trust** (1977), linked to St. Cuthbert's Church Centre in York. Other theatre groups include the **Footprints Theatre Trust** in Nottingham (1978) and the **Cornerstone Theatre Company** in Newcastle-upon-Tyne (1980). The **New Room Community of Creative Art** in Bristol (1980) enables people to work together 'in paint, clay, music, movement or writing' in order to realise 'their enormous potential for learning, growth and sheer enjoyment'. The **Carnhedryn Arts Trust** (1970) began by running a very successful arts festival in St. David's, South Wales, each summer and has been seeking to extend its work in order 'to help disturbed, under-privileged and mentally handicapped young people' through residential courses held there.

v. The environment and economics

Many associated with the basic Christian community movement have been concerned about environmental issues. The early 'seventies saw interest in ecology and conservation markedly increase, alongside growing public awareness of acute hunger and poverty in the Third World. Basic Christian groups appearing at that time responded in several different ways.

Residential communities set up in more rural parts nearly always sought to preserve the environment and had a commitment to the conservation of land and usually to animal welfare. The approach varied from modest small-holdings to advanced farming methods, as at **Commonwork** (1976) in Kent. The latter was a fully commercial enterprise, based on Christian principles, engaged in dairy farming and brick making, with a residential centre attached concerned with co-operative education. The co-operative principle was also prominent in a number of urban based projects, as with the **Daily Bread Co-operative** in Northampton which marketed muesli and packed wholefood products. This venture had its origins in a small house fellowship established in the 'seventies. It began trading operations in 1980 with a dozen or so members, some of whom were enabled to use the experience to help their recovery from mental breakdown.

Working mainly through small local groups, the **Life Style** movement was also active in this field[24]. Its members committed themselves to 'live more simply that all of us may simply live', and throughout the country undertook not only to exercise care in their own spending and consumption, but to engage in social and political action for a more just distribution of the earth's resources. Also concerned to press home this message was the staff of **Dartmouth House,** a diocesan conference centre in south-east London, who from 1974 to 1976 (when stopped by the diocesan authorities[25]) had worked as a close-knit team pursuing a life style for themselves and their guests which attempted to bring home the needs of a world facing ecological and economic crisis.

In 1981 the **Christian Ecology Group** was formed aiming 'to spread ecological insights among Christian people and churches, and to spread Christian insights into the consciousness of the Green Movement'. Their concern was not to set up another campaigning organisation, but 'to act as an informal network, supporting those already involved in campaigning on particular issues and persuading others to become involved'.

vi. Education

The basic Christian community movement was involved in new educational initiatives in a variety of ways. Throughout the 'seventies a number of groups formed to carry forward a ministry pioneered by the laity centres of previous decades. One important feature was a closely knit staff intent on working very much as a team. **Dartmouth House** has been mentioned above. **Lindley Lodge** (1970), a centre for training young employees in industry, was staffed by a small Christian community, also a feature of **Ammerdown** (1973) and **Hengrave Hall** (1974). The **William Temple Foundation** in Manchester, established in 1971, was supervised by a competent and energetic team and initiated numerous educational and community work research projects, of late especially concerned with the role of Christians in a high technology society facing large-scale unemployment.

A number of basic groups concentrated on imaginative training programmes mainly for clergy and religious, though lay people did attend the courses. The training was usually experiential in emphasis, as in the case of the **Urban Ministry Project,** originating in Morden (1968), which aimed to link field work and theological reflection. The **Urban Theology Unit** (1969), which started in Rochdale and then moved to Sheffield, was intent on bringing theology and sociology together in a new way in order to throw light on the mission of the church especially in the inner city. In 1976 **AVEC** (a service agency for church and community work) was set up as an itinerant training project based on non-directive principles of community development.

Basic groups also found a place at the centre of new educational ventures for young people. Examples were **Ringsfield Hall** in Suffolk (1972), where a small core community hosted parties from schools and churches coming for study and recreation; the **Ranch** Christian community in North Wales (1975) which provided residential facilties and adventure courses for young people; and from 1980 onwards, **Wick Court,** near Bath, whose residential centre was staffed by two families living as a small community.

At the beginning of the 'eighties basic Christian groups were becoming increasingly involved in the rapidly developing field of community education[26]. A pioneering project, the **Community Education Centre** in south-east London, had, from 1972 until its closure in 1976, run an imaginative urban based programme for teachers in training. But in more recent years the spectrum has widened, ranging from basic groups working alongside the black population in Brixton, to those involved with unemployed young people in Glasgow. A major programme of community education has been undertaken by the **Corrymeela Community** at its Ballycastle centre in Northern Ireland. These initiatives were complemented by many small groups of Christians involved in educational projects for those wishing to acquire or share skills and experience, especially the unemployed, based on schools or church premises.

In 1980 **Dunamis** was established as an educational foundation based on St. James's, Piccadilly, 'to explore issues of personal, national and international security in the modern age', as well as of 'the widening gap between rich North and poor South'. It is playing a valuable role, through lectures, workshops and discussions, often involving prominent figures in public life, in promoting serious reflection on the crises of our time.

vii. Welfare

As such a large number of basic Christian groups was engaged in the field of social welfare it is only possible here to mention a few examples of the work undertaken.

Basic Christian groups developing new forms of caring ministry appeared rather earlier on the post-war scene than in other spheres, in large part due to a realisation that the welfare state had not brought all the benefits originally hoped for. In the late 'fifties and 'sixties, basic Christian groups were notably active in providing residential facilities for the elderly, with the rehabilitation of those who had been in prison or suffered some form of breakdown, as well as with setting up accommodation for the single homeless, all within the context of a caring community. Such social needs have continued to produce basic Christian groups in more recent years.

The late 'sixties saw new initiatives in counselling. The **Westminster Pastoral Foundation,** aiming to 'provide a counselling service and training programme on the basis of a continuing link between the religious outlook and the behavioural sciences', began operations in London in 1970. A year later the **Dympna Centre** opened its doors to offer 'care to the carers', especially clergy and those from the religious orders. Throughout the 'seventies other counselling services were set up, usually staffed by a close-knit team of helpers — such as the **Southwark Pastoral Counselling Scheme** (1971), **Crossline** (1974) in Plymouth, and **Compass** (1978) in Liverpool.

Concern to offer the handicapped a deeper quality of community life also came to the fore, prominent here being the activities of **l'Arche,** founded in France in 1964 to provide a caring home-life as well as work opportunities for mentally handicapped adults. The first l'Arche house in Britain was opened in Kent in 1974. In 1975 **Faith and Light** was established to promote the formation of local groups of (mainly Roman Catholic) mentally handicapped people and their families, with the purpose of facilitating the former's integration into the life of wider society. Concern for the physically handicapped was also evident, as seen for example in the close association of the **Family Tree Community** (1978) in London with a nearby day centre for handicapped children.

From 1963 the **Simon Community** had pioneered work with the single homeless, a ministry which expanded steadily during that decade. The London based **St. Mungo Community Trust** began in 1968. In 1970, the **Cyrenians,** an offshoot of the Simon Community, was set up and established many homes throughout the country. More localised involvement in this field was typified by **Link-Up** (1976), a project for single homeless men and women based in Nuneaton. The latter was also concerned with homeless young people, many in acute personal need. Also aimed at this age group was **Centrepoint** (1969), providing temporary accommodation and assistance to young people at risk in London's West End and the **Boot Night Shelter** (1971), fulfilling a similar function in central Birmingham.

viii. Health

Basic Christian groups have been deeply involved in enriching the ministry of healing. The establishment of 'homes of healing' dates back to the early years of this century, but their work as basic Christian communities has continued. In 1982 another such home **Spennithorne Hall,** North Yorkshire, was opened by the North of England Christian Healing Trust (1981). Meanwhile, the Christian hospice movement was again coming very much to the fore, concerned to nurse the terminally ill within a caring Christian community. In this period **St. Christopher's Hospice** (1967) in the south-east London led the way. Others soon followed, such as **St. Mary's Hospice** (1979) in Birmingham and **Helen House** (1982), for seriously ill children, in Oxford.

Working more within an institutional framework was the **Ombersley Road** general medical practice (1977) in Birmingham, which based its activities on Christian principles relating to community health[27]. The **William Temple Foundation** actively supported the Ombersley Road experiment and promoted other similar endeavours related to the health service during this period.

ix. Justice and peace

Basic Christian groups were actively engaged during these years in the fields of justice, reconciliation and peacemaking. Groups involved in this area had arisen from time to time over earlier decades, notably the **Iona Community** in Scotland (1938), **Christian Action** (1946) and the British section of **Pax Christi** established in the early 'sixties. However, other groups soon began to proliferate.

Of immediate concern were the troubles in Northern Ireland. The **Corrymeela Community** began with the purchase of its Ballycastle house on the Northern Antrim coast in 1965, since then the setting for innumerable gatherings of those from all sides involved in the conflict. Throughout this period many other projects for reconciliation in Northern Ireland were launched, such as **PACE** (Protestant and Catholic Encounter) in 1969 with its aim of promoting 'harmony and good will between religious and political communities in Northern Ireland'. Also noteworthy was the **Centre for Christian Renewal** in Rostrevor, set up for fellowship, prayer and study, and **All Children Together** (1974), a group working for an integrated school system. In recent years one or two ecumenical community houses have been established, the latest being the **Columbanus Community** (1983) in Belfast committed to the work of reconciliation. In 1981 the **Fellowship of Good Counsel** came into being in Derry, dedicated to prayer for peace, and with an especial interest in prisoners and ex-prisoners, and their families. Over the last year or two the number of small (non-residential) **Christian Life Communities,** mainly involving Roman Catholics, but ecumenical in concern, has grown considerably.

Across the wider field of justice and peace, basic groups have emerged with very varied aims. **Christian Concern for Southern Africa** began in 1972 and **End Loans to South Africa** in 1974. **Keston College** was established in 1974 to undertake research and study into the 'state of religious communities in the Soviet Union and Eastern Europe'. The **Pilgrims of St. Francis** (originally set up to foster reconciliation in Europe in 1927) held their first international pilgrimage in Britain in 1976.

The end of the 'seventies saw a dramatic resurgence of the peace movement in Britain, a phenomenon the repercussions of which are likely to be of continuing significance for church and society alike. The impetus for disarmament gave a new lease of life to numerous older Christian groups and associations concerned with the peace issue, including the various **Quaker peace projects,** the **Fellowship of Reconciliation** (1914) and **Pax Christi**. In 1981 **Christian C.N.D.** came into being, as a distinct section with the wider C.N.D. movement, typifying involvement in peacemaking as a matter rapidly rising to the top of the agenda of many basic Christian groups. Scores of Christian peace groups have emerged over the last year or two operating at both national and local level, **Clergy Against Nuclear Arms** (1982), the **Leeds Inter-Church Peace Group** (1982) and the **Peace Chariot** in Sheffield (1982)[28], to name but a few.

b. The religious orders

It will be realised from what has already been written that the origins and apostolates of basic Christian groups have a good deal in common with those of the religious orders. That the latter are committed to poverty, chastity and obedience for life, and live and work in accordance with a formal rule, should not obscure the many similarities between them and basic Christian groups of more recent times. Both are founded on a search for, and active expression of, the richest possible forms of Christian community. They involve deep personal commitment over a considerable period. They are motivated by particular apostolates (be they 'contemplative' — in the field of prayer and spirituality — or 'active' — in the affairs of church and society). They are highly mobile, in the sense that their ministry often takes them well beyond the confines of a single parish.

In fact the similarities between the religious orders and basic groups have grown even greater since the Second Vatican Council. Ruth Duckworth, at that time Provincial of the Daughters of the Holy Ghost, writing in 'Community' in 1978, drew attention to some of the ways the Council had influenced her own order:

'In 1966 the Second Vatican Council issued a decree entitled "On the Renewal and Adaptation to Modern Times of the Religious Life". It asked all religious to examine their way of life, using as their touchstone (a) the gospel values which it should express, (b) the original inspiration which had led to the founding of each particular congregation and (c) the needs of the modern world. The decree made it clear that each congregation or order was responsible for its own renewal, and that it was to be the work, not only of a few leading spirits, but of every member.'[29]

She then went on to list some changes in her own congregation — from 'stately mansion' to smaller houses indistinguishable from their neighbours; 'from large institutions owned, run and largely staffed by ourselves, to sisters working side-by-side with and on the same conditions as other people in state hospitals, state schools, the social services, offices, shops and factories'; 'from the long sweeping habit and the medieval coiffure and wimple to a style of dress owing more to Marks and Spencers' than to our medieval ancestors, and often distinguished from that of others only by a small cross or emblem'. With these changes went more open, expressive relationships; the decline in use of the word 'superior' and the emergence of a 'sister among sisters'; rules reduced to a minimum; and as imaginative a form of liturgical prayer as possible[30].

Other orders too were engaged in this disturbing re-appraisal of their purpose, structure and relationships. For many there was a time of considerable stress before a new form of community life gradually emerged, but Ruth Duckworth spoke for most when she concluded: 'We know that we are more alive, more vitally united, freer to love and to serve'[31].

This book cannot cover the many exciting new expressions of Christian community being pioneered by the religious orders as such[32]. What is focused on here are the ways in which the latter and basic groups are beginning to link up and to share their life and work.

Already a number of orders have houses where religious and lay people share something of a common life. At the Roman Catholic **Benedictine abbey at Worth,** a small lay community for young people was established in 1971. Residents stay for about a year to experience community as lived out according to that form of spirituality. In 1974 a mixed religious and lay community was set up at Hengrave Hall, Suffolk, in large part to maintain and staff the work of the conference centre there. The Catholic **Sisters of the Assumption** and lay members have overall numbered about fifteen. Likewise lay people have shared urban life with religious. By the late 'seventies nine lay people were living with the Anglican brothers of the **Society of the Sacred Mission** on the outskirts of Milton Keynes. 'Bethanie' in Highgate, London, a house belonging to the Catholic **Augustinian Sisters,** has had numerous lay residents. In 1979 an ecumenical group of nine, including two Roman sisters, took upon themselves to live as a Christian community in nearby flats on the Kirkby estate in Liverpool. Such examples of a shared way of life continue to grow steadily.

In other spheres, too, lay and religious have been closely associated. **The Anchorhold,** a centre for prayer and meditation in Sussex opened in 1969 by the Anglican **Society of St. John the Evangelist,** has had a number of lay members and many lay visitors over the years. An increasing number of orders pursue a very supportive open house approach to those seeking spiritual renewal — ranging from the large convent at **Fairacres,** Oxford, belonging to the Anglican **Sisters of the Love of God,** and the London community of the **Society of St. John the Evangelist,** to the small Catholic **Benedictine community at Barn House** (1978) just outside Liverpool. In 1981 a Roman Catholic **La Retraite** sister and her social worker colleague were the first in Britain together to conduct a planned retreat held in the homes of lay people.

A number of conference centres now have at their heart a small Christian community incorporating religious and lay. **Scottish Churches House** in Dunblane, Hengrave Hall, and **Ammerdown** near Bath, the latter with a Methodist warden and a number of **Catholic Sisters of Sion** as staff, are cases in point.

Increasing co-operation between religious and lay has also been in evidence in more apostolic kinds of ministry. Two examples only are mentioned.

In 1980 religious from five Anglican communities, several Anglican priests and a number of Anglican lay people came together for what was called **'The Vauxhall Project'**[33]. This was a week long experiment in community living and parish work in inner London intended to open up 'the spiritual riches' of the monastic tradition to local residents, as well as explore how a large redundant church could be used as a resource centre for a wide area. In 1982 the **Cornerstone Community,** embracing religious and lay, established their open house in Belfast as a sign of reconciliation and hope for the nearby Catholic and Protestant residents.

c. 'The oppressed'

It is necessary to examine here one other category of basic Christian group much less in evidence on the British scene; those, as defined by Kate Pravera, whose life and activities are 'centred on a collective experience of oppression'[34]. Why Britain has not produced many basic groups of this kind is an important issue, especially as (for example in the writings of Johann Baptist Metz[35] and José Marins[36]) the more 'oppressed' basic ecclesial communities of Latin America are often looked upon as normative.

In the sense that the basic Christian community movement in Britain seeks to stand over against the domination of institutions, it is a 'marginal' phenomenon. Yet it contains few of the oppressed, the poor or disadvantaged members of our society for a number of reasons which can only be touched on briefly here.

Historically, the 'lower orders' or 'new working class' population in Britain began to disengage from active participation in the life of the church from at least the Reformation, and in particular with the coming of the Industrial Revolution. During the latter, the massive movement of population from the land to the towns and cities not only broke ancient ties with village and church alike but, with a parish system quite unable to cope, meant that links were never again to be re-forged. Furthermore, as industrialisation and urbanisation continued apace, the church was found by those misused and exploited rarely prepared to champion their cause. Thus it was not long before new secular associations (such as trades unions) committed to social and political reform began to command far more loyalty, enthusiasm and energy than religious bodies.

At the same time, those towards the lower end of the social scale who had retained their Christian allegiance but opted to join the ranks of Nonconformity, most recently the Methodists, soon began to pull clear of their humble origins. With the Protestant Ethic as their manifesto, they steadily climbed the social ladder, their fortunes becoming increasingly intertwined with those of the already existing middle class. During this century the same process has continued amongst Pentecostals, Roman Catholic Irish living in Britain and, of late, members of the black churches. At the same time Nonconformity has been increasingly prone to adopt traditional forms of ecclesiastical organisation and social practice, rather than align itself with the cause of the disadvantaged or the poor[37]. *It Never was front-ranking/poor.*

As a result of these factors, the vast majority of the working class population of Britain has retained little regular or active contact with any form of church life (unlike Latin America where Roman Catholicism remains deeply rooted within the culture of the disadvantaged). The British working class, and others now forming an 'underclass' of the unemployed, are not found in basic Christian groups simply because the Christian religion as such means far less to them than other interests or concerns — occupational, social or political. Any protest against inhuman or unjust institutions to which they may give voice expresses itself not through religious but secular groups and associations. In Britain the oppressed are little bothered about a re-formed church because history has persuaded them that it has little relevance to their lot.

But if this is true for Britain, for Northern Ireland the position is surely different. Are not present there those very ingredients — an oppressed people with a deeply religious culture — which have made basic Christian groups such a feature of the life of the poor in other parts of the world? Yet in Northern Ireland, too, those at the bottom of the social scale have not come together into anything resembling the basic ecclesial communities of Latin America. Why?

The reasons are complex but some at least can be suggested. In the first place, the poor of Northern Ireland are themselves deeply divided both religiously and politically in a way not true of the poor of most countries in South America. Thus they find themselves struggling against each other rather than those injustices of which they are all victims. Secondly, few leading Roman Catholic or Protestant churchmen are in open opposition to the British Government as such. Critical they may be of its handling of the Irish situation, but there is little here resembling the Latin American position of a more progressive hierarchy supporting downtrodden people against a dictatorial and totalitarian regime. Thirdly, the shortage of Roman Catholic priests, which in Latin America has freed lower class laity to take more control of their own lives, is not evident in Northern Ireland where clericalism consequently remains very strong. Indeed, it is possible that an upsurge of a popular and secular Republicanism could herald something of a repeat of the British experience in the nineteenth century, and separate off an increasing number of frustrated Roman Catholics from any form of church life.

The special historical and cultural features of church life in Britain and Northern Ireland have led, therefore, to the basic Christian community movement being spearheaded mainly by progressives of middle class origin. It is they who have become most acutely aware of the church's captivity to restrictive structures and closed ideologies, and it is they who have had the incentive, the resources and the opportunity to attempt a communal breakthrough. They have found little response from amongst the working class and a growing underclass to their vision and their endeavours; in Britain because the latter are largely apathetic about religious matters, in Northern Ireland because of the dominance of sectarianism and a conservative clericalism.

Nonetheless, the basic Christian community movement in the United Kingdom has encompassed disadvantaged groups of a different kind. In 1976, the **Gay Christian Movement** came into being 'to help the church re-examine its understanding of human sexuality and to work for a positive acceptance of gay relationships', as well as to enable members to 'witness to their faith in the gay community'. One or two other basic gay groups (for example amongst Quakers) have also emerged in recent years.

Feminism has also stimulated the formation of a number of basic Christian groups. In 1977, the **Roman Catholic Feminists** was set up, aiming 'to unite and support women through a network of groups . . . in order that they may bring together feminism and Roman Catholic allegiance'. In 1978 a more broadly based association of **Christian Feminists** was established 'to look at Feminist issues from a Christian standpoint and challenge sexism'. Since then, other feminist groups and a resource centre have appeared, reflecting the concerns of various networks such as **Noah's Ark,** the mainly Catholic association of groups for single parents in the diocese of Arundel and Brighton.

As yet the basic Christian community movement has hardly touched the black population as such. Many black Christian groups exist but these are almost entirely an integral part of local black congregations. Likewise, basic groups are infrequently associated with organisations of mixed race. Nonetheless, a few basic groups have been set up explicitly to work for racial justice and better race relations. In 1970 in Birmingham **All Faiths for One Race** was established to work for 'a harmonious pluralistic society' through advice work and multi-ethnic educational projects. **Seva Sadan** began in 1971, the community house staffed by a small Irish and Asian team, in order to minister to the Gujerati community in inner city Birmingham. The **Zebra Project** (1975), based in the East End of London, was founded to work for closer links between black and white Christians, the **Centre for Black and White Christian Partnership** (1977), at Selly Oak, Birmingham, was set up to provide a community based theological education mainly for black church leaders, whilst **Christians Against Racism and Fascism** (1978) had the aim of harnessing Christian resources to oppose racist and fascist organisations. In 1982 a **Multi-faith Resource Unit** was established at Selly Oak as an educational project to 'enable groups of people from different faiths to create religious and cultural programmes which promote interfaith dialogue and understanding'.

As already noted, the latest section of the population of the United Kingdom to be counted amongst the oppressed, the unemployed, have formed few basic Christian groups, largely because Christians do not figure prominently in this category. Christian projects have been mounted to assist the unemployed, but these are dominantly parish based (in part because premises are available there), inspired mainly by more progressive clergy, and almost entirely dependent on external (Manpower Services Commission) funding. However, in 1982, a group called **Church Action on Poverty** was founded specifically to mobilise a 'campaigning alliance of Christians' to improve the lot of the poor (including the unemployed).

Finally, in this context a word must be said about the religious orders. Religious have always had a very close association with the poor and oppressed. Their apostolate to these groups continues on the United Kingdom scene, for example through work amongst the homeless, the disadvantaged elderly and young people at risk. The **Little Brothers** and **Little Sisters of Jesus,** followers of Charles de Foucauld, have deliberately sought to place themselves alongside the poorer sections of the population by taking up demanding manual employment. Many religious orders, such as the **Sisters of Notre Dame,** are continuing to re-appraise their priorities and seeking ways to place their personnel and resources more fully at the service of the disadvantaged, especially in the inner city. However, to associate *with* can never be the same as to be one *of* the poor, especially if the most pertinent definition of the latter is 'those having no chance to choose for themselves'. The religious orders take a vow of poverty, yet in common with the Christian community movement as a whole their own standard of living in the West remains well above that of 'the genuine poor'. They have benefited from the privileges of affluence (for example, educationally), have freely chosen their vocation and can, in the last resort, contract out if they so wish. Thus religious communities, as with most basic Christian groups in Britain, have to be counted amongst those 'opting for', rather than 'belonging to', the poor and the oppressed. Some of the issues raised by this situation are honestly faced in the CORA Report on the 'Collaboration of Religious' when it considers the vow of poverty:

'Poverty . . . probably presents the most difficult area for discernment, both for the individual religious and the institutes themselves. How far can one go in renunciation of material goods and still be in a position to lead a fully human life and work for the betterment of the poor and the improvement of society? On the other hand, how can one seriously and honestly denounce the consumer society, the exploitation of the poor and of the resources of the world when one is oneself a beneficiary of that affluent society? According to the light we have as individuals and groups we must choose our responses to the dilemma: certainly involving our care for the poor and our action for justice, but also a judgement on our own life style which must be such that it can witness to our beliefs. One might go further and say that without some measure of the hardship and deprivation associated with Christian poverty a man may become affected by a materialist world and his spiritual understanding dulled.'[38].

3. Networking

From the late 'sixties onwards the withdrawal and dispersal of basic Christian groups in the United Kingdom maintained its momentum. Yet this would have offered little hope of liberation and a new re-formation if it had not been accompanied by *networking*. The 'new dispersion', as Loren Halvorson describes it[39], had to go hand in hand with a new means of getting together.

In Chapter IV, I stated that the process of networking followed that of withdrawal and dispersal. In reality, networking often commences almost as soon as withdrawal and dispersal begin, though it becomes more prominent as the years pass. This was as true for the basic Christian community movement of this period as for earlier re-formation movements.

The networking of the basic Christian community movement can be divided into five *phases*, all of which overlap, but each of which shows something of the changing emphasis of the current re-formation process. The *first phase* (a. below) was the forerunner in that it involved the coming together of certain denominational 'renewal groups', out of which sprang a number of initiatives with important consequences for the basic Christian community movement as a whole. The *second phase* (b. below) saw the development of networks largely intended to help promote and support Christian groups involved in outspoken protest about key social and political issues of the day. *Thirdly,* (c. below) came a phase in which groups predominantly committed to some form of communal living (commune, community house, etc.) began to meet up and exchange experiences. The *fourth phase* (d. below) saw the emergence of networks functionally aligned with major areas of institutional life (education, welfare, health, industry, etc.*), though intent on offering alternative ways of doing things. In the *latest* (but by no means the final) *phase* (e. below) of the networking process many of these networks have themselves been linking up into what might be described as an embryonic national 'network of networks'. Throughout this period the religious orders have also been strengthening their own links, as well as beginning actively to associate with the basic Christian community movement.

a. The networking of denominational renewal groups

The ferment in the church of the 'sixties witnessed the rapid growth of a number of renewal groups, each closely associated with a particular denomination, but all very much committed to the cause of Christian unity. Two such Anglican groups — **Friends of Reunion** and **Parish and People** — had in fact begun many years before, but the **Congregational Church Order Group,** the **Methodist Renewal Group** and the **Baptist Renewal Group** started in the early or mid 'sixties. In 1969 the **Catholic Renewal Group** came into being, close on the heels of 'Humanae Vitae'.

In 1968 the Methodist Renewal Group meeting in Birmingham passed a resolution which stated: 'Since we are called to one mission and have declared denominations to be not only meaningless but a hindrance, this conference encourages the officers of the various renewal groups in their efforts to work out the formation of one group comprising Christians of all bodies'[40]. The latter came into being in 1970 and was called **'One for Christian Renewal'.** It incorporated all the denominational groups mentioned above (with the exception of the Catholic Renewal Group, which nonetheless supported the Birmingham initiative). However, when church unity failed to materialise out of top level 'conversations',

---

*These major areas of institutional life, most of which have developed as a result of an increasing division of labour since the industrial revolution, I henceforth refer to as 'sectors'.

the denominational sub-groups tended to re-emerge again. Typical of this situation was the **Alliance of Radical Methodists** which was established in 1971 as an association of Methodist lay people and ministers aiming 'to support, judge and strengthen each other with a radical view of the Christian gospel'. At the same time, One for Christian Renewal took on more the character of a loose-knit inter-denominational network of individuals, at its peak serving nearly 1,000 members.

Despite its aspirations, One for Christian Renewal in many ways represented the old order. Its leadership was dominantly clerical (and until very recently, male), it did not offer any real alternative to the parish system (team ministry apart), and its denominational ties remained strong. Yet, as its progressive 'Declaration'[41] shows, it did have a vision of a re-formed church living and witnessing for a more just and human world.

One for Christian Renewal has continued ever since as a network of modest size. But its significance has been far in excess of its membership. In particular it provided the springboard and support for a number of important initiatives which helped to give the basic Christian community movement increasing momentum. Not least of these was the launching of the magazine 'Community' and the establishment of the National Centre for Christian Communities and Networks, to be described more fully below.

b. Issue-centred networks

One of the clauses in the 'Declaration' of One for Christian Renewal committed its members 'to combat poverty, racialism and oppression through social and political action'[42]. This aligned it with many emerging basic Christian groups which demonstrated a passionate concern to right the wrongs of an inhuman world, if necessary by drastic means.

Such groups gave impetus to a second phase of the networking process. This began in the late 'sixties and reflected the upsurge of radical politics, especially amongst the young, on the secular scene. Prominent here were the **Roadrunners** (a community of young Christians initially established in London), the **Blackheath Commune**, the **Ashram community houses** and the student community set up at **Wick Court** near Bristol in 1974. But these were only representative of scores of other more ad hoc Christian groups which came into being during this period in order to pursue a range of social and political concerns. By and large, these concerns remained broad-based rather than specific. They were a protest against traditional institutions and the capitalist system in general rather than focused on particular causes.

One important body which came to the fore to support basic groups and encourage networking at this time was the **Student Christian Movement** (SCM). It took on this role under considerable pressure from its younger members and often against the better judgement of its older constituents, a situation which caused much internal conflict.

Networking had initially been promoted by the Roadrunners who for six years produced the 'Catonsville Roadrunner', a magazine brashly outspoken in its attack on both church and society. Certain members of the Roadrunners, as well as of the Blackheath Commune, were prominent in the Student Christian Movement. And Wick Court, to which some of them moved in 1974, became for five years the headquarters of SCM, the latter in due course also setting up community houses in Oxford, Birmingham, Bristol and Dublin[43].

The SCM sought to link up like-minded radical Christian groups in three ways. First, Wick Court provided a symbolic centre with, at its peak, some 200 people a month passing through. Conferences were held there on radical themes such as 'The Theology of Gay Liberation' and 'Feminist Theology'[44]. Secondly, much larger gatherings, mainly for students, were arranged annually. In 1972 an event entitled 'Seeds of Liberation', concerned with the spiritual dimension to political struggle, attracted 400 people to Huddersfield. In 1974, 250 people met in Birmingham for 'A Celebration of Free Communities'[45]. Thirdly, the SCM's publications helped in network building, in particular its magazine 'Movement' and its 'People's Church: A Directory of Christian Alternatives', first published in 1972 (with a second but more sparse edition in 1977).

This first attempt at Christian networking around key social and political issues had shot its bolt by about the mid-'seventies. It had been too sweeping in its critique of church and society, too closely tied to the radical youth rebellion of the late 'sixties and too dependent on one body (the SCM) for financial and administrative support. Nonetheless, it had done a good deal to stimulate the future growth of more *focused* issue-centred networks.

Networks of the latter kind had begun to appear as early as the mid 'sixties, when Coventry Cathedral set up its **Community of the Cross of Nails** (1967) to link together some 50 Christian centres of reconciliation around the world. In Northern Ireland, the **Corrymeela Community,** from its establishment in 1965, also sought to build reconciliation networks, a task later furthered by such organisations as **Protestant and Catholic Encounter, All Children Together** and the **Christian Life Communities,** amongst others. Networking around the problems of South Africa came to the fore again in the early 'seventies (**Christian Concern for South Africa** and **End Loans to South Africa**), whilst race issues at home brought Christians together throughout the decade (**All Faiths for One Race,** the **Zebra project** and **Christians Against Racism and Fascism** for example). There was a growth of networks linking basic Christian groups tackling such issues as homosexuality (from 1973), feminism (from 1977), and poverty (**Church Action On Poverty** was set up in 1982). In 1981 those concerned with the environment were brought closer together by the establishment of the **Christian Ecology Group.**

The most significant development with regard to issue-centred networks in recent years has been the field of peacemaking, the appearance of **Christian C.N.D.** in 1981 being the main focus for a host of Christian initiatives sharing a similar concern. In late 1983, eighty representatives from groups of progressive evangelicals meeting in Birmingham committed themselves 'to build a supportive network' (as yet nameless) to oppose the proliferation of nuclear weapons and witness for peace. 1984 saw the setting up by the British Council of Churches of a **'Peace Forum'** to enable Christian groups of all kinds involved in the peace movement to come together from time to time to exchange ideas and share resources.

Networks drawing issue-centred groups together *across* their dominant interests have been much less prominent. To some extent the SCM fulfilled this function in the early 'seventies. In more recent years, two other bodies have attempted to fulfil something of a similar role, **COSPEC** (Christian Organisations for Social, Political and Economic Change) and, on a more modest scale, **ECUM** (The Evangelical Coalition for Urban Mission). These two bodies represented different theological emphases, though in their social and political concerns they had a good deal in common. In 1980, **COSPEC** came into being as a left-wing, loose-knit federation of some twenty groups, embracing such bodies as **Christian Action,** Christians Against Racism and Fascism, **Christian Feminist Groups** (London), the Student Christian Movement and the **Urban Theology Unit** (Sheffield). COSPEC's aim was, 'Co-operating in the struggle for a just, participatory and sustainable society . . . of necessity involving a break with the existing social, political and economic order'. In 1981, ECUM was established, linking more closely together the **Frontier Youth Trust,** the **Evangelical Urban Training Project,** the **Evangelical Race Relations Group** and the **Shaftesbury Project.** Its purpose was to co-ordinate the activities of its associated bodies to foster a Christian presence and challenge 'oppressive demonic' powers evident within urban life.

c. The networking of residential communities

The opposition evoked by protesting secular groups in the late 'sixties drove many young people to withdraw into various forms of communal living, wherever possible far away from the madding crowd. Communes proliferated. Andrew Rigby writing in 1972 estimated that by that time as many as a hundred were in existence throughout the United Kingdom[46]. Networking soon began and by 1971 the secular Commune Movement had some 350 members and, more significant, its journal 'Communes' a circulation of some 3,000[47].

It was little wonder, therefore, that Christian experiments in communal living were prominent from this time onwards and that the third phase of networking saw bonds and alliances develop between them. There were soon four **Ashram community houses** and five **l'Arche homes** for the mentally handicapped. In 1978 **Root Groups** came into being to enable young Christians to live a year of their life in a community house, and at the same time serve within a local (Anglican) parish. Five or six such opportunities were offered each year in various parts of the country. In 1981 **Toc H** took a policy decision to establish a number of new community houses, a lead followed a year later on a wider scale by the **Iona Community.** Ad hoc meeting and sharing went on between these groups and the fifty or so other independent Christian community houses which existed by the early 'eighties[48]. In 1983 well attended gatherings of basic Christian groups, many involved in communal living, were held in Northern Ireland, Wales and Scotland.

More organised Christian networks consisting of residential communities were less in evidence, though certain moves to set them up occurred. In 1974 members of the Society of Friends established the **Towards Community Group**, which brought Quakers interested (though not necessarily actively involved) in new forms of communal living together for sharing and discussion three or four times a year. In 1980 they published a symposium of material on the theme of community life, mostly of a residential nature[49]

In 1976 a number of North American 'life style communities', as they called themselves, linked up to form a 'community of communities'. Involved in this network were the **Community of Celebration**, situated on the Isle of Cumbrae, and **Post Green** in Dorset. The reasons for their joining together were given by Bob Sabbath of Sojourners (Washington D.C.) and underline the importance of networking in general:

'Renewal movements need each other . . . Most renewal movements are the fruit of a vision for a part of the gospel that is minimised or lacking in the church. But the clarity of their bold vision does not keep them from imbalances and glaring lacks within themselves. So renewal movements must themselves be continually renewed by one another . . . It is not easy for us as individuals, communities or renewal movements to look past the incompleteness of those around us and learn from their strengths. There is often a community pride or corporate arrogance that in the excitement of new birth keeps us from learning from others who have not yet embodied the fullness of our vision. But as individuals and communities mature in God's life, we either begin to listen deeply to one another, even to sectors of the church which we see are imbalanced, or the vision that called us forth begins to suffocate, to harden, and sometimes to die.'[50].

d. Sector-based networks

Though the basic Christian community movement in the United Kingdom was founded on the small group, this had never pre-determined the form that community making should take. Communal living as such has produced a great deal of valuable experience and many important insights, both for those actively involved and for those looking on, but the beginnings of a new re-formation have also been pioneered by many other kinds of basic group. Indeed, Parker Palmer, amongst others[51], has warned against taking the commune as normative. He writes:

'As we consider the forms of community life, we run into the cultural arrogance of the recent (secular) commune movement and its assumption that the small, intentional community, withdrawn from the larger society, is the only worthy form of the common life. Clearly the emergence of such communes is important for us. They do provide models, and they serve as schools for less intensive forms of life together. But they are out of reach for many people. We need to help each other build community where we are, rather than encouraging dreams which turn to despair over a community which for many of us will never be. We need to foster the diverse forms of community which are needed if an urban, technological society is to recover its human roots'[52].

One of the features of the basic Christian community movement in the United Kingdom is that it has encompassed groups which have been seeking a new quality of community of immediate relevance to the mainstream sectors of a secular society. Many of these groups have been mentioned earlier in relation to family life, the arts, the environment and economics, education, welfare and health. Here I concentrate on the *networks* beginning to emerge around these concerns.

Amongst the earliest examples of this fourth phase of networking was the **Association for Pastoral Care and Counselling** set up in 1970, though only one of a number of networks earlier established in this field and dating back as far as the **Guild of Health** (1904). More typical of the newer networks was the **Arts Centre**, founded in 1971 to link up Christians engaged in the arts, the media and entertainment. From 1972 onwards, those working in the field of mental handicap began to work more closely together, a prominent role being played here by **l'Arche** and **Faith and Light.**

Sector-based networks were slower to emerge in the mid 'seventies but by the end of the decade the pace had quickened. Three networks concerned with education then appeared: in 1979 the **Christian Association for Adult and Continuing Education** came into being as a forum for adult educators; in the same year the **Association of Laity Centres** (in the United Kingdom) was formally constituted to 'participate in the equipping, formation and education of Christian laity for their role as agents of creative change in society and of renewal in the churches'; and in 1981 the **Family Life Education Ecumenical Project** was set up, a more mainstream church enterprise but with the aim of creating situations for learning through sharing of experience of family life across denominations.

In 1982 **Church Action with the Unemployed** was launched to help harness and co-ordinate Christian endeavours to support the unemployed. The same year the **Christian Council on Ageing** was established, with the intention of making all churches more aware of their increasing responsibility to an ageing population. Though it was decided to establish membership on an individual basis, the Council's intent was to facilitate as much co-operation as possible between Christian agencies working in this field. In 1983 the **Association of Christians in Planning and Architecture** was launched to bring evangelical Christian insights to bear on this sector. In the same year a **Federation for Rural Evangelism** came into being to share insights and experiences in rural evangelism and to stimulate an effective ministry, by encouragement, education and example, of churches and Christians throughout rural areas.

e. Towards a network of networks

In 1981 the **National Centre for Christian Communities and Networks** came into being as an independent charity and resources centre for the basic Christian community movement throughout the United Kingdom. Within a year it had well over 100 basic groups and religious orders formally 'associated' with it from every part of the country, many of these being the core or headquarters group at the centre of their own wider networks. In addition, numerous other groups and individuals were in contact with the National Centre to give or gain information and to make use of its facilities. The establishment of the centre illustrates the latest phase in the networking process, the gradual emergence of a national ecumenical network of basic Christian groups and religious orders of a kind not seen before in this country.

The emergence of this national network of networks had begun as far back as the early 'seventies. In origin it owed a good deal to **One for Christian Renewal,** mentioned earlier, which had provided a financial and administrative base for the launching of the magazine 'Community' in 1971. 'Community'[53] was a broadsheet of some twenty pages which set out to publicise stories of the life and activities of basic Christian groups around the United Kingdom. By the end of the decade 'Community' had carried over a hundred case studies, the large majority written by those actively involved in the ventures therein described. 'Community' quickly rose in circulation to 700 and has stayed around that level ever since. The 'Community' magazine greatly facilitated the process of networking between basic groups, especially after 1974 when a 'Switchboard' section was included to provide readers with an opportunity to 'advertise' activities and events in which they were engaged. It was not surprising, therefore, that by 1975 enough links had been forged to make possible a first national gathering of basic Christian groups. This took place at Harborne Hall, Birmingham, and attracted over fifty people representing some twenty new ventures.

Two years later a similar gathering was held at Hengrave Hall in Suffolk, attracting nearly sixty people representing nearly thirty basic groups. For the first time the religious orders were represented, a matter of considerable significance to which I return later. The Hengrave Hall conference moved the basic Christian community movement forward in two important ways. It warmly supported an initiative taken earlier in 1977, again sponsored by One for Christian Renewal, to set up a **Community Resources Centre** (the forerunner of the National Centre for Christian Communities and Networks) in Birmingham, the purpose of which was to gather and disseminate information about basic Christian groups throughout tl e United Kingdom. Secondly, the Hengrave Hall conference urged the holding of a national congress to enable as many representatives of basic Christian groups as possible to meet and exchange experiences.

The development of a national network of networks was probably also helped on its way by the opportunity afforded me during these years to travel throughout the country meeting those involved in new Christian initiatives, and where of value put groups closer in touch with one another. Between 1974 and 1976 I was able to visit most parts of the United Kingdom and, as a result, in 1977 wrote a full-scale account of the basic Christian community movement as I then saw it[54]. As editor of the 'Community' magazine I was also able to ensure that stories about the most interesting initiatives were regularly passed on to a wider audience. From 1978 onwards 'Community' deliberately took a more thematic line in each issue, bringing together accounts of groups involved in such fields as education, work, health, caring, the arts, peacemaking and so on. From 1982 'Community' began to include brief reports on networks as such.

The existence of a national network of basic Christian groups first became clearly evident at the Community Congress held at Westhill and Woodbrooke Colleges, Birmingham, for five days in September 1980[55]. 250 people attended, representing 106 basic groups (53 of a residential and 53 of a non-residential kind) and 42 religious orders (13 Anglican and 29 Roman Catholic). The congress focused on 'sharing groups' and interest based 'workshops'. There were three main speakers, Jean Vanier (of l'Arche), Jim Wallis (of Sojourners in Washington D.C.) and Rosemary Haughton (from Lothlorien). The congress gave a unique opportunity to members of a wide variety of groups and communities, many of whom had never met before, to talk to listen and to share their experiences at depth.

The response of participants to the congress was very positive as the many comments received afterwards bore out. A small selection of these must suffice[56]:

'The Congress opened my eyes to the extent of what you call the alternative church. It is most encouraging to know just how many Christians are being called to valid ministry outside the parish.'

'A living experience of the dynamic work of the Holy Spirit in the world. A challenging experience of what it means to be a Christian in the world today. A rewarding experience of meeting up with so many marvellous people. An enriching experience which I hope will become fruitful in the years ahead.'

'Loved meeting all the "rainbow" of different Christian communities and individuals. Longing for something more "concrete" to emerge but I think the Holy Spirit's doing it all the time! This network is helping to bring in God's kingdom and root it here on earth.'

The 1980 Community Congress gave its full support to the establishment of the Community Resources Centre on a more permanent footing. Just over a year later the latter re-emerged as a registered charity, re-named the **National Centre for Christian Communities and Networks,** located in two small rooms on the campus of Westhill College, Birmingham. Since then the centre has been helping to service the basic Christian community movement in a variety of ways. Its magazine 'Community' (taken over from One for Christian Renewal) continues to carry case-studies of basic groups, religious orders and networks. The centre has a resources unit which has files on the origin and development of over 300 groups. Many enquiries reach it by letter or 'phone and visitors are frequent. In 1980 the centre published the first 'Directory of Christian Communities and Groups'[57] in the United Kingdom with nearly 400 annotated entries (a second updated edition appeared in May 1984).

The National Centre has set up a number of conferences and day consultations in recent years, the latter drawing together representatives of basic groups and religious orders pursuing a diversity of interests. The findings of these consultations, supplemented by other case studies and comments, have been published in the first six booklets of the 'New Christian Initiatives Series' entitled 'The Family in Transition', 'Christian Community and Cultural Diversity', 'Christian Initiatives in Community Education', 'Christian Voluntary Organisations in a Secular Society — Where Next?', and 'Christian Initiatives in Peacemaking'[58].

The National Centre has a management committee of twenty four members, drawn from a cross-section of basic Christian groups and the Roman Catholic and Anglican religious orders. The work of the centre itself is currently undertaken by myself as Honorary Director and three part-time administrative and resources staff, together with considerable voluntary assistance.

The National Centre is funded from three main sources. It has been given valuable assistance by a number of secular trusts, especially in its earlier days. It has received generous donations from both individuals and groups, not least from the Anglican and Roman Catholic religious orders. It is also maintained by the subscriptions of its associates, though these have never met more than a third of the centre's modest annual budget. Since its inception (as the Community Resources Centre in 1977) the National Centre has as yet received no financial support from any of the major denominations. The development, and indeed continuation, of the work of the centre will depend on more substantial long-term funding becoming available.

An important development since 1980 has been the establishment of a number of regional **'contact centres'** in close touch with the National Centre. These have begun to build links between, and arrange gatherings of, basic Christian groups in their own areas. Notable here was a meeting held early in 1983 at Corrymeela's Ballycastle house in Northern Ireland attended by over fifty people of many denominations and representing some twenty basic Christian groups. A similar gathering in the spring of 1983 was held at Coleg Trefeca in South Wales attended by some thirty people representing a wide cross-section of Christian groups and religious orders from all over Wales. Other regional meetings of like kind were held in 1983 for the Leicester area, the South-West, East Scotland and the West Midlands.

One other significant development has been the gradual strengthening of links between basic groups on the United Kingdom scene and those overseas. A number of the former, such as the lay Catholic **Volunteer Missionary Movement** (1969), Post Green, **Christians Aware**, (1975) and l'Arche are already very much involved abroad as well as in Britain. But overseas contacts through other basic groups are also growing. The National Centre itself receives many enquiries and visitors from abroad. In 1983 'Community' began to carry reports on basic groups in other countries.

f. Numbers

At the end of 1983, the National Centre for Christian Communities and Networks had 75 groups and 275 individuals (not including religious orders) formally associated with it. The 1980 'Directory' published by the National Centre listed 211 groups (not including religious orders). In 1984 the second edition of the 'Directory' listed 252 such groups, 80 of those included in 1980 not appearing (some were no longer seen as appropriate inclusions, others failed to return forms and a few had ceased to exist), and 91 being new entries. (In both 1980 and 1984 long established and often explicitly denominational associations or societies were not listed in the 'Directory' as details about these frequently appeared elsewhere.)

These figures very much understate the total number of groups currently in existence, especially as many of those included only once in the 'Directory' are the 'core groups' or 'headquarters' of wider networks. For example, the Cyrenians, the Ashram Community and l'Arche embrace numerous associated community houses. In addition, there are many groups without a name, or not wishing to advertise their existence beyond a very limited range of people, about whom the National Centre knows little or nothing. If all these are counted in together with the large company of individuals who are linked to basic groups as 'companions', 'partners', 'friends', etc., *the total number of people involved in the basic Christian community movement at the present time runs into tens of thousands.*

The development of the basic Christian Community movement is currently most evident in the growth of community houses or flats, in connection with groups engaged in community work, community education, the arts, work amongst the elderly and the hospice movement, and in relation to groups taking up the issues of poverty, unemployment, women's rights, and peacemaking.

At the end of 1983, 43 religious orders, 21 Anglican and 22 Roman Catholic, were group associates of the National Centre. The 1980 'Directory' listed 144 religious orders, 35 Anglican and 109 Roman Catholic. The 1984 edition included 132 religious orders, 42 Anglican and 90 Roman Catholic (the difference here being entirely due to whether or not forms were returned to the National Centre). A report published in 1982[59] shows that (in England and Wales) the Roman Catholics have 286 congregations and 17,225 religious; the Anglicans 56 communities and some 2,000 religious.

In 1983 the management committee of the National Centre felt the signs of growth encouraging enough to initiate plans for a second National Congress to be held in Birmingham in July 1984. The aim was to enable 'basic Christian groups and religious orders together to clarify their vision of what church and society might be in the rest of the 'eighties and to explore their own role in helping to turn that vision into reality'. The 1984 congress was modelled on the 1980 event, except that there was to be more concentration on small-scale meetings and less on main speakers. A new addition was five 'centres' — a women's centre, an under 25s' centre, a justice and peace centre, an interfaith centre and an arts centre — to be open throughout the congress to give those with a strong interest in these fields of Christian concern a place to meet as and when they wished.

g. Religious orders networking

After Vatican Two the Roman Catholic religious congregations had increasingly begun to link up and share resources around a number of common apostolates. An **Association of Sisters in Pastoral Ministry** came into being in the 'seventies concerned mainly with parish work, and an **Association of Senior Religious** in 1973 to support and help utilise the gifts of those retired. Also of note here are the two sector-based networks, the **Association of Nursing Religious** (1962) and the **Association of Religious in Education.** The latter changed its name in 1983 from that of the Association of Teaching Religious (1969) because many congregations were moving away from school teaching as such into other forms of educational work.

Roman Catholic congregations had begun to forge closer links amongst themselves some years before Vatican Two. Following a large congress of Catholic religious in Liverpool in 1956, and initiatives from the Sacred Congregation of Religious in Rome a year later, a **Conference of Major Religious Superiors of England and Wales** was formally constituted in 1959, with separate men's and women's sections. Pre-eminent amongst its defined purposes was that of communication and co-operation. By the mid-'seventies, however, it was felt that the men's and women's sections should operate more closely together and a joint executive, joint secretariat and male and female co-presidents came into being from 1978.

Closer association between the Anglican orders began with three major conferences for religious, at Oxford and York, held between 1965 and 1974. These led to increasing contact between superiors and ultimately to the setting up of a **Communities Consultative Council** in 1975, with its annual meeting of representatives from all orders, and gatherings in between of communities in local areas.

Both the Roman and Anglican orders were themselves networking internationally by the mid-'seventies and, in 1980, a **Permanent (International) Ecumenical Consultation of Religious** was formally established with its secretariat in Rome. The Consultation was committed to 'share an experience of the gift of unity we have received in Christ, and to be a living witness to that hope of perfect unity for which he prayed.'[60] A number of the members of this Consultation (especially Anglicans) were from England. A smaller **English Consultation** of Roman and Anglican religious had been meeting since 1978 and was given further impetus by the formation of the international Permanent Ecumenical Consultation. In 1983 the English Consultation unanimously passed a resolution urging 'that wherever possible Anglican and Roman Catholic religious should co-operate, particularly at the practical level' and come together in ecumenical gatherings of 'bursars, formation teams, parish sisters, teachers and other groups'[61].

Of great significance for the basic Christian community movement in the United Kingdom was increasing contact between the religious orders and basic Christian groups during this period. In 1976, Alan Harrison, Secretary of the Advisory Council for (Anglican) Religious Communities, wrote in the 'Community' magazine about 'Missing Links'[62]: 'Religious communities are notoriously reluctant to change direction once the tradition has evolved. Tradition is good; it has a cohesive effect in community. But when tradition obscures the vision it is no longer cohesive; it gums up the works altogether.' He saw close contact between the established orders and younger groups as vital in helping to 'ungum the works', concluding that the traditional orders need to be able to share the insights being gained by basic groups. Yet, 'Similarly the new forms of community life at their peril neglect to learn from the experience of centuries enshrined in the traditional communities now being modified in the light of renewal. It is time those who bear witness to the common life of faith talked to each other.'

Alan Harrison's word soon bore fruit. The second gathering of basic Christian groups held at Hengrave Hall in 1977 included male Anglican religious from Mirfield, Nashdom and Alton Abbey; sisters from Bede House, St. Teilo's Priory (Cardiff) and the Community of St. Francis at Compton Durville. Amongst the Roman religious were priests from Douai Abbey (Reading) and Glencree (County Wicklow); sisters from St. Mary's Convent (Cambridge) and 'Bethanie' (Highgate, London). The impact of this encounter was summed up by one sister who wrote: 'I left Hengrave thanking God that I have been born right now and not a century ago!'

Contacts between the religious orders and basic Christian groups continued to grow stronger in succeeding years. The orders occupied about a third of the places at the 1980 Community Congress. They readily supported the setting up of the National Centre for Christian Communities and Networks. Two Anglican and two Catholic religious currently serve on its management committee. A number of religious communities have also offered their services as regional contact centres.

Over the past year or two it has become commonplace for religious and members of basic Christian groups to participate on equal terms in events concerned with the renewal of community. In 1982, for example, religious and lay groups shared together in the Wells Festival, a spectacular day event of worship, workshops and exhibitions in and around the cathedral, to celebrate the 800th year of the birth of St. Francis, and attended by about a thousand people. At regional gatherings in 1983 in Northern Ireland, South Wales, Scotland and elsewhere religious and those from basic groups of all denominations have also mixed freely and enthusiastically.

VII: CLARIFYING THE MESSAGE

The first three stages of past re-formations — protest, withdrawal and dispersal, and networking — have usually brought home to Christian groups the need to reflect on and clarify their message to church and society. The basic Christian community movement in the United Kingdom today is no exception.

At the outset, the movement's message was expressed in many different ways by many different groups, each one emphasising the particular concern which had originally impelled its members to protest about the quality of community within church and world. In the early years of the basic community movement most groups were so intent on pursuing their own interests that they rarely took time off to listen to the concerns and experiences of others. Thus to outside observers the message which came across often seemed clamorous or incoherent.

As the initial furore died down certain themes became more prominent, and the diversity of groups witnessing to them strengthened rather than weakened the overall message. The latter was clarified in two main ways. First, and most important, it was given substance and shape by what Christian groups actually *were* and *did*. The medium became an essential way of declaring and authenticating the message. Thus in this chapter I often refer to the ongoing life and work of groups and networks in order to illustrate the message they were seeking to communicate.

In the second place, the message was given greater lucidity and coherence by the speaking and the writing of a number of leading figures in the basic Christian community movement, both in this country and abroad (some of whose comments I use later in this chapter). Notable here were Jean Vanier (the founder of l'Arche), Rosemary Haughton (of Lothlorien, but her work now spanning the Atlantic), Jim Wallis (of the Sojourners community in Washington D.C.), Edwina Gateley (founder and first Director of the Volunteer Missionary Movement), Loren Halvorson (a founder member of ARC in Minnesota, U.S.A.), and Ian Fraser (formerly Dean of Mission at Selly Oak Colleges, Birmingham).

'Community-life uncovers a prophetic possibility that was there all along, but hidden'[1], writes John Davies. So it has been with the basic Christian community movement. The message which came to the fore was about 'the emergence of something very odd, very important — and strangely familiar as well as altogether new'[2], as Rosemary Haughton puts it. It has been a message conveyed both by basic Christian groups and by religious orders. The former were described by Rosemary

Haughton as, 'The emergent church, a re-born church, arising, unevangelised, unplanned (and unwanted!) in all kinds of unexpected situations and people'[3]. Of the religious orders Alan Harrison wrote, 'The signs are that with the freedom from the dead weight of over-institutionalisation the religious life is refinding its identity in the school of the prophets'[4]. '(We) by our calling are intended to be among the radical followers of Jesus,'[5] wrote Catherine Hughes, Provincial of the Sisters of Notre Dame. 'All that we can be sure of is that the basic role of religious life in the church . . . is to be a sign and a sacrament, a continuous challenge by the radical living of the gospel',[6] stated the CORA Report on the collaboration of (Roman) religious.

The heart of the message that basic Christian groups and religious orders began to declare in deeds and, through its spokesmen, also in words, was that of a deep and widespread need for a new quality of community. It was a message of contradiction, but also one of hope, for a world facing choices of life or death, wealth or poverty, justice or injustice and meaning or despair. 'Community', wrote Jean Vanier, 'helps people . . . to find inner freedom in order to give their lives for justice and peace'[7]. The message was a call for people to claim their freedom and give their lives to the building of one church and one world in Christ; it was a call to 'liberation in solidarity'[8], as Loren Halvorson described it.

For such liberation to become a reality the basic Christian community movement had to bear witness to the possibility of liberation and another re-formation; to credible and practical ways in which the people of God could be delivered from restrictive ideologies and structures in order more effectively to undertake an apostolate of reconciliation and salvation. Basic groups had to show that Christians need no longer be prisoners of a captive church, but had a new vision of community which by God's grace could become a reality even in a secular world. Message and medium had to come together into a dynamic synthesis.

1. From secularism to faith

Basic Christian groups have been no less exposed to the influence of secularisation, and indeed secularism, than any other part of the church in the West, past or present. As a result, a number of groups whose founders were committed Christians now disassociate themselves from an *explicitly* Christian commitment. Amongst these are such bodies as the Samaritans, the Richmond Fellowship, Centrepoint and the Compassionate Friends.

Other basic groups have oscillated over the years between an overt affirmation of Christian faith and agnostic humanism. The pioneering

Blackheath Commune, for example, was originally based on 'a Christian understanding of life'. Yet towards the end of its existence one member wrote, 'We differ now in the relevance of Christian thought and structures to our continuing development and understanding'[9]. A similar ambivalence characterised the life of Taena in Gloucestershire, which in forty immensely rich years encompassed beliefs ranging from atheism through Roman Catholicism to eastern mysticism.

By and large, however, basic Christian groups have not only been born out of, but have continued to be nourished by, a passionate Christian faith which has given purpose and depth to their lives, activities and message. Such groups have repudiated the 'bloodless intellect' of secularistic rationalism in favour of an openness to God's revelation in and through the many and varied forms of human experience.

This faith commitment of basic Christian groups draws on manifold traditions of spirituality to nurture and sustain it.

Some existing groups have again emerged in places where Christians have been gathering and worshipping for centuries, and from which their forefathers have gone out to proclaim the gospel to a hostile world. The Iona Community, Scottish Churches House in Dunblane, Marygate House on Holy Island, the Community of Christ the Sower at Little Gidding and groups around Glastonbury, are all sustained by the memory of a long Christian heritage of prayer and worship in the places where they are located.

The spirituality of the Julian Meetings looks to the classical Christian tradition stemming from such people as Julian of Norwich. That of the Christian Life Communities and the At Home Retreat movement draw on St. Ignatius' exercises. The Jubilee Group derives its spiritual inspiration from 'the Catholic movement' in the Church of England[10]. Post Green, the Barnabas Fellowship in Dorset, the Community of Celebration, and the Katimavik gatherings amongst others, are associated with the charismatic tradition.

Basic Christian groups express a passionate 'Yes' to God in both quiet waiting, like the Servants of Christ the King which meet in small companies for this purpose, as well as through music and song, like the Fisherfolk at Post Green. Basic groups utilise stillness and silence, as in the case of the 'Shalom' retreats at Ammerdown, as well as drama and mime, as at Scargill House in Wharfedale[11], and dance, such as the Tai Chi Chuan at Taena[12].

Many in the basic Christian community movement come together to celebrate their faith not only in small groups but in large and exciting festivals, like that held in 1982 at Wells Cathedral to celebrate the 800th anniversary of the birth of St. Francis. Of note here is also the biennial week's 'Summerfest' held at Corrymeela's Ballycastle centre in Northern Ireland: in 1983 over 2,000 people attending 'workshops, creative expression, a market place of ideas and special interest groups, children and youth programmes, crêches, concerts, ceilidhes, and bands (which) made it a kaleideiscope of colour and events'[13].

The basic Christian community movement is also a sign of contradiction within a world subservient to secularistic materialism. In 1977 I wrote that the 'Yes' to God of basic Christian groups was typified by a willingness 'to endure cold, rain and mud at Keveral Farm and Lothlorien; to cope with hard manual work at Pilsdon and Scoraig; to take the wear and tear of being on hand to deal with the needs of broken families at Bystock Court, of the homeless in the Cyrenian shelters, and of those disoriented by violence at Corrymeela'[14]. The years since then have shown basic groups no less ready to put the needs of the kingdom of God first, and the desire for material well-being second. Groups are situated in inner city areas, on vast outer ring council estates, and in villages suffering from 'rural retreat'[15]. Groups are active amongst ethnic minorities, the homeless, the handicapped and the terminally ill. All bear witness to the fact that people not possessions come first.

The message of the Christian community movement is that basic groups could not live the life they live and undertake the work they do without the conviction that if they say 'Yes' to God they will be given the vision of what community can be and the strength to make that vision a reality.

2. From sacralism to the secular

The temptation to sacralism does not spare basic Christian groups. Indeed the history of the church is littered not just with large institutions but small groups which have become arrogant in their claim to represent the only true way of salvation.

The basic Christian community movement in the United Kingdom brushes shoulders with a number of strongly sacralistic groups. Amongst these some would put the 'New Age' communities, like Findhorn in north-east Scotland, and many of the groups represented at the bizarre Festival for Mind-Body-Spirit held regularly for some years at Olympia. Within the more explicitly Christian tradition a few basic groups with a strongly sacralistic ethos also exist, though these often have more in common with the house church movement (described in Chapter V) than with the Christian community movement as such.

However, the large majority of basic Christian groups are of a very different kind. They shun imperialistic dogmatism and seek to engage as positively as possible with a secular society. Those involved in counselling, such as the Dympna Centre or the Westminster Pastoral Foundation, are committed to professional skills training. Those concerned with homes of healing or with hospices know that medical expertise and experience are essential.

Christian groups involved in education are more than aware of the necessity of holding their own within an informed secular world. This is as true for the Teilhard Centre, acting as advocate for the insights of that famous Jesuit explorer with his passionate desire to bring together the discoveries of science and religion, as it is for the laity centres much of whose work is focused on key secular concerns of the day. Prominent in their Christian concern about social and political, as well as technological and industrial issues are the Audenshaw Foundation, Woodbrooke College, Scottish Churches House, the William Temple Foundation and Ammerdown. In 1981 the Luton Industrial College published 'Shaping Tomorrow'[16], a report in which matters such as genetic engineering, nuclear energy, the electronics revolution and the future of work were important themes.

Issues-centred groups, for example the Catholic Institute for International Relations, Christian C.N.D. and Church Action on Poverty, are likewise fully cognisant of the need to base their advocacy on accurate and relevant data.

The religious orders are developing an increasingly informed engagement with a secular society. In 1973, the Roman Catholic Conference of Major Religious Superiors in England and Wales commissioned a full scale 'Pastoral Investigation of Social Trends'[17]. The published studies were deliberately intended to stimulate the thinking and guide the work of religious on such topics as 'The Care of the Elderly', 'The Church and Social Work', 'Poverty in Britain', 'Housing Need' and 'Community Health'.

Nonetheless a great deal still remains to be done. The involvement of basic Christian groups in the affairs of a secular society often remains superficial and tentative, not least in the fields of industry, commerce and government. The ability of some basic groups to say a wholehearted 'Yes' to man in his strength as well as his weakness is still limited, even if commitment to a well informed secular apostolate is characteristic of many others.

3. From priest to people

'The structure of the church is being stood on its head. The "we and they" church is giving way to "our" church'[18], writes Rosemary Haughton. The basic Christian community movement bears witness to a new conception of authority within the church, and of the necessity of moving from a priest to a people-centred understanding of Christian community. Terms such as 'partnership' and 'co-responsibility' are not cosmetic, but practices lived out in everyday affairs.

Leadership within the basic community movement is a matter of function before status, of need before office. Because basic Christian

131

groups are part of a dynamic missionary movement, it is the requirements of the situation, rather than tradition or custom, which shape the nature and the style of leadership.

This does not mean the exclusion of the clergy, who remain prominent within basic Christian groups. Out of those groups mentioned in the previous chapter nearly half have at some stage had ordained ministers in positions of leadership. Some of these, such as Ray Davey of Corrymeela, John Vincent of the Sheffield Inner City Ecumenical Mission, Tony Hodgson of Little Gidding, Cecil Kerr of the Christian Renewal Centre in Rostrevor, and Graham Pulkingham of the Community of Celebration, have been the actual founders of basic Christian groups. But considerable lay involvement and democractic control remain very much the order of the day.

The missionary task of basic Christain groups has brought four key aspects of leadership to the fore. The first has been a *prophetic function,* a role fulfilled by both clergy and laity. Of the clergy, George MacLeod, the founder of the Iona Community, and of the laity, Jean Vanier, founder of l'Arche, are probably amongst the best known figures. Their pronouncements have been both inspirational and challenging for many within the basic community movement and beyond. Such prophetic leaders have possessed what Vanier himself calls 'a true gift of discernment'[19], knowing where God is leading his people and how they can follow the signs without losing their way. Thus they have enabled the basic Christian community movement to bear witness to the prophetic made practical.

A second important function of leadership has been that of *gathering the dispersed and the isolated together;* the ability to identify and bring into contact those who have caught the vision of what Christian community is all about. Both clergy and laity have also been active in this connection, the latter represented by founders of basic groups such as Carol Graham of the Farncombe Community, Faith and Tom Lees of Post Green, Cicely Saunders of St. Christopher's Hospice and Roger Sawtell of the Daily Bread Co-operative. Some basic groups have come into being through the endeavours of families who have formed the nucleus of a wider circle, as at Lothlorien, Ringsfield Hall, Commonwork, Albert Road in Birmingham and the West Pilton community.

A third aspect of leadership within the basic Christian community movement has been that of *corporate responsibility and decision making.* Here the shift from priest to people, a move from authority exercised by the one to that shared by the many, is particularly in evidence. Jean Vanier writes, 'A community can only become a harmonious whole, with "one heart, one soul, one spirit", if all its members are exercising their own gifts fully. If the model of their relationships to authority is worker to boss, or soldier to officer, then there is no understanding of what community means'[20]. There still remain basic Christian groups whose leadership and organisation are more autocratic, bureaucratic or charismatic than corporate[21], but the continuing trend is towards what the Community of the Word of God call taking decisions according to 'the common mind'[22].

Reflecting this move toward corporate leadership are the increasing number of Christian self-help groups and co-operatives. These include the Association of Interchurch Families, set up in the late 'sixties for the mutual support of families where husband and wife are committed to different church allegiances (usually Roman Catholic and a different denomination), the Compassionate Friends for peer counselling amongst bereaved parents, Glencolumbkille, a communalised parish in County Donegal[23], and the Daily Bread Co-operative.

The religious orders too are moving steadily in this direction. 'Yesterday's religious life', writes Alan Harrison, 'gives the impression of a monolithic structured hierarchy, monarchical and pyramidical'[24]. But many orders are now changing their constitutions to achieve a more corporate mode of operation; though some would still contend along with Alan Harrison that, 'A religious community (is not) a democracy ruled by a popular vote'[25].

A fourth important, but still developing, function of leadership within the community movement is that of '*making creative connections*'. This is the task of linking person with person and group with group, thus building networks of one kind or another to facilitate the sharing of experiences, ideas and resources. It is a role fulfilled in two main ways; by certain *groups* which take on the function of 'assembly points', and by particular *individuals* who move from place to place keeping people in touch with one another. In the former case, laity centres such as Scottish Churches House, Trefeca and Hengrave Hall, as well as a number of conference and retreat centres such as Centre Space in Kent and the Skreen in South Wales, play such a role. In the latter case, it is those able to be more mobile, for example the staff of the National Centre for Christian Communities and Networks or the provincials of religious orders, who have helped groups to link up on a geographical or apostolic basis.

The fact that basic Christian groups have sprung up 'where the action is' helps to ensure that leadership as well as membership has an indigenous quality. 'Indigenous' in this context means not so much that leaders have been born and bred where their group is located, though that can certainly happen especially in places like Northern Ireland, but that they have for many years been dedicated to and actively involved in the *concerns* of the groups with which they are associated. As a result, leaders often serve their groups, in one capacity or another, over decades rather than years. Indeed, an implicit life-long commitment to the group and its work is not uncommon, as, for example, with Iona, l'Arche, and Post Green.

All these factors underline that entry into a leadership role within the basic Christian community movement is very much a matter of a calling to a particular apostolate expressed through the life and witness of a basic group (or network), akin to belonging to a religious order. Whether leaders are ordained or not is in practice secondary to whether they are committed and equipped to undertake the responsibilities of leadership. Nonetheless, there is a growing feeling that ordination should be open to all those called to and fitted for such leadership roles, even if their functions are not the traditional liturgical, pastoral or catechetical ones. *WHY?*

Women play an important part in the leadership of many basic Christian groups, for example in the Grail, St. Julians, the Farncombe Community, the Volunteer Missionary Movement, Post Green, the Julian Meetings, Faith and Light and Christian C.N.D. The basic Christian community movement as a whole (though still with a few unfortunate exceptions) shares the conviction that women should be not only equal partners with men in the exercise of leadership, but that the female contribution towards a new quality of community should come far more to the fore. The most outspoken amongst basic groups seeking to upgrade the status and strengthen the contribution of women are those directly associated with the feminist movement. They are not numerous, yet are a constant reminder of the issues at stake.

Other groups contain those deeply concerned about liberation from male clericalism in order to free both women and men to make their distinctive contribution to church and world. It is imperative for the future of the church that, 'the masculine and feminine ways of being human, the two ways in which the divine life is experienced . . . complement and perfect each other'[26], writes Rosemary Haughton. In an article written for the 'Community' magazine she states:

'What is emerging as the new being of the church is linked to the emergence into cultural consciousness of the feminine principle in human community, which has always been there, but not as consciously assimilated and therefore "available". While it was unconscious (and therefore known as dark, threatening, numinous, and too dangerous to let loose) it worked only through symbols, often as "goddesses", whilst real women, inevitably carrying that symbolism, tended to be either suppressed or sacralised. They could be priestesses or possessions but seldom people. They could be poets, sages, war-leaders, matriarchs, prostitutes, slaves, but not companions. The human community could not yet cope with the dynamic of its own feminine nature, and if, at last, it becomes possible for humanity to "withdraw its projection" and actually live, consciously, its feminine aspects, the consequences must be so enormous that we cannot begin to guess at them.'[27]

Rosemary Haughton takes Jung's archetypes of 'the animus' and 'the anima'[28] to throw light on the profound change slowly taking place in the history of the West[29]. She sees Jung's anima principle as part of the biblical concept of Wisdom, the feminine aspect of the Godhead which has been negated by church and society over the centuries with devastating consequences[30]. The shift from the dominance of the animus, the male element in life, to greater acknowledgement of the anima, the female element, is thus part of a rediscovery of the nature and purposes of God.

Nonetheless, some basic groups living communally report a tendency for the traditional sexist division of labour to reassert itself. Within the religious orders the struggle to reaffirm the equality of female and male, in pre-Renaissance and pre-Reformation times widely recognised, is also a continuing one. Alan Harrison's sentiments regarding Anglican religious are wholehearted when he writes: 'It seems to be a literal matter of life and death that woman's spiritual priesthood should be given back to her'[31] — though it must be added that most women within the basic community movement do not regard their role as primarily related to 'priesthood' and, even where they do, they take it for granted rather than wait to 'be given it back'. Liberation from male clericalism is seen not so much as a matter of ordination (though that remains important), but as a major shift in attitude and practice towards validating the feminine as an essential component in the rebuilding of community.

A small number of basic Christian groups incorporate the shift from priest to people into their apostolate of training ordinands. Of note here has been the work of the Urban Ministry Project, the Urban Theology Unit and AVEC. Some centres, such as the Luton Industrial College, Ammerdown, and Scottish Churches House, include in-service clergy courses of an imaginative kind in their normal programmes. The Roman Catholic Movement for a Better World conducts training on a long-term basis with priests and their congregations in the parish itself. The aim of many such ventures is to enable clergy to learn side by side with laity, to make use of real life situations and experiences, and to develop the skills of corporate leadership.

Basic Christian groups also attempt to carry over their understanding of authority into the *secular* world. They cannot seek liberation from clericalism within the church and rest content with the 'clericalism' evident within secular institutions. Though basic groups are often found on the margins of society, their attitude to authority thus raises important questions for those secular sectors to which they most directly relate. Those such as the l'Arche houses in connection with the mentally handicapped, Corrymeela in its work of community education in Northern Ireland, Noah's Ark in its support of single parents and

Christian C.N.D. in peacemaking, point to the need for power to be transferred from 'priest to people' in the secular world. As such they are not only signs of contradiction, but also of hope that a new kind of authority is both workable and liberating, and that community can thereby be enriched and strengthened.

4. From community of place to community of concern

Edwina Gateley writes:
'In March 1980 the U.S. Catholic Centre for Volunteer Ministry encouraged the religious communities and congregations "to look carefully into the spirit of your founders and see the great potential for community renewal to be found by including laity in your ministry". Good Lord! The laity can't be used in that way! We don't want to be "included" in anybody's ministries. We want to fulfil our own ministry in partnership and equality with the religious orders and with ordained members of the church. We don't want to be co-opted in, or under, or through, anything: we want to be ministers in our own right.'[32]

She might have been a little more encouraged if she had been able to read the words of Catherine Hughes, Provincial of the Sisters of Notre Dame, writing in 'Community' only six months later: 'Whatever the future of the hierarchy in the church, the religious is placed with the laity, receiving from and giving to any human being on an equal basis'[33]. Basic Christian groups are likewise pledged to the apostolate of the laity having the utmost significance in its own right.

The last chapter documented the wide diversity of work in which basic Christian groups are involved, a demonstration of how they have begun to take very seriously the need to move from preoccupation with community of place towards deliberate involvement in communities of concern. Their apostolate bears witness to how the basic Christian community movement has broken clear of the straight-jacket of parochialism in order to be able to respond to the fact that Christians today live in a cosmopolitan world.

Basic Christian groups are acting as harbingers of a new lay and ecumenical apostolate especially in relation to the institutional sectors and in response to key issues of the day.

With regard to a *sector-based apostolate,* basic groups are notably active in education, welfare and health — for example, at Seva Sadan through language and literacy tuition for Gujeratis in inner city

Birmingham, at Link-Up through its work with the homeless in Nuneaton, and at St. Christopher's Hospice in south-east London. Here they are able to draw on many lay people already trained and experienced in the teaching or helping professions. Basic groups have also formed in sectors concerned with the arts, publishing, agriculture, alternative technology, co-operatives and politics.

However, in other sectors, such as government and administration, industry, commerce and the media, basic Christian groups are as yet few and far between. The reasons for this are not hard to find. First, secularisation has gone furthest in these sectors. In these sectors Christians are not just thinner on the ground, but bearing an often isolated witness in the face of considerable cynicism or apathy. Secondly, the pace of life in these sectors means that the time and energy available for Christians to meet, share experiences and ideas, and support one another, are at a premium. Thirdly, some Christians have been put off too public a witness by the past formation of 'holy huddles' in various places of work, the members of which seem to be seeking to escape from, rather than engage with, a secular world. Consequently, if progressive laity do attempt to form basic Christian groups, they fear being tarred with the same brush, and being taken by their fellows to be establishing exclusive religious cliques.

Basic Christian groups are particularly active, in connection with *issue-centred concerns,* for example conservation, minority rights, justice and peace, and third world poverty. Of all basic Christian groups, those pursuing key issues of the day sit lightest to community of place. They are highly mobile. They multiply (and die away) rapidly. This does not negate the value of their apostolate; issue-centred groups can only survive whilst the cause they pursue remains a live one. Issue-centred groups, being the pioneers they are, often pursue false trails: they need freedom to explore, experiment and fail, as well as to succeed. But win or lose, they have come into existence because a church captive to parochialism cannot respond freely or quickly enough to break the mould of a privatised faith.

There exists some tension between sector-based groups and issue-centred groups. Sector-based groups keep a lower profile politically and are more dependent on, even if still critical of, the social system as it is. Issue-centred groups stand over against many traditional forms of institutional life and are more outspoken about the necessity for radical change. Consequently, they sometimes express doubts about other Christian groups which invest time and money seeking to make faith meaningful within and through the existing system.

Basic groups have been active in promoting reflection and discussion on a lay apostolate in a secular society. In the van have been many of the laity centres already mentioned. One of these, now sadly no longer in existence, was for me an outstanding example of what could be achieved in this connection.

From 1961 to 1962 I spent a year as a student at the William Temple College, Rugby. The college, an independent Anglican foundation, was a brilliant achievement in Christian community education, due in large part to the inspiration of its one-time chairman, Bishop Hunter of Sheffield, and its dynamic Principal, Mollie Batten. It brought together theology and the social sciences, clergy and lay people of all denominations, the church and secular institutions, British and overseas students, in a remarkably creative educational encounter. At the heart of the college was a residential community of some twenty staff and students engaged in an ordered life of study and worship. This core community helped to maintain a supportive Christian life-style into which short-term students and conference participants were welcomed. The association of a continuing residential community with a wider learning programme, open to people from different secular institutions, gave full credence to the declared intention that, 'The College hopes . . . to promote the integration of contemporary society in the light of the Christian faith by sending back into everyday life and work those who have . . . studied in a community in which all give and receive from one another'[34].

The William Temple College failed to survive very long after the departure of its first principal in 1966. But its corporate life-style and educational programme contained many of the ingredients essential for furthering a lively lay apostolate. The establishment of such centres of Christian community education, in forms relevant to each sector, remains of immense importance for a new re-formation and for effective engagement with a secular society.

Nonetheless, many basic Christian groups continue to help the laity undertake a meaningful apostolate. Regular consultations about the latter are held at places like Iona, Othona, Glencree in the Republic of Ireland, Corrymeela, Commonwork and the William Temple Foundation in Manchester. L'Arche has spent a considerable time, including one six week international 'retreat', reflecting on the issues of mental handicap and community in a theological context. In 1979 the Christian Association for Adult and Continuing Education came into being to provide a forum for those concerned to explore the Christian perspective on adult continuing education.

The exercise of both sector-based and issue-centred apostolates enables the basic Christian community movement to be a sign of contradiction and of hope not only for the church, but in relation to the 'parochialism' evident in *secular* life. The movement's message is that *every* institution needs to validate and liberate the skills and experiences of all its members, as well as widen their horizons, in the name of community, if a more human society is to be achieved. Despite their present marginality and sometimes fragility, basic Christian groups bear witness to the meaning of an incarnational faith and to the significance of the contribution of each individual within every part of society.

5. From meeting to encounter

'We have to create a base that is internally strong enough to enable us to survive as Christians and to empower us to be actively engaged in the world',[35] writes Jim Wallis of Sojourners, Washington D.C. Basic Christian groups are attempting to demonstrate a new quality of community through their life together which can be both example and message to a wider society.

Residential Christian communities have in many respects led the way in overcoming a restrictive congregationalism and moving from meeting to encounter. They have gone through many of the trials and tribulations known to those, like the religious orders, living continuously together, but this has neither obliterated their enthusiasm for community life nor destroyed its benefits.

In my book on 'Basic Communities' I examined at some length the profile of those participating in, the size, the organisation and the activities of, residential communities[36]. Those involved in the latter are often in their 'twenties or middle-aged, though of late there has been a move by the more elderly to seek a communal way of life. Residential groups contain a considerable proportion of single people.

Residential communities can offer a very strong sense of solidarity to their members. It is an experience born of sharing and caring in an intimate yet open way. Members of the Beeston Community house write: 'The concept of sharing is fundamental to the life of any community — it is an axiom of the family lifestyle which we aim to have, and without which we would be merely a collection of individuals who happen to live under the same roof'[37]. Sharing takes many forms. Incomes are often pooled. Eating together is very important, the members at Little Gidding commenting that, 'Our commitment to God and to each other is symbolised in our common meals'[38]. There is always a domestic division of labour.

Few basic Christian groups of a residential kind have a formal rule of life though there is a set time in most for corporate worship, be that a formal liturgy as at Hengrave Hall, or 'together every evening for a brief encounter with Christ in prayer'[39], as at Lindore Road in south-west London. Many communities, like that at Beeston, report that 'the focal point for our worship together is our weekly communion service'[40]. Worship and related events, particularly festivals and celebrations, can

139

open up a new dimension of Christian living. Of the l'Arche households Jean Vanier writes: 'Our communities are places of growth for all, founded in some way upon Jesus and his Spirit. At the heart of the community are relationships, fidelity and forgiveness, rooted in God. For some this rootedness flowers in prayer and thanksgiving, for others in a searching for the meaning of life in community'.[41]

Residential communities at their best offer an impressive example of nurture and support not only to their own members but to all comers. Such groups have taken the need to move from meeting to encounter very much to heart. The ideal of openness and warmth is aptly summed up in the words which met those entering Bystock Court, when it was a community caring for disadvantaged mothers and their young children:

'And the Lord said —
"Behold, I have set aside this house and have blessed it,
That it may become a resting place and a refuge for the weary.
Peace is to be found within its walls,
And friendship.
All who cross the threshold shall find welcome,
And a comforting hand to give fresh courage
In place of dark despair.
In this house shall My Name be glorified,
For that which is shattered
Shall be made whole."'[42]

On the other hand, all such groups have had to weather periods of strife and upheaval. Intimate caring and sharing are demanding. But 'staying with relationships' and living through the difficulties brings its own rewards. Jean Vanier writes: 'The times of trial which destroy a superficial security often free new energies which had until then been hidden. Hope is reborn from the wound.'[43]

Growth in the ability to nurture and sustain one another in love has also typified the life of many religious orders. Prior to the Second Vatican Council the orders suffered from constraints akin to congregationalism. Their convents were often large and impersonal. 'Poverty could easily become an attitude of irresponsibility, chastity could easily become the denial of humanity and ultimately of the Incarnation itself, and obedience could result in childishness instead of childlikeness'[44]. The last two decades have seen the orders changing steadily, if not without pain, and a move away from congregationalism. There has been a switch to smaller and more intimate households, relationships have become freer and less formal and open friendships between women and men religious have increased. A decisive shift from meeting to encounter is well underway.

The move from meeting to encounter is, however, in evidence far beyond those able to share in the life of any residential community. A wide range of non-residential groups has offered a new experience of the interpersonal dimension of life to many others. The expression of a personal encounter with God expressed through art and music at the Netherbow in Edinburgh, an ecumenical prayer meeting convened by a small Christian Life Community in Belfast, work together at the Daily Bread Co-operative, fellowship in a company of the Servants of Christ the King, the shared creativity of making children's jigsaws at Keveral Farm, being nursed as persons rather than as patients at a Christian hospice — these and many similar experiences within basic groups have brought koinonia to life.

The strengthening of the family as a major factor in the renewal of community has also been an important aim within the basic Christian community movement. Basic groups have encompassed a number of new patterns of family life (such as 'the joint family', 'the shared home' and 'a circle of families'[45]), but always in an attempt to increase the quality of marriage and sustain the home in a time of rapid change. Some groups have been active in building family networks so that more families can relate easily and creatively to one another. The Grail have led the way here, one of their current ventures being a 'Family and Community Week' run each August, 'ideal because there are enough people to choose from to make friends and a sufficient variety of activities, with the freedom "to do just nothing at all"'[46].

There has been some tension between those who see the nuclear family as *the* foundation of community, and those who feel that residence within a larger group is essential for the full possibilities of personal growth to be realised. There has been a temptation for members of nuclear families to view residential communities as over intense and even as a threat to traditional family life. On the other hand, there has been a temptation for those living in residential communities to feel that theirs is the model of 'real' community, and to assume that the nuclear family living on its own is inevitably second best. More mature judgement within the basic community movement would reflect the view that *both* the nuclear family *and* the residential community are important and indeed complementary, meeting the needs of different people at different times of their lives.

I described in Chapter II how congregationalism could help perpetuate 'the suburban captivity of the church', that is the latter's confinement to areas of relative affluence and security. To break with congregationalism and move towards a new experience of solidarity and a greater degree of ecumenicity, can be an important step in the loosening of this stranglehold. Many basic groups, of both a residential and non-residential kind, are able to offer a 'base camp' for laity and clergy alike working in less privileged and less secure situations. Such groups can serve inner city neighbourhoods, like the five Christian couples living in six flats in Pilton in 1981, 'the most neglected and depressed council house scheme in Edinburgh'[47]. They can support those pursuing key issues of the day, such as members of Life Style or Christian C.N.D. Basic groups can also offer nurture and encouragement to those involved in sector-based ministries and help put an end to the church's subservience to suburban captivity.

As yet training for those involved in the establishment and development of basic groups of this kind is extremely limited, though the Grail, Movement for a Better World (focused on parish life), Marriage Encounter and the Family Life Educational Ecumenical Project are amongst those pioneering the way.

The search by basic Christian groups for a new quality of solidarity is a sign of both contradiction and hope for those who are captive to forms of 'congregationalism' within *secular* society, be that within neighbourhood or institution. The solidarity basic Christian groups seek to discover and manifest calls into question the impersonality and inhumanity of many secular organisations serving a cosmopolitan world. As such *the life style of basic Christian groups challenges a society which is increasingly losing sight of the human scale and devaluing the human foundations on which its very future depends.*

6. From division to unity

Jim Wallis writes: 'There is growing evidence of new alignments in the churches, a new coming together which is deeply ecumenical. It revolves around a radical response to Jesus Christ and his kingdom and the call to community. A new community is emerging from diverse traditions and strands in the church's life.'[48] Breaking the grip of denominationalism in its various forms is perhaps the most demanding task that the basic Christian community movement faces. Without a breakthrough here, its witness will be compromised and its message seem hollow.

The commitment of basic Christian groups to *one church* is seen first and foremost in the ecumenical nature of their membership and the constant contacts made between those from different denominations. In the 1984 edition of the 'Directory of Christian Groups, Communities and Networks'[49], 151 out of 252 basic groups listed describe themselves as 'ecumenical' or 'interdenominational'. However, from the very beginnings of the movement co-operation between basic groups of different denominations has been the general rule; the early example of One for Christian Renewal having been affirmed in principle and taken a good deal further in practice. Across the whole movement Roman Catholics, Anglicans, and members of the Free Churches figure most prominently. Quakers play a significant if numerically limited part. Little is seen of members of the Salvation Army, Pentecostal and independent churches. The many networks cited in the previous chapter also traverse traditional denominational allegiances, though the latter have by no means ceased to matter. Basic Christian groups and networks still solidly of one denomination are most often Roman Catholic , though in virtually all cases there is still considerable openness to those of other denominations.

Basic Christian groups and networks continue to come into existence on an ecumenical basis, recent examples being the Cornerstone and Columbanus community houses in Belfast, and the Iona Community's Columban flats and houses in a number of Scottish cities. New networks too, such as Church Action with the Unemployed and the Christian Council on Ageing, are usually of an ecumenical nature. The National Centre for Christian Communities and Networks was itself established on a fully ecumenical basis, its trustees and management committee currently consisting of eleven Anglicans, six Roman Catholics, four Methodists, four Quakers, three from the United Reformed Church and two Baptists. Its entire operation is based on the paramount importance of ecumenicity.

The religious orders have also been opening themselves to an increasing degree of sharing across denominational boundaries. The message of this new ecumenism is clearly and cogently summed up by Ruth Duckworth, writing when Provincial of the Daughters of the Holy Ghost:

'Twenty years ago — and I blush to say it — I thought of ecumenism in terms of praying that everybody might come into the Roman Catholic Church. My idea now is totally different. What I now mean by ecumenical hope is a hope that we may come together in our common faith in Christ and the gospel, conscious of the richness of our diverse traditions, accepting the joy of variety, respecting the diversity that comes about when men stammer to express the little they think they understand of the ineffable mystery of God, prepared to hear each other, to learn from each other, to allow the limitations and the bias of traditions to be corrected and enriched by sharing with others, to celebrate our unity in Christ, and to work and pray together for the coming of the kingdom.'[50]

The basic Christian community movement's deep concern for the building of one church brings it to seek not only greater co-operation between denominations but greater rapport between those holding differing theological viewpoints. Theologically speaking, the movement is diverse. Biblical fundamentalists are nowhere in evidence. Conservative evangelicals are few and far between, but progressive evangelicals are increasingly ready to see themselves as part of a wider Christian community movement (a matter I return to in the following chapter). Many basic groups and religious orders have been strongly influenced by the charismatic movement. A large part of the basic Christian community movement would associate itself with a 'new liberal' theology, though there is a strongly radical minority.

The community movement has encompassed this wide spectrum of theological viewpoints with some success. Most groups would agree with Kenneth Wilson that, 'Unless theology can be freed from identification with confessional points of view, it will not engage in its true activitiy which is to enable human flourishing, as opposed to sectarian survival'[51]. As yet, however, a distinctive theology of community (see the next section) which could in the long-term hold together more firmly those with traditionally diverse outlooks is only slowly emerging.

The message of the basic Christian community movement is not only about the unity of the church, it is about the necessity of creating *one world*. It is this commitment that brings together so many basic groups with different convictions. Jim Wallis writes, 'We have learned at Sojourners that we have nothing more to share with the world than we are sharing with each other'[52]. The desire for the building of one world is especially manifest amongst groups concerned with issues of economic justice, human rights and peacemaking. Their activities have already been mentioned in the previous chapter, though they would be the first to acknowledge that they themselves often fall victim to persistent *secular* forms of 'denominationalism' — such as militant nationalism, the class system, racism and sexism.

It is here that the basic Christian community movement comes up against the testing task of finding some way through those political differences which frequently lie behind disagreements over matters of faith and religious practice. Joe Holland, of the Centre of Concern in Washington D.C., comments on this task as follows:

'For many the crisis of our age appears predominantly as a series of "social" issues, each part of a loosely knit network of causes:
— the suffering of the poor of the earth;
— the threat of nuclear destruction;
— systematic violations of human rights;
— a world wide attack on labour movements;
— continuing oppression and exploitation of women and people of colour;
— deepening ecological damage.
For others, the crisis appears predominately as a series of "moral" issues, also forming a network of causes:
— the secularism of progressive politics;
— the collapse of traditional values;
— the crisis of family;
— the celebration of promiscuous sexuality;

144

— the promotion of abortion;
— the loss of spiritual depth in a sterile culture.
Sometimes these two clusters, one "social" and the other "moral", take shape in antagonistic political projects. Those who favour the first often are drawn to the Left. Those who favour the second often are drawn to the Right.

But are either of these two conventional ways of thinking, divided into Left and Right, sufficient to carry us through the crisis of modern civilisation? Or does each, in different ways, partly reflect the crisis of our age? Does each carry a partly distorted social and spiritual vision? Do we have in effect a crisis of ideologies — not of one particular ideology (Right or Left or Centre), but rather a crisis of the common cultural foundation of all modern ideologies?'[53]

These two classic political positions are inevitably reflected within the basic Christian community movement, though less starkly than indicated by Joe Holland. In the second category often fall those basic groups working mainly in a face-to-face relationship with individuals in personal need. In the first category come most sector-based groups, and groups responding to issues such as women's rights, poverty or peacemaking. As a result, divisions can develop between basic groups which see the immediate meeting of individual human need as the top priority, and those which believe that unless the social system as a whole is radically changed then all is in vain.

The message coming from a growing number of groups and networks within the Christian community movement is that such polarisation, and the eternal round of confrontation politics it brings, has less and less to offer to a world in crisis. A new way forward has to be found — and found urgently. *It has to be a way which upholds the unique value of the individual as a person and allows and encourages his or her growth towards autonomy. But it has also to transform sectarian and divisive forms of both religious and secular solidarity into a full-blooded ecumenicity.* In short, the basic Christian community movement is seeking *a new style politics* whose aim is the freeing of people for the building of one world in Christ, founded on social justice, reconciliation and peace. But a new style politics will need a new style theology, not to mention a liberated and re-formed church. *and a lot more knowledge of human nature I fear!*

6. A theology of community

The basic Christian community movement demonstrates that for a new theology of community to emerge message and medium must interlock. Programme and process have to be one. For the basic community

145

movement, theology is founded on 'the inductive method'[54], it is built out of open-ended reflection on the Christian experience of each generation. If this appears as 'heretical', theologising in this way simply becomes (for basic Christian groups) an 'heretical imperative'[55].

A theology of community being mined from everyday life and work by basic Christian groups is not something that can be neatly packaged and parcelled, and then delivered up to academics for analysis and codification. For one thing, it comes from deep within the joys and fears, the achievements and failures of human experience. It is intensely personal and richly interpersonal. Much is manifest, but much remains, and will always remain, hidden, like the leaven or the mustard seed. For another thing, this process of theological discovery is a continuing round of 'seeing, judging and acting'. To interrupt the story can make possible a form of stock-taking, but meanwhile the drama moves on.

Nevertheless, the basic community movement is faced with an increasing need to give open expression to its theological reflections, if only to help communicate its message more clearly to a wider world. A number of basic groups are beginning to do this. For some it means using their own regular community gatherings. As Ruth Musgrave puts it, 'Doing theology must be done in the context of a shared group life, as that life is the material out of which theology is made'[56]. The thinking of such groups emerges directly from the encounter of person with person and not as a matter of solitary academic study.

Numerous groups, such as the Iona Community, the Servants of Christ the King, the Firs Christian Community in Manchester and the Volunteer Missionary Movement, set aside particular times and occasions to reflect together on the relation of faith to life. Members of other groups face questions of a more ethical nature in their everyday work. For example, of a section of the Arts Centre Group, Veronica Zundel writes: 'The photographers are meeting with a fashion model. This could raise issues of sexuality; of "art" photography versus "commercial" photography; of how we value different arts and distinguish between "art" and "craft"[57]'. The women's movement has been active in seeking to work out a feminine theology of community[58]. The Oxford Christian Women's Writing Group describe this process as an attempt 'to heal the split in our lives between Christianity and feminism . . . to articulate more clearly what sort of community we are, and to express our commitment to each other in more definite ways'[59].

The experiences of different basic groups are also being shared and explored theologically through networking. In 1982 the National Centre for Christian Communities and Networks set up a project entitled 'Theology in the Making'[60]. This drew on the first-hand experience of half a dozen basic groups and religious orders and was a preliminary step to finding a way of working towards a more explicit theology of community. Also offering a similar facility are certain laity and retreat centres, as well as such groups as the Urban Theology Unit and a number of 'institutes of Christian studies'.

As a result of these and other developments, it is already possible to discern something of the theology of community evident in the life and experience, and through the insights, of the basic Christian community movement as a whole. If we do take the liberty of interrupting the story, *the message underlying this theology might be summarised as follows:*

It is a message about the nature of the kingdom of God, in particular about the lived experience of koinonia, of Christian community, which lies at the heart of the kingdom. It is about the hall-marks of community — autonomy and ecumenicity, freedom and togetherness in Christ.

The basic Christian community movement witnesses to the vital need for secular faith, the continuing divine promise of revelation, meaning and grace for those who have the courage to be open to the truth found in and through a secular world. Secular faith acknowledges 'the glory of man'[61]; but simultaneously affirms the majesty and providence of God.

Secular faith is an earthed faith. It is about passionate engagement. This means confrontation with closed structures, and those principalities and powers on which they rely, as much as with closed ideologies. *an awful lot of cliché here.*

Thus the basic Christian community movement embraces a new understanding of authority wherein power is seen as belonging to and shared by the whole people of God, laity and clergy, women and men, young and old, black and white, as equal partners in Christ.

The basic community movement affirms the divine significance of each person and values his or her unique concerns, experience and skills in the service of the kingdom. Its message is about a new apostolate in which every person has a distinctive part to play. It is about men and women growing to be fully human persons, about autonomy in Christ.

The basic Christian community movement has sprung out of a conviction that the small group and the human scale are the foundation on which all healthy institutions, as well as society itself, are built. It bears witness to a new quality of caring and sharing, of intimate yet open relationships, made possible through the nurture and support offered by human groups.

At the same time, the Christian community movement bears witness to the conviction that a deep sense of solidarity must be matched by an all-embracing ecumenicity which can still welcome differences and diversity. The experience of the community movement is that an ecumenicity of this kind can only flourish when the needs of all sorts and conditions of men and women, above all the poor and disadvantaged, in whom Christ is made manifest, are placed at the centre of human concerns. True unity comes when the whole people of God, with any of similar convictions, seek to further justice, reconciliation and peacemaking in Christ's name.

In brief, *the message of the basic Christian community movement is about the liberation of all people to live for one world in Christ.* It is a prophetic message of both contradiction and hope. If heard and acted upon, it challenges the domination of current ideologies and structures, sacred *and* secular, yet opens up the possibility of an exhilarating journey of immense promise for human kind.

The community movement's theology of community is being built on this message and these themes. Its continuing evolution will require not only the insights of basic Christian groups themselves, but all the expertise and wisdom that trained theologians can offer. A quite new partnership in, new language for, and new way of 'making theology' are now called for.

Such a theology of community is also a theology of the kingdom. This will mean a new theology of the church, liberated to be the true servant of the kingdom. The basic Christian community movement is the herald of a theology of liberation for our culture and our nation. We could, in the words of Alan Ecclestone, be catching the first notes of 'the dawn chorus of a new creation'[62].

8. A whole new beginning

To be true to its calling, the basic Christian community movement has to embrace and declare *all* facets of its message. It cannot forget the need for secular faith, or the centrality of the whole people of God, or the importance of autonomy, or the necessity of ecumenicity. *The movement's message is about a whole new beginning in Christ, about the meaning of salvation in the fullest sense of the word.*

Because this message and this theology are born *out of* a lived experience, they can only be adequately expressed *through* a lived experience. The word has to be made flesh.

But the basic Christian community movement is not only a community movement. *It is the forerunner of a new missionary movement.* It exists to declare to Christian and non-Christian alike the nature of the kingdom of God.

This will involve passionate engagement with a secular world. It will entail bearing witness to a new model of church and of society. It is an undertaking which will have to take priority over other loyalties and commitments, ecclesiastical and secular, many still precious. As such it will at times be a very lonely and costly task. The community movement is called to show the way, setting aside old ideologies and structures which hold Christians captive and make it impossible to turn the crises of our time into opportunities for redemption. The community movement exists to enable Christians to 'choose life'. *Not just a partial but a whole new beginning has to be made.*

This task requires of basic Christian groups a continuing commitment to Christ and to one another in a way which can break the present impasse without destroying that experience of community which holds the movement together. It means solving the problem that has beset all past re-formations, that of finding a unity in diversity which can weather the storms of internal disagreement and external opposition.

One way forward for past generations was covenanting, based on mutual pledges of loyalty. The covenant relationship between God and his people, and amongst the people themselves, lies at the heart of the story of the old and new Israel. It has been central to many movements of Christian renewal throughout history. It is still available today, not least to those associated with the basic community movement. 'Community is the place of safe covenant relationships founded on forgiveness, where trust is nurtured',[63] writes Jean Vanier.

Loren Halvorson believes that the strength of many basic Christian groups lies in the fact that they are 'covenant communities'[64], a microcosm of the rich koinonia offered by God to all his people. For many this is implicit in their corporate life and worship, not least in celebrating together the eucharist, though here some groups are still caught between loyalty to their own denomination and their desire to share in holy communion with their fellows in the community movement.

However, this has not prevented basic groups making a more explicit corporate affirmation or agreeing together some form of covenant, for example in the case of the Iona Community, the Corrymeela Community, Coventry Cathedral's Community of the Cross of Nails and the Community of Christ the Sower at Little Gidding. Some time ago the Grail described their own mutual commitment as follows:

'Our basic purpose is to help ourselves and other people towards true growth and freedom. This means living a full Christian life ourselves and as a group; striving to become a working model of what Christian community could be: a community that exists not just for itself but for others . . .

It involves us in the breaking down of barriers between people generally, between clergy and laity, between classes and cultures. And this process includes in its dynamism healing, the building of bridges, and building communion . . .

It calls us to accept our responsibility for the world, for helping to transform it into a world of peace and fellowship; for making Christ present and active wherever we live and work, and in so doing to see the value of all created realities and, supremely, the value of the human person. In a word, it calls us to take our share in extending the work of Christ, in making all things new.'[65]

More recently, the Cornerstone Community in Belfast entered into a covenant which included the following:

' . . . We resolve to listen with our living God, to walk where we can, knowing He will lead us where we cannot at the moment go. We resolve to pray and wait, sharing with each other the vision He is giving us . . . We want to bind ourselves to each other and to His promise through a simple commitment in love — to hold each other constantly in our hearts before the Father . . . We will take the Beatitudes as our guide for our desire to live a Gospel way of life . . . We will continue to hunger and thirst for justice, for wholeness, for true peace for all our people . . . We entrust our future steps into the hands of the living God, in whom we live and move and have our being.'[66]

It may well be that the basic Christian community movement will in the future find such particular covenants pointing the way to a wider covenant embracing many different groups. If so, a wider covenant would have to both 'free and unite' those who entered into it. In 1982 the Permanent Ecumenical Consultation of (Roman and Anglican) Religious held at Canterbury gave some indication of what could lie ahead when they made this declaration:

'We are committed by the vows of obedience, poverty and chastity to promote the dignity and rights of each person, and the responsible sharing of the world's resources in the fulfilling of God's plan for his creation. In a world torn apart by political and socio-economic injustices such as the evil use of power, the accumulation of wealth, and the exploitation of sexuality, we are bonded to each other and the whole people of God in building a world of freedom, justice, and love. By the conversion of our lives and by our response to the needs of the churches and the world, we are called to be·a sign of hope and a sacrament of God's loving presence among his people. In a world becoming increasingly secular, we bear witness in worship and prayer to Jesus Christ as the source of life.'

For the moment, however, it may well be that Philip Potter's reminder to the Sixth Assembly of the World Council of Churches that the First Assembly 'started timidly and with much mutual suspicion by covenanting to stay together'[67], should be taken to heart. For basic Christian groups to covenant to 'stay together', welcoming the differences and disagreements mentioned in this chapter, would be a major step on the journey. Where that journey might lead, and its practical implications for Christian community movement and institutional church alike, I consider in the final two chapters.

This suffers from too much stifling cliche, not always clearly defined.

VIII: THE MISSIONARY STRUCTURE OF THE CHURCH

In England?
What of Africa?

'The overriding message to the churches is — "You are a minority. You are declining not reviving. You are not purveying the gospel of Jesus Christ. You must learn again to do it in new ways".' (Director of a voluntary organisation) *What We?*

'A new reformation is going to be forced on the church whether it wants it or not.' (City planning officer)

So far in this book I have been describing and reflecting on the significance of events and experiences past and present. In these last two chapters I attempt to look forward, and to offer some thoughts about the shape of things to come.

I base my future scenario on what we have learnt so far about the impasse in which the church in this country now finds itself and about the nature of a new re-formation. I put forward explicit suggestions for the future simply to give more point and purpose to the debate which must ensue.

In this particular chapter I look at the future task of the basic Christian community movement. I contend that such a movement must not become an end in itself or it will lose impetus and slowly fade from the scene. I suggest that the most vital role for the basic Christian community movement now to play is that of catalyst, 'conscientising' the whole people of God, but above all the laity, and seeking to inspire them to work for the liberation and re-formation of the church.

This will mean the emergence of a new lay and ecumenical missionary movement, some features of which I then explore. I here owe a considerable debt to the study launched in 1961, on the initiative of the Third Assembly of the World Council of Churches, called 'The Missionary Structure of the Congregation' (though because of my problems with 'congregationalism' I have changed that word in the title of this chapter). The findings of that study remain as relevant as ever. In particular Colin Williams' two books 'Where in the World?' and 'What in the World?'[1], written over twenty years ago, are compulsory reading for all concerned with the issues discussed below.

Finally, in this chapter, I take a look at two Christian bodies (apart from the religious orders) having a strong affinity with the aims of, and a

Oh dear! This rather gives the game away.

potentially major contribution to make to a future re-formed, lay and ecumenical missionary church.

1. Re-entry

All re-formations have begun on the margins of church and society. But no re-formation has been achieved if its pioneers have remained there. Protest, withdrawal and dispersal, and the clarifying of their message, have always impelled genuine re-formers to re-enter and re-engage with the major institutions of their day. That this has often been costly simply goes to underline the fact that a prophetic ministry brings no escape from the intransigence and condemnation of a captive church and an alien world.

If the basic Christian community movement in the United Kingdom is to be true to itself and its message, then the task of re-entry and re-engagement must be taken up in earnest. This does not ignore the fact that many basic Christian groups have been engaged in the fray almost since their inception. Nor does re-entry demand that new groups immediately plunge back into the thick of things without an opportunity to withdraw and work through the meaning of their own call and apostolate. However, *lasting re-formations only occur when the prophetic individual gives way to the prophetic group, the prophetic group inspires a prophetic movement and that movement begins to turn the world upside down*[2]. This means that the basic Christian community movement *as a whole* has to seek to communicate its message to church and society. Re-entry must be a *corporate* undertaking. It must involve a collective and continuing witness to the need for a new quality of community in Christ.

The basic Christian community movement has many limitations. Withdrawal and dispersal have meant just that; perhaps typified by the Iona Community with its base on a remote island off the West coast of Scotland and with a widely scattered mainland membership. Despite 'the tens of thousands' (Chapter VI) in some way linked to the Christian community movement, the active core is relatively small. Financially, many basic groups have a bare minimum of support. As with any genuinely prophetic movement, wealthy patrons are few and far between. Funds available to spend on travel, publications and communicating their concerns to a wider public are minimal. Thus, for those outside the movement, it is often difficult to discover which groups actually exist, and even to keep in touch with what those groups which are known about are doing.

Despite these difficulties, there are three requirements which the basic Christian community movement must fulfil if it is to re-enter and re-engage with church and society. First, *its message has to be declared*

153

passionately and clearly. The key themes of this message I have already attempted to outline, though the movement itself will be the final judge as to whether I have described them accurately. In any case, it is a living message and as such will be redefined and further clarified as time goes by.

Secondly, basic Christian groups are called *to act as 'base camps'* for those sharing the vision of a new community in Christ and wanting to express that vision through their life and work. Basic groups have the task of giving support, directly and indirectly, regularly or occasionally, to all those wishing to participate in new forms of apostolate.

Thirdly, and of vital importance, the basic Christian community movement is called to be *a catalyst for change*. It exists to challenge a captive church in an age of crisis. It is a sign of contradiction within a society which denies many the opportunity of human fulfilment. As a catalyst, the community movement's responsibility is to seek to awaken and harness the energies of Christians, as well as of non-Christians sharing similar ideals, to work together for the liberation of the church and the salvation of the world.

In this task *the religious orders* also have a key role to play. I stress again here that I see the religious orders as a distinctive but integral part of the basic Christian community movement. In the liberation and re-formation of the church their contribution is indispensable.

The religious orders, called as they always have been to the task of community building in church and world, can be seen as historic forerunners of today's basic Christian groups. They have come into existence on the foundation of a passionate faith impelling them to engage actively in prayer and service. They offer a wealth of spirituality, much needed by basic Christian groups so caught up in the thick of things that 'struggle' often overwhelms opportunities for 'contemplation'.

The religious have long years of experience of working out the meaning of faith within an often hostile world. They have been amongst the first to pick up the signals of changing times and to respond sensitively and boldly.

The religious have as profound an understanding of community as any. They have wrestled with the meaning of authority and the proper exercise of power. The religious life has validated the vocation of both women and men. It has offered a wide diversity of apostolates which have taken them into every sector of life, and enabled them to pursue major issues of the day with vigour and persistence. The religious have been involved in a continuing experience of living together and have thereby gained deep insight into the strengths and weaknesses of human nature.

The religious realise that community has to be shared. They have a vision of one world in Christ which has sent them to the far corners of the

154

earth to preach, teach and serve. They are amongst the most active missionaries of the church.

This does not mean that the religious have escaped the dangers of assimilation by an institutionalised church or secularistic society. They too have often succumbed to closed ideologies and structures. Even after the summons by the Second Vatican Council to renew their life, many remain diffident and dependent. Some congregations and communities have lost the inspiration of their founder's convictions and others, though aware of this, are still struggling to find a new understanding of their vocation. Nonetheless, *the religious in the United Kingdom, Roman Catholic, Anglican and Orthodox alike, remain a unique resource for a new missionary church.*

Yet even the combined endeavours of basic Christian groups and the religious could never be enough to achieve the full liberation of the church. *It is the whole people of God who have to free the people of God.* This means that, though ministers, priests and clergy also have an important role to play, nothing less than a massive ground swell of lay concern and involvement can now suffice if the church is to be transformed into the true servant of the kingdom. The hope for the future is that laity of all denominations will be so quickened by the example and message of the basic community movement that they themselves will begin to give their energies to the task of bringing a new missionary church into being.

This is wholly true but· how ?

2. 'God's lively people'[3]

'The issue', writes Metz, 'is no longer whether this person or another should come forward in an élite kind of way as critic of the church and as reformer. Today the reform must encompass everyone, or else it will not succeed.'[4] — *sheer utopianism / fear.*

There is a misapprehension present amongst some Christians, mainly Protestants, that the mobilisation of lay resources is a mainly Catholic problem. There is a belief that the historic Reformation has already taken Protestant churches as far along the road of lay participation and responsibility as is necessary. Nothing could be further from the truth. The message of the basic Christian community movement is that *all* churches remain the victims of clericalism, and that, if anything, it is more of a hindrance in non-Catholic churches because there it seems at first sight less apparent. The liberation of the church is necessary across the board — it is a whole new beginning — and it will not come about unless it brings into play the shared experience and resource of lay people of *every* denomination.

The basic Christian community movement declares that the liberation

155

and re-formation of the church will require the talents and abilities of all lay people. It is not just those currently active in parish affairs who need to be involved, though they may have a significant role to play. A new re-formation means the liberation of laity in every sector, sacred and secular, in every walk of life, and at all levels of public responsibility. It has to embrace those at the top as well as the bottom of the social scale, in positions of strength as well as weakness. As David Sheppard reminds us, there are many influential laity 'caught in the trap of a divided society'[5] who, given the vision and support, could help greatly in transforming the status quo.

The basic community movement bears witness to the hope that men and women can be freed to build one world in Christ. But that hope has to capture the hearts of a laity often far removed from the places where basic groups currently operate. *It is a hope which has to be carried into the very heart of institutional affairs, and brought to bear on key issues of the day.* If this does not happen, it will remain the utopian dream only of the few. *Nothing less than a new ecumenical missionary endeavour is required; a new and dynamic missionary movement; a new form of missionary church, founded on the faith, experience and skill of lay people fully engaged in every aspect of the life of our society.*

3. Lessons from the past

If basic Christian groups and religious orders, as catalysts, do begin to evoke a response from lay people at present largely unaware of their own power and responsibility to liberate the church, the scene will be set for the emergence of a major new missionary movement within the United Kingdom. It will be a *missionary* movement, in the sense of it being Christians 'on the move, taking fresh initiatives, exploring new beginnings',[6] as John Tiller puts it. If it takes a lead from the basic Christian community movement, it will not only proclaim a liberating message but seek to live this out through an apostolate of prayer, critical reflection, sharing, service and the pursuit of justice and peace. 'Mission is in the heart of God: it is therefore the church's true vocation.'[7]

For a new lay and ecumenical missionary movement to come into being some form of organisation and structure is inevitable in order to facilitate communication, decision making and the sharing of resources. The question is not *whether* to organise; that the liberation and re-formation of the church could come about without this is wishful thinking. It is *how* to organise, in a way true to the ethos and message of the basic Christian community movement. Nevertheless, Alan Ecclestone's words of warning must be heeded: 'Any organisation can do no more than put men and goods into certain places. It is the servant of certain assumptions about the nature of men and their good life. It usurps the place of the divine when it hides from men the engagement with God that has pronounced them to be his people and related them to one another as members of one body, when it ignores or denies the transcendent element in each man, and imposes its own categorisation upon their lives'[8].

A new missionary movement will have to respond easily and immediately to the circumstances of life today. Without compromising its message, its structures will need to facilitate active and continuous involvement in the affairs of a cosmopolitan and secular society.

In this context it is interesting to compare our situation today with that of Britain in the sixth century. The fall of the Roman Empire in 410 A.D. resulted in Britain being overrun by invading Angles, Saxons and Jutes. Christianity was all but obliterated as pagan tribes swept across the country, leaving only 'the Celtic fringe' where faith survived in any strength at all.

The Celtic Church was essentially monastic, consisting of virtually autonomous communities which became not only refuges but spring-boards for long and arduous missions into alien territory. In the middle of the sixth century the fulcrum of Celtic evangelistic endeavours became the island of Iona, from where, after Columba's arrival in 563 A.D., missionaries fanned out rapidly across much of the mainland. For the rest of that century nearly half of Britain looked to Iona as the source of a renewed Christian faith.

Not until Augustine landed in Kent in 597 A.D. did a Roman form of church life again appear on the British scene. The Roman Church gradually reasserted its authority, taking advantage of a land in large part re-Christianised by the Celtic missions, as well as of the gradual growth of a feudal, territorially organised and more settled society. The Celtic missions were symbolised by their temporary churches constructed of wood and rushes; Roman Christianity by permanent churches built of stone.

To some observers[9], it seems that the situation in which the United Kingdom finds itself today has a good deal more in common with the Britain of the sixth century than of later centuries. Forces alien to faith, though of secularism rather than of paganism as such, have invaded our culture. They appear to have pushed Christian belief to the very margins of our society. Thus there are now new mission fields in which the gospel must be proclaimed, though these are of an institutional and associational, rather than territorial, nature. The old Roman and feudal model of church seems ill-equipped to meet the missionary challenge of the present day. A missionary form of church is required, akin to the Celtic, to make possible active engagement with a cosmopolitan and secularistic world.

157

The appearance of the basic Christian community movement has come as a response to the inability of an institutionalised church to meet this challenge. Like the Celtic Church, basic Christian groups have had to find ways of surviving and living out their message in an alien environment. But in the process the community movement has gained a great deal of first-hand experience, indicating what the shape of a new missionary movement might look like. The next section draws on this experience.

4. The shape of things to come?

what if post-industrial areas?

A missionary church in the 'eighties has to relate to a highly industrialised and technological, not feudal and landed, society. The former is characterised by an advanced division of labour and by high mobility, social as well as spatial. In Merton's words, the 'cosmopolitan' has taken priority over the 'local'[10], and the life of institutions (the sectors) come to overshadow life in the neighbourhood.

other? always?

Any new missionary movement has also to come to terms with the fact that the secular, and the accompanying secularism which characterises today's cosmopolitan institutions, has for centuries been allowed to push the sacred into the local and domestic realm. 'At the moment', states a report from the William Temple Foundation, 'the church is only effectively geared to intervention at the neighbourhood level . . . We see the need to engage with groups, movements and institutions at the various levels of government operations and decision taking, if the limitations associated with local community involvement are to be overcome. This implies a radical reshaping of the Christian understanding of what it means to intervene.'[11] 'To intervene' in this way requires a lay and ecumenical missionary church actively to engage with the major sectors of modern society and their related organisations and associations.

It could be argued that, though the sectors will be an important arena for future missionary activity, the most obvious initiatives for change occur in response to key issues — peace, unemployment, racism, sexism and so on. There is a good deal in this. But to attempt to build a new missionary movement wholly around one or two immediate issues, however vital, is doomed to fail. This is not just because salvation is about the whole of life. It is because the demise or decline in the prominence of such issues would then mean the end of all missionary endeavour. Furthermore, no issue can ever be fully resolved unless action is taken by those controlling society's institutions. Thus, *although any future missionary movement must be keenly concerned with topical issues, its engagement with the life of the sectors remains of crucial importance.*

It must be stressed again that this new movement will be

predominantly *lay,* for it is the laity who are *already* deeply involved in the institutional life of society. It will also be *ecumenical. To talk of a denominational missionary movement in a cosmopolitan and secular age is not only to deny the message of the basic Christian community movement but to attempt to deal with society in a currency which is no longer of any value.* Ec…o n…u ?

The main organisational features of a new missionary movement will closely resemble those of the basic Christian community movement (especially its basic Christian groups and networks, though in a developed and extended form). The possible shape of such a new movement is outlined in the diagrams on pages 160 and 161.

a. The role of basic Christian groups

The core unit of a new missionary movement will be the basic Christian group (represented diagrammatically by the small circles) consisting of lay people. Such basic groups (defined in Chapter VI) can appear anywhere at any time, They can spring up quickly (and end quickly). They are diverse. Their members are highly mobile. At the same time basic groups can offer and communicate a powerful sense of community. This makes them, as in re-formations past, an essential component of a new missionary church.

A new missionary movement within the sectors (represented diagrammatically by the triangles) will in time require a plethora of diverse basic Christian groups operating for various lengths of time. These groups will embrace laity exercising responsibility at all levels. The task of a new missionary movement is to ensure that their experience, expertise and influence are validated and fully used for the building of a new quality of community life of benefit to all.

Basic Christian groups will continue to spring up on the boundaries of institutions, for sectors do not have clearly defined edges. Here they will often have a more critical function, frequently being involved with pioneering alternatives to current institutional practice. Here too their interests will overlap with more explicitly issue-centred concerns (represented diagrammatically by the letter 'I').

Some basic Christian groups will relate directly to the local neighbourhood (represented diagrammatically by squares). Those with a nurturing or pastoral apostolate will have immediate relevance to the life of the parish as a whole. But others, for example those engaged in education, though based in the neighbourhood, will normally be as concerned with some form of institutional or issue-centred apostolate as with the parish as such.

It is in no way assumed that to be part of a new missionary movement all lay people will have to become card-carrying members of basic Christian

THE MISSIONARY STRUCTURE OF THE CHURCH

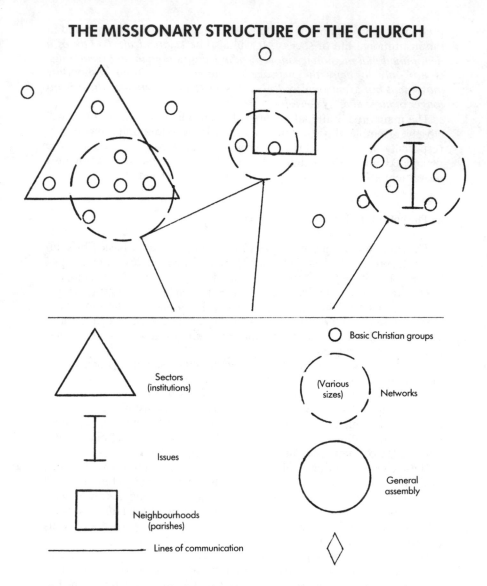

Basic Christian groups

(Various sizes) — Networks

General assembly

Sectors (institutions)

Issues

Neighbourhoods (parishes)

Lines of communication

The diagrams on page 160 and 161 represent the possible shape of a new missionary church. Some basic Christian groups (small circles) are active within the sectors (triangles); some gather around key issues ('I's); a few are closely related to the neighbourhood (squares); some spring up in the space between all these.

Basic Christian groups link up through networks (broken circles). Networks maintain contact (lines) with one another, and sometimes come together in a general assembly (large circle). All are served by a resources unit (diamond).

THE MISSIONARY STRUCTURE OF THE CHURCH
'Diocesan' or national level

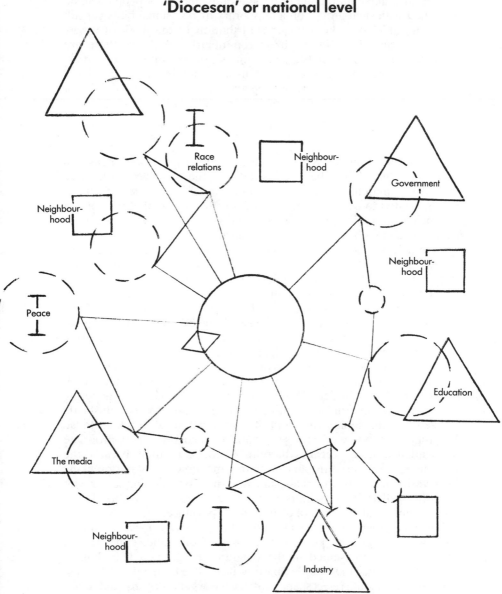

Note: Only a very limited number of possible networks and lines of communication are shown.

groups. Although there will need to be those prepared to serve at the heart of and maintain the life of basic groups, many lay people will be associated with such groups on a temporary or occasional basis yet still ready and able to make a major contribution to the work of a new missionary church (as in the basic community movement there are concentric circles of 'friends', 'companions', or just interested parties, linked to a core group). It is important in a mobile society that basic groups allow Christians to relate together in any way that can be of mutual benefit yet, at the appropriate moment, move on.

b. The role of networks

I have argued that unless basic Christian groups appear within, as well as on the edges of and beyond institutions, the message of the basic Christian community movement cannot in the end be effectively communicated to a secular society. It is for this reason that the coming into being of basic groups of laity engaged in the *mainstream* of institutional life is of such major significance for the future.

Nonetheless, a new missionary church will still not emerge unless this process is complemented by that of *networking* (networks are represented diagrammatically by broken circles of various sizes). 'Most people belong to networks without having to call them by that name',[12] writes Nancy Foy. A missionary church needs to make the most of this fact and, instead of 'letting the devil have all the best networks', begin to utilise some of those already in existence, as well as fostering the creation of new ones, in the service of the kingdom.

The Celtic model of church was in many respects that of a network of networks. Each network, with a monastic community or minster church at its centre, had considerable independence, yet through its wandering missionaries retained links with those operating in other parts of the land.

Likewise a missionary church of the future will need to acknowledge the proper autonomy of each sector and to recognise the appropriate independence of any network therein. At the same time, because the message of the basic Christian community movement is about breaking down vested interests, the establishment of networks linking sector with sector (as well as linking sectors with issue-centred and neighbourhood-based groups) will be a task of continuing importance.

A new missionary church will need to be *very well informed* if it is to make a meaningful response to the crises of our time. (The flow of information is represented in the diagrams by straight lines linking different networks.) David Sheppard writes: 'The demand of Christian love is that we should reject snappy catch answers and slogans, and refuse to withdraw when the subject becomes difficult. We must stay with it until we do understand, as best we can, what are the causes of a particular situation and what are the options for a way out.'[13] 'The purpose of a network is the flow of informal information',[14] states Foy. It is also to enable Christians to 'stay with it until we do understand as best we can', to respect, not ignore or reject, the expertise and insights offered by a secular society.

A second purpose of networking is to facilitate the *human encounter* of Christian with Christian and basic group with basic group. Such encounters will arise from a need for the exchange of information to be accompanied by a greater sharing of experiences, ideas and resources. How often and where such meetings will occur will be dependent on the circumstances, though if such gatherings are too few and far between, the sense of solidarity and ecumenicity, essential for any missionary movement to sustain its morale and momentum, will be weakened.

A third purpose of networking is to enable those involved to make *corporate decisions,* though this will be less important than getting together for the purpose of sharing concerns and the facilitation of a good flow of information.

If a new missionary movement is to get underway, an occasional general assembly (represented diagrammatically by the large circle) of all those involved in sector groups, in issue-centred groups and in neighbourhood-based groups, and their respective networks, will be necessary. Nancy Foy writes, 'A network needs . . . a symbolic gathering of at least a critical mass of the faithful . . . an opportunity for . . . (a) mutually accepted symbol of their occasional but ongoing togetherness'[15].

'A network needs a good list of members more than it needs a set of bylaws.'[16] 'A network needs a 'phone number rather than a building.'[17] 'A network needs a note or newspaper more than it needs a journal.'[18] This means that any effective network, though seeking to retain its spontaneity and informality, will require some kind of co-ordinating administrative 'unit', however modest. This could be one person working on a voluntary or part-time basis. In other circumstances, and especially to facilitate networking on a wide scale, an office, or resources centre (represented diagrammatically by the small diamond) may be necessary.

The degree to which a new missionary movement will eventually need to formalise its organisation and structures is as yet hard to predict. The more it does so, the more basic groups and networks may lose something of their initial ethos. On the other hand, a missionary engagement with an alien and powerful world (as faced by the Celtic Church) will undoubtedly call for more than enthusiasm, spontaneity and informality. *The challenge will be to develop an organisation and structures which can sustain an effective engagement with a secular society whilst remaining true to the original message of the basic Christian community movement.*

If premature assimilation into a secularistic system does occur (something that has often happened in times past), then we will have to await another liberation movement, the responsibility for which will then become that of a future generation. However, Nancy Foy's belief that, 'A formal organisation or group can also be a network, so long as it respects the separate needs of the network'[19], offers at least some hope that those re-forming endeavours already underway and still to come will have rather more impact and tenacity than has sometimes been the case in the past.

There remains the question of the geographical area on which a new missionary movement should be based. If a missionary church is to engage effectively with a secular society then it will need to interlock with significant units of secular government and administration. Decision making within all institutions, the family excepted, normally takes place in relation to an area far greater than the parish. Thus the geographical zone covered by the large diagram on page 161 would most obviously fit that served by a local authority, though in some cases it might relate to a major town or part of a city.

The same diagram could also be taken to represent the structure of a national missionary movement, which some features of the basic Christian community movement, such as its national congresses and national resources centre, may already reflect in embryonic form.

5. Facilitators

A missionary church will require leaders. Such leadership will be predominantly of an enabling kind. Thus I prefer to speak of leaders within a new missionary movement as *'facilitators'*, though at times directiveness will be necessary. Unfortunately the term 'facilitator' has in recent years become associated with an easy going, or even laissez-faire, kind of leadership. But I use 'facilitator' here to denote a person with considerable skills and undertaking a very demanding type of responsibility.

The overall concern of such facilitators will be to help form and maintain a missionary movement committed to freeing men and women to live for one world in Christ. Their responsibility will be to serve all the people of God in this calling, ensuring that each person's experience, abilities and skills are used to the full.

The more focused functions of facilitators will be similar to those currently exercised by many in the basic Christian community movement. The first priority will be *the validation of the whole life, occupation as well as the home reponsibilities, of the laity.* With this will come the major long-term responsibility of *awakening lay people, whose apostolate has for centuries been neglected, to their prophetic role;* to the essential part they have to play in the liberation and re-formation of the church and in the service of the kingdom.

164

The facilitators of a lay and ecumenical missionary church will have the task of *locating and identifying those who are or might be in sympathy with the message of the basic Christian community movement.* This will be no easy undertaking in the present circumstances with few ways, other than through the denominational press or the parish priest, of communicating with the large majority of lay people.

Facilitators will then need *to foster the formation of basic Christian groups* in order to provide the personal support and encouragement needed to sustain the often lonely apostolate of lay people in a secular society. Within such groups facilitators would seek *to stimulate full and open discussion of lay concerns,* ensuring that appropriate biblical and theological resources were available. But they would also encourage basic groups *to work out their own theology of liberation and theology of community.* The extent to which such groups would pray and worship, and celebrate the eucharist together,would be for them to decide in the light of their own loyalties and convictions.

An important task for facilitators of a new missionary church will be *to ensure that basic groups can operate effectively without them.* A new clericalism imported into a missionary church would be a crippling denial of both the message and medium of the basic community movement.

Facilitators will have a major part to play in the creation of networks. 'A network needs a spider at the centre of the web',[20] writes Nancy Foy. 'The spider's role is to build internal links, to keep the web touching enough different elements to retain its strength and balance, and to keep the information flowing across the network. The spider works not from a power role but more as a helpful assistant to the members.'

Facilitators in a new missionary movement will in many respects be taking on *the role of 'community educators'*[21]; helping individuals and groups to establish and use networks to promote the sharing of ideas, expertise and skills in order to inform and develop their apostolate of community building. One major resource here, as it has been for the community movement, will be the present laity centres and Christian institutes. But many more of these will be needed, even if of a relatively modest kind, so that each region of a missionary church can have access to facilities and accommodation to provide for the meeting of members of basic groups and networks away from the immediate pressures of their daily lives.

From where will such facilitators come? Whatever may be the outcome of what Jan Kerkhofs calls 'the fight to the death over the widening of the scope of the ministry'[22], one thing is certain. Missionary facilitators will need to have first-hand experience of the secular mission field. Lesslie Newbigin describes the situation as follows:

'Modern industrial society is a highly complex system of differentiated but overlapping communities in each of which men and women have to

165

live their working lives, interact with others and take daily and hourly decisions on highly complex and difficult issues. The ministerial leadership of the church in such communities must be part of their life, understanding its pressures and its complexities and its ethical ambiguities. Only with such leadership can there develop in each of these communities — be it factory, university, city council, professional association or whatever — living Christian cells which can function as a sign and foretaste of God's reign for those communities. Only in this way can we expect to see visible expressions of the life of the church where the powers of evil are recognised, unmasked and challenged, where the sin of the world is borne, where the power of the resurrection is made credible, where a sign of the kingdom is erected.'[23]

The role of facilitators may be exercised within a single basic group or may operate across a wider field, serving one or more networks. But in all cases their authenticity will rest first and foremost, as Schillebeeckx reminds us, on 'the vitality of the community in terms of the gospel'[24], that is on the quality of that life in Christ to which basic groups and networks are actually bearing witness.

This factor in itself goes a long way to answering the question of *what authority* such facilitators will have, and whether or not they should be ordained. Schillebeeckx makes it clear that the practice of the church of the first few centuries after Christ was that the basic Christian group (community) itself decided the matter. In fact any form of 'absolute consecration' from above, without reference to the calling of a potential ordinand by a particular Christian community, was declared to be invalid by the Council of Chalcedon[25]. Thus, given the appropriate testing of vocation and training by the wider church, there would seem to be no reason today why any basic Christian group with reasonable stability and continuity of life should not call and present its facilitator, male or female, for ordination. If this happened, as Schillebeeckx argues, 'the modern so-called shortage of priests', for whatever task and not least that of serving a new missionary movement, would, as in the case of the early church, be 'an ecclesiastical impossibility'[26].

This is not to underestimate the problem of our acceptance of and adaptation to a new understanding of ordination and the role of facilitators in a missionary church. The model of ordained ministry currently dominating the scene is that of the priest, clergyman or minister appointed from outside, sent to offer word and sacrament to, and to teach, have pastoral oversight and administer the affairs of, an unknown congregation. When those ordained move into the sectors today, notably as chaplains, it is thus their traditional status and functions which most take with them. It will take a long time before the key role of facilitators

within a new missionary movement, be they ordained or not, is
understood, valued and utilised to the full.

By whom?

Facilitators, from wherever they come, will need *training*. They will
need both theological and secular qualifications. They will also require
the knowledge and expertise to equip them to develop and maintain the
life and witness of basic Christian groups and networks. This will be a
pioneering task demanding considerable skill — in group dynamics,
network building and resource provision, to name but three fields — as
well as sensitivity to the all-important human dimension of such work.

Forms of training for launching a new missionary church are already
being developed here and there, not least by a number of basic Christian
groups and networks already mentioned. But major programmes of
initial or in-service training to prepare facilitators for the role described
above do not yet exist. Setting these up will be a matter of top priority.

For the facilitators of a new missionary movement the concept of *team
ministry* (see Chapter III) should come to life in an exciting way. Teams
can provide personal support for facilitators working in demanding
situations. They can help bring together in useful encounters those
operating *in and across* the sectors, issue-centred groups and
neighbourhood groups. *Re Moorcall it a way!*

Facilitators will require *a salary and material support*. It seems likely
that many will in the future earn at least part of their living in the sectors.
This would help to give them standing in a secular society. However, care
would have to be taken that this did not detract from their main
missionary responsibilities. At the same time a significant number of
facilitators would need to be free to undertake the more mobile and time-
consuming task of servicing a wider range of networks. Given lay people
who had caught the vision of the basic Christian community movement,
there seems no reason why those working in each sector would not be
willing to pay, support and house facilitators called to serve their own
sectors. *This also our Var attvents 1960 -ish.*

6. Fellow travellers

Here I need to make mention of two bodies, the Society of Friends and
the evangelicals, whose relation to the basic Christian community
movement has hitherto been touched on only in passing, but who have a
potentially very important part to play in a new lay and ecumenical
missionary movement.

a. The Society of Friends

'Feel the power of God in one another, drawing you together as he
draws you to himself.'[27] 'The main function of religion (is) to maintain

human community.'[28] These statements, the first from the 'Advices' of the Society of Friends, the second made at the Yearly Meeting at Warwick in 1982, underline the affinity that Quakers have with the ethos and message of the basic Christian community movement.

Since George Fox descended Pendle Hill in 1652, filled with enthusiasm to establish a life-giving society of Christian people to save the soul of a nation, the Friends have often occupied the role of a basic Christian community movement in English church history. In our day that role remains prominent, though Quakers, as with other long established bodies, have experienced ideologies and structures closing in on them and threatening to conventionalise the liberating ideals of Fox and his notable successors.

For example, the desire of Friends to equate the 'renewal of the Society with the renewal of society'[29] has been impressive. Yet such a close engagement with the secular can produce amongst Friends what Tony Brown calls 'an isolationist and negative theological attitude sometimes . . . so reductionist as to exclude entertaining the possibility of theology'[30]. This can open the way for Christianity to slide into secularistic humanism and for faith to be submerged by works. Nor are Friends free from clericalising tendencies, however democratic overseers, elders and 'an army of clerks'[31] may attempt to be. Conformity can be imposed through 'consensus' almost as easily as through autocracy or charisma. Meetings for worship which lie at the heart of Quaker solidarity do not always escape the formality and impersonality of congregational worship evident in other denominations. 'Participation' can become routinised, silence become oppressive and the spontaneous and the emotional frowned on. *actually if it is highly formal and elitist.*

Yet these hazards only help to highlight the great heritage which the Society of Friends has to offer for the encouragement of the basic Christian community movement today, and in the service of a liberated and re-formed church to come.

Quaker spirituality at its best challenges the church's captivity to secularism. The Friends' practice of the presence of God offers a vital means of grace in a society that does all it can to drown out the still, small voice. Their awareness of the living and energising power of the Spirit is crucially important in an age which faces the crisis of meaninglessness and helplessness. At the same time, because 'the core of the Quaker tradition is a way of inward seeking which leads to outward acts of integrity and service', as Parker Palmer writes[32], this journey in can also be a journey out, to match doing with being, to link contemplation and struggle.

Friends have attempted to live out in practice what 'the priesthood of all believers' really means. They have viewed the equality of all men and women under God as central to their understanding of Christian community. They have discerned more clearly than most the dangers and abuses that status and privilege can bring, inside and outside the church.

Thus, as a Society, they have refused to accept a separated or life-long form of leadership.

Friends have been freer than most from the presumption that the laity exist first and foremost to serve the church. As many famous, and less well known, names in the world of business and industry show, Quakers have seen their work in society as of a piece with their weekly worship. They have been in the forefront of those validating the wide variety of interests and concerns of Christians, wherever pursued. They realise that 'whatever kinds of community the world needs it surely needs the kind that embraces human diversity'[33].

Friends have sought since the beginning to be an open fellowship. They have come to an appreciation not only of the value of the individual as a person with a name, but of the wholeness of church and world. They have held on to a belief that true unity comes when we meet around the needs of men and women; not when we strive in abstraction to integrate our doctrines and dogmas. This has pushed Quakers to the edge of official ecumenical discussions about church unity; but it has placed them in the forefront of movements committed to feed the hungry and to bring peace to those whose lives have been ravaged by war. Friends know that 'the freedom of the kingdom of God involves membership one of another and responsibility towards God and man', as the 'Advices' say[34].

Friends have been thinkers. Centres such as Woodbrooke College, Birmingham, have over the last eighty years played an invaluable role in not only enabling Quakers and others to reflect on a wide spectrum of issues relating faith to life, but to do so in the context of a caring community. Woodbrooke symbolises how passionate engagement and secular faith can come together in thought and practice for the deepening and furtherance of community.

What is now all important is that Friends become increasingly aware of what they have to give to, as well as receive from, a new missionary church. Tony Brown writes:

'To the rest of the church, we must at times seem simply to be the intransigent minority, even though other Christians are generally more charitable and complimentary to our face. An intransigent minority within the body of Christ is a group to be reckoned with, but as long as we persist in isolationist attitudes, we may be safely disregarded as an irrelevancy. If, however, we genuinely possess part of the treasure from the Reformation, then we have a clear duty to place it at the disposal of the whole communion of God. We need to share it, not only for the common good, but also for our own survival . . .

The genuine humble learners in the school of Christ (need to) be making a pilgrim journey back towards the common centre along with other right-minded pilgrims pursuing their separate paths. The alternative seems to be that we shall sit talking endlessly to ourselves about the rightness of our convictions, until we dwindle from irrelevance into nothingness about the middle of the next century.'[35].

The basic Christian community movement, and the wider missionary movement it heralds, look with eagerness to having many more Friends as fellow travellers.

b. The evangelicals

For nearly 150 years the Evangelical Alliance and those associated with it have claimed to represent a major missionary movement, evangelising in the name of 'the true faith'. The Alliance was formed in 1846 as 'an inter-denominational' association, largely of Anglicans though also including many members of the Free Churches and independent congregations, to 'concentrate the strength of an enlightened Protestantism'[36]. The Alliance became very influential during the nineteenth century, though in this century its original impetus faded somewhat until the 'sixties. Since then it has gradually gained ground, and is now once more a movement whose contribution to the future of the church in this country must be reckoned with.

The Evangelical Alliance's strength lies in two main areas — doctrine and organisation. Its basis of faith[37] is short, definitive and personal. It is precise about the attributes of God and the meaning of Christ's life and death. It upholds the 'entire trustworthiness and supreme authority of the Holy Scripture'. It emphasises the necessity of individual conversion and 'the priesthood of all believers'. Such a basis of faith lends itself to a powerful sense of personal vocation and strong commitment to mission.

At the same time, the Evangelical Alliance is organised in a way well suited to link up with the secular structures of modern society. Its local base consists of some 500 affiliated congregations and fellowships[38], together with 'personal' and 'group members'[39]. The Alliance has helped to facilitate the emergence of numerous apostolic groups and networks, for example consisting of those in business, architecture, the police force, nursing, social work and the arts. It has become adept in its use of the media: evangelical magazines have enjoyed a boom over the past decade[40], the Alliance's involvement in radio and television has grown apace, and evangelicals lead the field in the manufacture and distribution of cassettes and video films. It has a number of influential and wealthy supporters who are prepared to give very generously to support its work.

As a result, the Alliance has been able to promote its own means of Christian outreach in an impressive way in recent years. Notable here has been its work amongst young people, from Youth for Christ to the rapid expansion since the last world war of the Universities and Colleges Christian Fellowship[41]. The now annual Greenbelt rock festival attracted nearly 30,000 young people in 1983[42]. The Alliance has also been very

170

active in the promotion of Mission London, Mission England and Christian Heritage Year, all operations requiring substantial organisational and financial resources.

The Evangelical Alliance is serviced by a number of full-time staff, many of whom undertake the support of local groups and networks. Its central office produces the magazine 'Idea', with a circulation of some 4,500, and has recently shared in the publication of a comprehensive directory of Christian organisations in the United Kingdom[43].

The evangelical movement is now facing the rapid emergence of two 'wings': conservative (in the traditional theological sense) and progressive. *The conservative wing* has been so bound to a literal interpretation of the Alliance's basis of faith that it almost forms another denomination. Many conservatives see their Christian faith as legitimating, or even necessitating, what Steve Bruce describes as 'the creation and maintenance of a parallel world'[44]. Bruce writes:

'The conservative Protestant milieu offers alternatives to most voluntary and leisure activities. Although conservative Protestants work in the secular world — often in professions and small businesses — church-related activities take up a major part of leisure time. As already mentioned even secular occupations are to some extent sacralised by conservative Protestant associations. There are conservative Protestant holiday camps, tours of the Holy Land, boarding houses for born again travelling salesmen, insurance policies for total abstainers, and an array of Bible study courses to match secular further education. Instead of 'Time', the conservative Protestant can read 'Family' or 'Today'. Instead of secular rock music, there is Gospel rock. For live entertainment there are crusades. In brief, while the liberal Protestant attempts to minimise that which separates the faith from the secular world, the conservative erects barriers.'

Thus conservative evangelicals are particularly vulnerable to the closed ideology of sacralism, on the one hand, and their own form of denominationalism, on the other. Any desire they may have for the renewal of the church is generally expressed from an uncompromising position as a 'take it or leave it' option.

Conservative evangelicals currently face two major challenges. One is the growing evidence that mass evangelism 'does not represent a major channel of recruitment to Christianity. Rather it offers an opportunity for young Christians publicly to commit themselves to a faith into which they have gradually been socialised.'[45] Bruce goes on to observe that, 'Evangelicals are in the main produced by evangelical parents, Sunday schools, youth fellowships, seaside missions and camps, Christian Unions in universities and colleges, and membership in one or more of the many inter-denominational evangelical organisations.'[46] It is a view corroborated by Jim Graham who reporting in early 1984 on his apparently very successful Gold Hill Baptist Church writes, 'One of the major weaknesses is that . . . the majority of people who join the church are either keen Christians who have moved into the area, or nominal (dormant) Christians who now have a living faith in Jesus'.[47].

The other major challenge comes from what Ian Coffey describes as the increasing fragmentation of the conservative evangelical ranks in recent years: there now being numerous groupings such as 'charismatics/ non-charismatics, house churches/denominational churches, black/white churches'[48]. Thus there seems some reason to doubt whether even the Evangelical Alliance's definitive basis of faith can prevent centrifugal forces leading to the proliferation not just of independent but of separated Christian bodies. (Note here the fate of the Nationwide Initiative in Evangelism discussed in Chapter III, and the separatist tendencies evident within the house church movement described in Chapter V.)

However, another wing of the evangelical movement is now coming to the fore. This consists of a smaller but growing number of *progressive evangelicals* who are moving in a very different direction. They remain committed to the Evangelical Alliance's statement of belief and are as concerned as any to stress the biblical basis of faith, the necessity of personal conversion, the centrality of prayer, and the imperative of mission.

But they acknowledge the dangers of imbalance. 'We see one-sidedness in a preoccupation with "contending for the faith" while ignoring a world going up in flames,' states the 'Open Letter' from evangelicals present at the Sixth Assembly of the World Council of Churches[49]. The move towards open engagement with a secular world is summed up by Ronald Sider in his general preface to a series of evangelical publications on 'contemporary issues in social ethics'[50]. He writes:

'An historic transformation is in process. In all parts of the world evangelical Christians in growing numbers are rediscovering the biblical summons to serve the poor, minister to the needy, correct injustice and seek societal shalom. The Chicago Declaration of Evangelical Social Concern (1973), the Lausanne Covenant's section on social responsibility (1974), the Evangelical Fellowship of India's Madras Declaration on Evangelical Social Action (1979) and the Evangelical Commitment to Simple Lifestyle (1980) are symptomatic of far-reaching change. A fundamentally new world-wide movement is emerging. It seeks justice and peace in the power of the Spirit. It consists of biblical Christians passionately committed to a new search for social justice that is thoroughly biblical, deeply immersed in prayer, and totally dependent on the presence of the Holy Spirit.'

On the United Kingdom scene, progressive evangelicals are taking a similar stand. Late in 1983 a network of evangelicals committed to peacemaking came into being, a development reported in Post Green's magazine 'Grass Roots'[51] which has for some years been strongly advocating this and related concerns. Progressive evangelicals are also giving considerable attention to issues such as unemployment, racism and urban deprivation, as in the case of the Frontier Youth Trust, the Evangelical Race Relations Group and the Shaftesbury Project, groups which themselves came together in an Evangelical Coalition for Urban Mission in 1980.

For this wing of the evangelical movement, there is an ardent desire to respond positively to the needs of a world in crisis and to explore at depth the relation of faith to a secular society. In the latter connection, a valuable role is being played by the London Institute for Contemporary Christianity set up in 1982, which through lectures, seminars and courses is seeking to help lay people 'relate their Christian faith to their work and home, their public or civic life and the complex problems of today'[52].

These developments are now bringing progressive evangelicals to question conservative views on the issue of ecumenism. The 'Open Letter' from evangelicals at Vancouver states:

'Because we have seen evidence of God at work here, we cannot but share our growing conviction that evangelicals should question biblically the easy acceptance of withdrawal, fragmentation and parochial isolation that tends to characterise many of us. Should we not be more trustful of those who profess Christ's lordship? Should we not be more concerned with the peace, purity *and unity* of the people of God in our day? And if God thereby grants the church renewal for which many pray, shall this not forever demolish that all too popular evangelical heresy — that the way to renew the body of Christ is to separate from it and relentlessly criticise it?'[53]

It is not, therefore, surprising to find a number of progressive evangelical groups, some mentioned here or in previous chapters, who increasingly see themselves as part of a world-wide basic Christian community movement. Openness not only to fellow Protestants, but to Roman Catholics, is growing apace. One of the lead speakers, alongside two Roman Catholics, at the Community Congress of 1980 was Jim Wallis from the evangelical Sojourners community in Washington D.C. The Evangelical Coalition for Urban Mission currently has a representative, together with a number of Roman Catholic groups, on the management committee of the National Centre for Christian Communities and Networks.

All progressive evangelicals in this country may not as yet be aware of or committed to a new kind of missionary movement. But the signs are encouraging. If and when this happens, they will bring to such a movement not only a living Christian experience, fresh ideas and skills, but a passion for the proclamation of the gospel, a deep concern for the poor and a desire to be active in peacemaking, which will immensely strengthen it, and make the liberation of the church all the more imminent.

IX: ONE IN CHRIST

'If we are going to survive as a church the emphasis has simply *got* to be on what unites us, and *not* on what divides us.' (Councillor)

'The Christian life is meant to be a pilgrimage, an adventure and an exploration, rather than being certain about where we're going. It's the company you're in that matters.' (Headmaster)

↳ Keep the elite together, boys!

In this final chapter I argue that new missionary movement and historic institution, as different expressions of the life of the one church, must work in partnership if the people of God are to be liberated to build one world in Christ. I look at existing points of contact and suggest some 'next steps' in the re-formation process.

In all this, the question of the future shape of the church *as a whole* (as opposed to its missionary form discussed in the last chapter) remains an open one. But I contend that it is imperative that the historic institution welcomes the birth of a new lay and ecumenical missionary movement, formed around basic groups and networks, as an essential prerequisite for Christian mission in a secular society. I affirm my conviction that to such a movement the historic institution should give all the support it is able, at the same time seeking to work out the implications for its own future function and form.

Finally, I look at the significance of what is happening in the United Kingdom in relation to the growth of basic Christian groups in other parts of the world.

1. Getting it together

The Celtic Church of the sixth century saved England from paganism. 'Its burning missionary zeal'[1] carried the gospel across the length and breadth of the land. This, together with the Celtic Church's 'love of simplicity, poverty, and humility, its often exaggerated asceticism (and) its stress on pilgrimage and voluntary exile for the love of God', left an indelible mark on the future of English religious life.

Yet the Celtic Church as it stood was 'too haphazard, too dependent on the fervour of the individual preacher, to supply the permanent religious needs of the population when the first stage of the conversion was over'[2]. It could not for ever maintain the momentum of its missionary endeavours, adequately nurture the converted or offer a comprehensive system of pastoral oversight to the faithful. Another form of church was needed to play a more stabilising and sustaining role. The Roman system, which gradually re-established itself after the arrival of Augustine in 597 A.D., fulfilled just such a function.

As I have noted, the Roman Church aligned itself much more closely with territories ruled by local lords, foreshadowing the emergence of the parish system. Growing co-operation between the secular authority and an hierarchically structured church provided the population of medieval England with a sense of security and permanence. The new beauty and dignity of church buildings and rituals awakened the faithful to a calmer and more immutable dimension of the spiritual life. Above all, the Roman Church offered experience of organisation and government, and organic ties with a universal ecclesiastical body.

A new lay and ecumenical missionary movement today, empowered by the energy and enthusiasm of basic Christian groups has, like the Celtic Church, an essential role to play in communicating the gospel to an alien society. But, like the Celtic Church, it cannot in the end go it alone. Rosemary Ruether writes: 'The continued vitality of the (whole) church depends on a creative interchange between converted community and historical institution in which both recognise the specific role of the other, in which the committed community does not become strangled by trying to replace the historical institution, and the historical institution does not rebuff the self-actualisation of community.'[3] A new missionary movement carried forward by 'converted community' needs to be complemented by the stability and continuity of 'the historic institution'.

The historic institution offers word and sacrament to all comers at appointed and regular times and places. It has the wherewithal to socialise the young and instruct them in the essentials of the faith. It provides rites of passage which remain important for non-Christian and Christian alike. It offers ongoing pastoral oversight to the faithful, especially in times of personal crisis. It provides a system of church government and administration which ensures the maintenance of the religious sector within the life of society. It is a reminder of the church's long and precious heritage.

The liberation of the church does not mean the end of the historic institution. Liberation is neither a denial of the church's past nor a rejection of the church present. It means holding fast to what is still of value, whilst freeing Christians to fulfil a missionary calling which has been all but lost. *If the people of God are to bring hope to a world in crisis, then historic institution and new missionary movement must work as true partners in the service of the kingdom.* There must be what Werner Stark calls 'an inspired synthesis'[4] in the name of one Lord and one people of God.

This is precisely what failed to happen in seventh century England. In

664 A.D. at the Synod of Whitby, ecclesiastical differences were settled, and the eventual shape of the church in Britain decided (by the secular authority in the person of the King of Northumbria let this be noted). The Celtic pattern of Christian life and witness was suppressed in favour of the Roman model. Ever since that time new missionary movements of any consequence have been pushed gently or violently to the edge of institutional church life (and often over the edge, where they have been obliged to form separate sects or independent denominations).

In our generation, the liberation of the church depends on our doing what Whitby failed to do. It means our retaining the distinctive character and contribution of *both* institutional church *and* missionary movement, enabling them to work together in a way which can offer an unbelieving world a living example of what it means to be a new community in Christ.

2. Points of contact

A prior condition for the development of any such partnership is that both parties concerned are *fully aware of each other's existence*. The basic Christian community movement knows a great deal about the institutional church; the latter as yet knows very little about the basic community movement.

Some church leaders are now conscious of the existence of basic Christian groups, for example where such groups are involved in peacemaking and have ruffled the surface of ecclesiastical affairs a little, or where leaders of basic groups (like Jean Vanier of l'Arche) have become international figures of repute. The Bishop of Birmingham was chairman of the committee which organised the 1980 Community Congress. For this event, and for the inauguration of the National Centre for Christian Communities and Networks in 1981[5], the heads of the main English churches conveyed their greetings. A number of dioceses and districts sent representatives to a conference in September 1983 when a first attempt was made to explore the significance of the basic Christian community movement for the United Kingdom[6]. These links apart, however, church leaders generally have little knowledge of the work and the message of the basic Christian community movement and their implications for the future. Basic Christian groups thus face a major task in re-engaging with the historic institution, let alone with a secular society.

A second condition for a liberating encounter between a new missionary movement and the institutional church is that both *remain open to one another*. There is a possibility that the present basic Christian community movement could again retreat into the wilderness or the ghetto. There is a possibility that the institutional church could finally reject the basic community movement. But as the realisation dawns that each needs the other to ensure that the whole people of God are freed for their apostolate of building one world in Christ, it is to be hoped that the commitment to give time and energy to meet and to listen to one another will grow.

Here and there this process of encounter has already begun. Despite widespread ignorance of the basic community movement, there have already been meetings and exchanges of an encouraging kind. The need now is for these to grow in number and frequency, as well as for new ways of co-operation and the sharing of resources to be explored.

a. Links at neighbourhood level

The activities of basic Christian groups are currently touching the life of the local church in a number of ways, though the significance of these contacts is largely unrealised. Some basic groups are operating in a nurturing capacity, especially family groupings and community houses. Some are more involved in a serving ministry, for example in connection with the mentally handicapped, homeless, or terminally ill. Others are involved at the local level in issues such as peacemaking or human rights.

The number of such basic groups in any one parish is usually small. Nonetheless, those groups that exist do provide an opportunity for local congregations to experience alternative ways of building Christian community in a secular society. It would be valuable if each congregation sought to keep in close touch with, and spread news about, the work of basic Christian groups in their locality. One useful way of strengthening links could be to offer those involved in basic groups the chance of making regular contributions to weekly worship. A major step forward would be taken if one community house were eventually opened in every parish.

b. Links at 'diocesan' level

As indicated in the last chapter, it is over an area much wider than the parish that the encounter of new missionary movement and institutional church promises to be most fruitful. Effective mission to the sectors can only really make sense in relation to meaningful secular units of government and administration. Thus it is the 'diocese', ecclesiastically speaking, that offers the most relevant arena for the emergence of a new missionary church.

The term 'diocese' is here used in a non-denominational sense; 'district', 'area', or any other ecclesiastical term with a similar meaning could just as well be used. It is the relevance of such ecclesiastical units of government to secular structures of decision making that matters. (John Tiller argues that the Anglican deanery, or its equivalent, may sometimes be as significant as the diocese for missionary purposes[7].)

Problems abound of course in that dioceses, districts, and areas vary so enormously in size and rarely coincide with one another; or indeed with secular units of government and administration (which themselves also fail to match up neatly). But the fact remains that a new missionary church must engage with secular structures as effectively as possible, and this first becomes a viable proposition at the diocesan/local authority level.

The liberation of the church will require the efforts of liberated bishops, chairmen, moderators, area superintendents, overseers, or other church leaders in similar positions. John Tiller believes that the bishop, 'Is of all Christian ministers the one best placed to bring together the institutional church and the outreach of pioneering ministries, so that the two are not separated and moving in different directions'[8]. It is possible that the process of co-operation between the historic institution and a new missionary movement would be facilitated by the appointment of more suffragan or assistant bishops, or their equivalents, *specifically to support 'pioneering ministries' within each sector;* and possibly by the formation of 'episcopal teams' to encourage the growth and multiplication of such ministries. However, it would be essential that basic groups and networks retain the opportunity to develop their own distinctive (lay and ecumenical) apostolates under the guidance of those chosen by them for that purpose.

The institutional church has many personnel with a diocesan-wide brief who could act as useful facilitators, especially in the early days of a new missionary movement. Amongst those already ordained, ministers now employed within the sectors would be a major resource. As yet these remain very scattered and their efforts almost entirely unco-ordinated. However in 1983 a group of Methodist sector ministers, deaconesses and lay people took a step forward by beginning to meet twice yearly for discussions on a national basis. Many chaplains are also in a key position to help create and support basic groups and networks.

Non-stipendiary ministers, and those of similar standing outside the Anglican church, whose main concern has hitherto been to exercise a parish-based ministry (and of whose existence Mark Hodge reports the TUC, CBI and British Institute of Management, amongst other bodies, to be quite unaware[9]), could yet prove valuable facilitators for a missionary church within the sectors.

Diocesan authorities could help by encouraging more of the religious to act as facilitators to a new missionary movement, though many of the latter are already actively engaged alongside members of basic Christian groups in this kind of apostolate. The potential of the various deaconess orders as facilitators within a new missionary movement is also considerable. A number of them, following their international 'Diakonia' conference in 1983, are now beginning to look seriously at such forms of ministry. Some full-time lay church workers, for example Church Army officers[10] and community and youth workers, could also play a useful part as facilitators in a missionary church of the future.

Nonetheless, *it is the laity as a whole who remain the indispensable source of leadership for a new missionary movement in the years ahead.* Each diocese, district, or area could render an invaluable service by seeking in every way possible to encourage suitable lay men and women to prepare for this role.

There will be the need for some recognised meeting ground between historic institution and new missionary movement. This could be a diocesan synod or similar kind of body. As yet no synod gives attention to the work of basic Christian groups, and few give serious consideration to the apostolate of the laity in the sectors, with the occasional exception of education, health or industry. But if normal church business gets in the way, then special sessions of synod ought to be arranged to receive and consider reports from sector-based and issue-centred groups.

One great asset which the Anglican diocese possesses is its cathedral (Free Churches sometimes have equally well-sited central halls or missions). Tiller emphasises the potential of the cathedral as a focus of the life and work of the whole people of God[11]. In a missionary church the cathedral could become as important an ecumenical meeting point as any. Some cathedrals are already active in opening their doors in this kind of endeavour, the lively festival held at Wells Cathedral in 1982 to celebrate the birth of St. Francis being but one example. But many more exciting possibilities exist for Anglican cathedrals (or their Roman Catholic or Free Church equivalents) to encourage, enrich and celebrate the encounter between a new lay and ecumenical missionary movement and the historic institution.

c. Links at national level

At a national level a number of links have already been established between the major denominations and the basic Christian community movement, in this case often represented by the National Centre for Christian Communities and Networks.

The Church of England's Board of Education, National Society for Religious Education and Children's Society are group associates of the National Centre. The latter's project on 'The Family in Transition'[12] was set up in 1982 with the help of some funding from the Board for Social Responsibility. Giving outstanding and continuing support to the basic Christian community movement has been the Communities Consultative Council representing the Anglican religious orders. A still dormant but potentially very valuable opportunity for future co-operation lies in links with the 'voluntary societies' of the Church of England, their origins reflecting in some ways those of the beginnings of basic Christian groups today.

Likewise, within the Roman Catholic Church, co-operation between the National Council for the Lay Apostolate and the basic Christian community movement could well open the way to a deeper awareness of the meaning of a new ecumenical missionary movement. One problem here is that many Catholic associations are still engaged in serving mainly the needs of Catholics, rather than in wider community building. The emergence of a parallel religious world, akin to that established by conservative evangelicals, has been one result. However, the National Council for the Lay Apostolate is seeking a deeper understanding of its task in a secular society, as well as stronger ecumenical links. The Newman Association, Christian Life Communities, Pax Christi and the Volunteer Missionary Movement are members of the Council for the Lay Apostolate as well as group associates of the National Centre for Christian Communities and Networks.

At present by far the strongest bond with the Catholic Church has been forged through the many ties now linking the Roman religious orders and the basic Christian community movement, with the Conference of Major Religious Superiors here playing a very important part.

The Methodist Church's Home Mission Division and Division of Social Responsibility are group associates of the National Centre. So too is the Baptist Union of Great Britain and Ireland.

Links between the basic community movement and the Society of Friends have so far been limited but encouraging. The National Centre has a close working relationship with Woodbrooke College, Birmingham, which has hosted numerous gatherings of basic Christian groups. Several Quaker associations have taken a lively interest in the basic Christian community movement.

Unfortunately, contacts between the basic Christian community movement and black independent Christian churches in the United Kingdom have been few and far between. One reason for this seems to be that the ministry of the black churches has so far been exercised largely at neighbourhood level. Few black church leaders have as yet seen an active sector-based or issue-centred apostolate (other than opposing racism) as possible or even necessary. Motivation to link up with the majority of basic Christian groups and networks has, therefore, remained weak. What about the Silem university Project in this area.

Nevertheless, there are signs that the black churches are beginning to take greater interest in the concerns and ways of working typical of the basic Christian community movement as a whole. For example, in 1981, a Federation of Black Alternative Schools, in which black Christians were very active, was set up. In 1984 Christian Concern for the (Ethnic Minority) Elderly was formed[13], and has already established a working partnership with the Christian Council on Ageing. From the other side, a number of basic Christian groups and religious orders (as mentioned in Chapter VI) are seeking to strengthen links with the black churches. Thus growing black participation in a new missionary movement begins to look more of a possibility.

On the national ecumenical scene, the British Council of Churches has been very positive in its support of the establishment and work of the National Centre for Christian Communities and Networks. The Council for World Missions is a group associate of the latter. There has been regular and valuable contact with the staff of Christian Aid. Several members of the staff of the British Council of Churches have been involved in arrangements for the 1984 National Congress. Other ecumenical bodies in touch with the National Centre include the Family Life Ecumenical Education Project, Church Action with the Unemployed and the National Council of Y.M.C.As.

Contacts between the basic Christian community movement and the institutional church outside England have not been detailed here as developments in Wales, Scotland and Northern Ireland have been taking a direction particular to their own regional situations. In Wales, Coleg Trefeca, the laity centre of the Presbyterian Church of Wales, is proving an important meeting ground. In Scotland the Iona Community has long-standing ties with the Church of Scotland. Scottish Churches House is playing an increasingly important role in helping link historic institution and new missionary movement (a resource centre containing material on basic Christian community movements around the world currently being set up there by Ian Fraser). In Northern Ireland links with the mainstream churches are maintained through a wide variety of basic Christian groups, the recently established Columbanus Community having committed the major denominations to involvement at a more official level than hitherto. These regions will undoubtedly continue to develop further the partnership between missionary movement and institutional church very much in the context of their own historical and cultural situation.

3. Where next?

It is neither helpful nor possible to attempt to prescribe in detail what form of church will eventually emerge from the encounter of new missionary movement and historic institution. The process of liberation and re-formation necessarily remains dynamic and unpredictable, open to the guidance of the Spirit and the response of those 'with eyes to see and ears to hear'. However, I suggest here a few possible *next steps*.

a. The basic Christian community movement

The basic Christian community movement itself now needs to give birth to some form of national association (with a membership), which can help to strengthen its own identity and corporate endeavour without compromising its ethos and message. (The National Centre for Christian Communities and Networks has associates, ie., those who subscribe to its mailings, but no formal membership as such.) Such an association would benefit from a national gathering annually.

The basic Christian community movement should explore the possibility of covenanting 'to stay together' whilst at the same time basic Christian groups and networks continue to pursue their own particular apostolates.

The community movement in each part of the United Kingdom should encourage the development of basic Christian groups and networks in ways appropriate to its own history, culture and present concerns. Regional gatherings should be held.

The National Centre for Christian Communities and Networks should develop further its distinctively national services to the present basic Christian community movement. It should also respond to the immediate needs of a new lay and ecumenical missionary movement by helping to train facilitators to foster the establishment and growth of basic Christian groups and promote the emergence of networks. For these tasks it will need to be staffed and funded far more adequately than at present.

Regional resources centres should be set up with a function similar to that of the National Centre.

b. A new lay and ecumenical missionary movement

A new missionary movement needs to come into being at both 'diocesan' (district, area, etc.) and national levels. This will in part be stimulated by, and built around, existing basic Christian groups and networks; in part consist of quite new basic Christian groups and networks established specifically for this purpose.

This process could be encouraged by the formation of ecumenical working groups at 'diocesan' and national levels, made up of lay people active in secular affairs, to advise and assist in the development of a new lay apostolate.

Laity centres and Christian institutes should give top priority to consultations and courses for the development of a new ecumenical lay apostolate.

c. The historic institution

To prepare *themselves* for their part in a new lay missionary movement consultations should be held by:
- national and 'diocesan' church leaders;
- ordained ministers working in the sectors or in issue-centred situations;
- members of the religious orders;
- those in the diaconate;
- other paid church workers exercising sector-based or issue-centred ministries.

Where possible such consultations should include representatives of all these groupings.

The British Council of Churches (or equivalent bodies in other regions) should take active steps to strengthen the links between the historic institution and the basic Christian community movement, and to foster the emergence of a new lay and ecumenical missionary movement.

Much work needs to be done on developing a theology of community and a theology of liberation for church *and* society in the United Kingdom. *This is a big task .*

Discussion of the significance of a lay and ecumenical missionary movement, and the need for the whole church to participate in its development, should be introduced into the training of all ordinands.

4. Free people for one world in Christ

'The change which is happening to the church, and the radical conversion which that demands, is not only on a greater scale than ever before, but has a different character from any previous changes which have called the church to a new baptism'[14], writes Rosemary Haughton. The points of contact already described offer the opportunity for an occasional linking of hands between historic institution and new missionary movement. But a continuing and deepening encounter is needed if a captive church is to be liberated and re-formed to serve the kingdom in today's world.

Such an encounter will cause much heart-searching and at times bring anxiety and fear. Fear of exchanging the Christian community we know, even if lacking in zeal and zest, for a journey into the unknown. Fear of our losing control over church order, and not believing that 'authority is neither being rejected nor destroyed — it is being rediscovered and redeployed'[15]. Fear of pluralism, of the complexity and confusion of what seems too much personal choice in matters spiritual and ethical.

Fear of our male presumptions being challenged by the upsurge of the feminine in human affairs. Fear of moving our resources out of buildings, where we have treasure on earth, to sustain the living stones, the members of the body of Christ building the kingdom out in an alien world. Fear of the consequences of confronting society's idolisation of the secular. Fear of upsetting our affluent way of life in order to uphold justice and peace. In short, *fear of freedom*[16].

Thus some may opt for the familiar surroundings of captivity rather than the new and disturbing challenge of liberation. Some, as in the 'sixties[17], may attempt to dismiss the signs of a new re-formation as trivial or temporary. Some may outwardly welcome such signs, whilst at the same time seeking to close ecclesiastical ranks even further. Some may try to co-opt and institutionalise the forces of a new missionary movement.* Some may even assume that the church can never change.

But the future of our world is at stake. 'Community means more than the comfort of souls', writes Parker Palmer. 'It means, and has always meant, the survival of the species.'[18]

We are being offered a choice which could lead to the promised land, or mean obliteration. *To be able to 'choose life', our whole world needs to be freed from secularism and sacralism, to be delivered from its own forms of 'clericalism', 'parochialism', 'congregationalism' and 'denominationalism'. It needs to be shown the way of salvation by a church able and eager to pioneer the journey.* This *get rather tires o me .*

Yet how can a church, itself captive to fears within and beset by foes (and cynics) without, answer this call? How can it prevent its condition worsening, its concerns becoming increasingly self-centred, and its message becoming ever more irrelevant?

'No institution can direct its own renewal by means of its formal structures'[19], writes Jos Vollebergh. The church's hope of liberation now lies in discerning and learning from the many signs of new life springing up around it. It is a hope which lies in its encouraging the growth and assisting the multiplication of basic Christian groups of many different kinds at present on its margins, yet already revealing a way through the impasse. The challenge is described nowhere more lucidly than by Karl Rahner:

'If such basic communities gradually become indispensable — since otherwise in the present situation and in that of the immediate future the institutional church will shrivel up into a church without people —

*The great weakness of John Tiller's often imaginative plans for the ministry of the Church of England over the next four (!) decades is not so much its almost inevitable captivity to denominationalism. It is its attempt to graft a new missionary endeavour onto an old parochial system which Tiller himself describes as 'already in large measure broken down'[20].

185

the episcopal great church has the task and duty of stimulating and contributing to their formation and their necessary missionary activity. The episcopal great church must not regard them suspiciously as a disturbing element in a bureaucratically functioning organisation. If the basic community is really Christian and genuinely alive, the result of a free decision of faith in the midst of a secularised world where Christianity can scarcely be handed on any longer by the power of social tradition, then all ecclesiastical organisation is largely at the service of these communities: they are not means to serve the ends of an ecclesiastical bureacracy defending and wanting to reproduce itself.'[21]

If the historic institution insists on wanting 'to reproduce itself', then basic Christian groups must press on with their appointed task, proclaiming their message openly and fearlessly. *The people of God can no longer collude with secularism and sacralism. They can no longer surrender to the enslaving power of clericalism, or parochialism, or congregationalism, or denominationalism. The future of church and of world is too precious a matter for that.*

If, however, historic institution and new missionary movement can find and learn from one another, can realise the God given power of their combined resources, then the hope of a free people living for one world in Christ will begin to become a reality.

5. The United Kingdom in a world perspective

If the basic Christian community movement is heralding the emergence of a new missionary church in the United Kingdom, what then is our role in relation to other countries around the world?

I left the global scene as such behind in Chapter IV. I return to it here because we need to remember that what is occurring in such places as Latin America, Africa and the Far East remains of continuing importance to us in the West. Latin America has in particular been a pioneer in this respect, the politically as well as spiritually inspired message and activities of basic ecclesial communities making the emergence of the community movement there far-reaching in its implications.

Yet it is essential that any world-wide movement of basic Christian groups remains true to its own principles. *Each nation has to discover the meaning of liberation and re-formation for itself.* Each has to hammer out a theology of community and of liberation on the anvil of its own historical, cultural and political experience. Only then will the discoveries be worth sharing; only then can the mystery of a kingdom which brings

danger of
'Little Englandism'

186

wholeness out of human diversity be revealed.

Thus we in this land must work out our own salvation with fear and trembling. This does not mean we become 'little Englanders' again, nor ignore the call to an ecumenicity which transcends national boundaries. But it does require that we spend time and energy setting our own house in order. John Kent puts the point bluntly:

> 'It is time to end the favourite English middle-class game, no doubt a substitute for the lost empire, of vicarious imperialism, which is reflected at the religious institutional and pressure-group levels as an obsession with pseudo-action in South Africa or South America — any place which is a long way from the Welsh mining valleys or the quiet hell of outer London. It is time the English came home imaginatively and set about the transformation of their own society, which they have put off for a hundred years while they interfered with the societies of other races.'[22] *For or us I agree with John Kent.*

The pioneers of our liberation and new re-formation must begin with their own experience and their own culture. Unless they do they will remain parasitical on others, and will have little that is distinctive to contribute to their own, let alone the wider, Christian scene.

As a nation, we have been given some valuable assets. We are a people both religious and pragmatic; the discovery of the meaning of secular faith is a quest for which we are well suited. We are at heart a people who hold 'the amateur' and the lay person in high esteem. We have a long tradition of 'free churches' and voluntary religious associations which in times past have helped to remedy ecclesiastical and social ills. We are a small island whose inhabitants, though much affected by mobility and plurality, still remember the many benefits which close-knit communities can offer. We are a country in which numerous denominations exist in some strength, and within which an ecumenical future will of necessity have to embrace a wide cross-section of viewpoints. We belong to a nation whose history, despite many mistakes, has given us a global perspective and a genuine concern for the future of our planet.

With these and many more resources as our heritage, the Christian church in the United Kingdom, historic institution and new missionary movement together, has a unique opportunity to blaze a trail into the next century, of lasting significance not only for our own land but for many other countries across the world.

A great amount of interesting material but the argument is repetitious to the point of boredom and far too generalized with a 1960's than [to]? affliction to the horrendous problems of the 80's

APPENDIX:

Distinguishing Features of Basic Christian Groups in Latin America and the United Kingdom

	LATIN AMERICA	UNITED KINGDOM (as described in this book)
DEFINITIONS		
Name:	Basic ecclesial communities (Comunidades eclesiales de base – CEBs or BECs).	Basic Christian groups.
'Basic':	'Those at the lowest level of society'[1]. 'Popular'[2].	Primary (face-to-face) groups – usually informal. At all social levels.
'Ecclesial':	'Wholly the church but not the whole church'[3].	Term rarely used and then only of Roman Catholic groups[4].
'Community':	An observable human collective.	A quality of corporate life – 'autonomy' and 'ecumenicity' key components.
GEOGRAPHICAL SPREAD		
	'Number millions of participants, particularly in Brazil, but also in Central America, Chile, Peru, and in lesser numbers in nearly all countries'[5].	Active in comparatively limited numbers throughout the UK.
SOCIO-RELIGIOUS CONTEXT		
	'Profoundly religious'[6]. Roman Catholicism 'the strongest social influence'[7]. Pentecostalism 'the most important religious force after Catholicism'[8].	Considerably secularised (often secularistic). Denominationally pluralistic. Growing multi-faith dimension.
ORIGINS		
Date appeared:	Late 'fifties.	Late 'sixties.
Founders:	'Most of them began as lay-led bible study groups, compensating in some way for	Half lay, half ordained. A few by the religious.

	chronic shortage of priests'[9]. Priests (majority from the religious[10]) and nuns[11, 12] as catalysts. Many of these foreigners[13, 14].	Indigenous
AIMS **In relation to the church:**	'To renew the church at the grass roots'[15].	A new community to free people for one world in Christ. A liberated church re-formed for mission. A challenge to sacralism. Passionate faith.
	Lay participation. Ecclesiastical democratisation	*A change of priorities –* from priest to people, from community of place to community of concern, from meeting to encounter, from division to unity.
	'Share everyday experience in the light of the bible'[16] Pastoral rejuvenation.	
In relation to society:		A new community – free people for one world in Christ. Secular engagement. A challenge to secularism.
	'Pursuit of justice'[17]. Social change – 'political spinoff'[18].	*A similar change of priorities* (see above) in secular affairs.
WORSHIP	'The life of grassroot communities moves between the twin poles of celebration and community action'[19]. Top-priority — eucharist the central event[20], though often very infrequent[21] due to shortage of priests[22]. 'Liturgy of the Word' increasing in significance[23].	Worship together varies from frequent to occasional. Eucharistic practice according to the convictions of each group. Some new liturgical forms.
THEOLOGY	'The people's religion with the theology of liberation'[24].	Seeking a theology of community. Seeking a theology of liberation for the United Kingdom.

'Liberation theology cannot
be understood apart from
the life of the Christian grass-
roots communities and of
other Christian groups
engaged in the liberation
movement'[25].

GENERAL CHARACTERISTICS

'Limits' of participation:	'Geographic proximity'[26].	Common concerns or interests.
Size:	20 to 30 families – 100 to 150 people[27]. 'Up to ten families' (Paraguay)[28].	Varies – usually between 5 and 15 members, though a few much larger.
Social composition:	'Predominance of groups of people economically weak'[29]. 'Growth of a more educated Catholic lower class'[30].	Mainly middle class, though many in socially marginal situations.
Ecclesiological composition:	'At bottom a lay move-ment'[31].	Predominantly lay.
Denominational composition:	Roman Catholic. 'In some places non-Catholics take part'[32].	Many groups ecumenical or 'inter-denominational', though some denominationally uniform.
Family involvement:	Many families involved[33].	Families most prominent in residential groups and in family 'clusters', 'circles', etc.

LOCATION

	On the outskirts of towns and cities[34, 35]. Many in rural areas. Neighbourhoods within large parishes. A few issue-centred.	Both urban, especially inner city, and rural areas. Some neighbourhood based. Many clustered round issues. Many related to the sectors (in-stitutionally based).

MEETINGS

Venue:	Homes[36] – huts – church halls.	Homes – residential centres – church premises – offices – any-where practical.

190

Frequency:	Weekly or more often[37].	Varies – from daily (residential groups) to monthly.

ORGANISATION

Leadership:	'Lay people assisted by a priest'[38]. 'Priests, sisters and lay people . . . serve as pastoral agents and "animators" of the communities'[39]. Lay pastors and 'presidents'[40]. Mainly male.	Lay and clergy. Majority male – women's influence growing.
	Indigenous – taking over from foreigners.	Indigenous.
Internal organisation:	'Participatory'[41]. Modestly structured. Collective[42] management.	Participatory. Moderately structured. Collective management usual.

WIDER CONTACTS

Inter-group contact:	Occasional local and national gatherings (Vitoria 1975)[43]. Networks vary from country to country – eg. the Liga Agraria (Agrarian League) in Paraguay[44], and 'Faith and Action in Solidarity' in Peru[45].	Occasional regional and national gatherings. Networks numerous and growing. Contacts facilitated by the National Centre for Christian Communities and Networks.
Relationship with institutional church:	Encouraged by National Pastoral Plans[46, 47], Officially recognised and 'monitored' by the bishops – from Medellin, 1968[48]. Bishops helped provide 'visible communities with legitimate pastors'[49]. Support of many theologians[50, 51]. 'A fluid relationship with the "normal" structure of the church'[52].	Little known about them by the mainstream churches. Contacts largely ad hoc and informal. Very few theologians in touch.
Ecumenical involvement:	Difficult and minimal – 'at a very early stage'[53].	Considerable and well advanced.

REFERENCES

I: CRISIS AND COMMUNITY

1. Bowden, J., *Voices in the Wilderness,* SCM Press, 1977, p. 30
2. Attenborough, D., *Life on Earth,* William Collins, 1979
3. Cf. Leakey, R.E. and Lewin, R., *Origins,* Futura Publications, 1982
4. Many books now deal with this theme but note especially: *The Church and the Bomb,* Hodder and Stoughton and Church Information Office, 1982.
5. *The Guardian,* 2/12/82
6. *North-South: A programme for survival,* Pan Books, 1980, p. 16
7. *Community,* no. 33, NACCCAN, Summer 1982, p. 1
8. Ecclestone, A., *Yes to God,* Darton, Longman and Todd, 1975, p. 109
9. *North-South,* op cit., p. 14
10. Tillich, P., *The Courage to Be,* Fontana, Collins, 1962
11. Berger, P.L., *The Heretical Imperative,* Anchor Books, Doubleday New York, 1980, p. 22
12. Ibid., p. 9
13. Capra, F., *The Turning Point,* Wildwood House, 1982
14. See for example, Bonhoeffer, D., *Letters and Papers from Prison, Fontana, Collins,* 1959, p. 108
15. Williams, R., *Keywords,* Fontana, Croom Helm, 1976, pp. 65-66
16. Toennies, F., *Community and Association,* translated and supplemented by Loomis, C.P., Routledge and Kegan Paul, London 1955 (first published 1887)
17. Williams, op. cit., p. 65
18. Clark, D., 'The Church as Symbolic Place' in the *Epworth Review,* vol. 1, no. 2, May 1974
19. Clark, D., 'The Concept of Community: a Re-examination', in *The Sociological Review,* vol. 2, no. 3, University of Keele, August 1973, pp. 397-416
20. *The Book of Job,* ch. 28, vs. 12, RSV
21. Williams, op. cit, p. 66
22. Jenkins, D., *What is a Man?,* SCM Press, 1970, p. 81
23. Tillich, op. cit., p. 30
24. Furlong, M., *The End of Our Exploring,* Hodder and Stoughton, 1973
25. Tillich, op. cit., pp. 114-151
26. Wright, D., *The Psychology of Moral Behaviour,* Penguin, 1971, p. 222

27. Driver, T.F., *Christ in a Changing World,* SCM Press, 1981, p. 149
28. Tillich, op. cit., pp. 89-113
29. Ecclestone, op. cit., p. 112
30. Halvorson, L., *Primary Enterprise,* Luther Northwestern Seminary (typecript), 1983, p. 49
31. *The Final Report,* Anglican-Roman Catholic International Commission, SPCK and Catholic Truth Society, 1982
32. Ibid., p. 6
33. Ibid.
34. Halvorson, op. cit., p. 147
35. Driver, op. cit., p. 162

II: THE CAPTIVE CHURCH

1. Stark, W., *The Sociology of Religion, Vol. V. Types of Religious Culture,* Routledge and Kegan Paul, 1972, p. 248
2. Wallis, J., *The Call to Conversion,* Lion Publishing, 1981, p. 109
3. *The Guardian,* 30/11/82
4. Kent, J.H.S., *The End of the Line?,* SCM Press, 1982, p. 79
5. Williams, C.W., *Where in the World?,* National Council of the Churches of Christ, New York, 1963
6. See on 'differentiation' and 'disengagement', Glasner, P.E., *The Sociology of Secularisation,* Routledge and Kegan Paul, 1977, p. 27f
7. Newbigin, L., *Your Kingdom Come,* John Paul The Preacher's Press, 1980 p. 29; cf. Newbigin, L., *The Other Side of 1984: Questions for the Churches,* British Council of Churches, 1983
8. Tillich, P., The Courage to Be, Fontana, Collins, 1962, p. 86
9. Newbigin, Your Kingdom Come, op. cit., p. 5
10. Gilbert, A.D., *Religion and Society in Industrial England,* Longman, 1976
11. Ibid., p.203; cf. Gilbert, A.D., *The Making of Post-Christian Britain,* Longman, 1980.
12. Ecclestone, A., *Yes to God,* Darton, Longman and Todd, 1975.
13. Rahner, K., *The Shape of the Church to Come,* SPCK, 1974, p. 86
14. Tillich, op. cit., p. 167
15. *The Guardian,* 17/12/83
16. Robinson, J.A.T., *The New Reformation?,* SCM Press, 1965, p. 95
17. Ecclestone, op. cit., pp. 119-120
18. Newbigin, op. cit., p. 11
19. Berger, P.L., *The Heretical Imperative,* Anchor Books, Doubleday, New York, 1980, p.58.
20. Ibid.
21. Ibid., p.57.

22. Ibid., p.58
23. Bethge, E., *Bonhoeffer,* Fount Paperback, Collins, 1979, p.155
24. Ibid., p.156
25. Newbigin, op. cit., p.35
26. Tillich, op. cit., p.182
27. Bethge, op. cit., p.151
28. Tiller, J., *A Strategy for the Church's Ministry,* Church Information Office, September 1983, pp.97-100
29. Cross, F.L. (ed.), *The Oxford Dictionary of the Christian Church,* Oxford University Press, 1961, p.779
30. Schillebeeckx, E., *Ministry — a Case for Change,* SCM Press, 1980
31. Robinson, op. cit., p.56
32. Russell, A., *The Clerical Profession,* SPCK, 1980
33. *Why can't a woman be more like a man?,* The (Roman Catholic) Laity Commission, 1982, p.10
34. Halvorson, L., *Primary Enterprise,* Luther Northwestern Seminary (typescript), 1983, p.128
35. Kerkhofs, J., 'From Frustration to Liberation?' in *Minister? Pastor? Prophet?,* SCM Press, 1980, p.26
36. Paul, L., *The Deployment and Payment of the Clergy,* Church Information Office, 1964
37. Russell, op. cit., p.294
38. Tiller, op. cit., p.98
39. Grierson, J., *The Deaconess,* Church Information Office, 1981
40. Hodge, M., *Non-Stipendiary Ministry in the Church of England,* Church Information Office, 1983
41. Ibid., p.21
42. Tiller, op. cit., p.24
43. Perman, D., *Change and the Churches,* Bodley Head, 1977, p.129
44. Russell, op. cit., p.270
45. Ranson, S., Bryman, A. and Henings, B., *Clergy, Ministers and Priests,* Routledge and Kegan Paul, 1977, p.170
46. Rahner, op. cot., p.56
47. Bettey, J.H., *Church and Community,* Moonraker Press, 1979, p.13
48. Merton, R.K., *Social Theory and Social Structure,* The Free Press, New York, revised edn., 1957, pp. 387-420; cf. Gilbert, *The Making of Post-Christian Britain,* op. cit., pp.84-85
49. Beeson, T., *Britain Today and Tomorrow,* Collins, 1978, p.268
50. Tiller, op. cit.
51. Bettey, op. cit., p.21
52. Ibid., p.23
53. Gilbert, op. cit., pp.92-94
54. Ibid., pp.110-111
55. Bettey, op. cit., p.23
56. Halvorson, op. cit., p.172

57. See for example the recent endeavours of the Family Life Education Ecumenical Project, c/o 86 Tavistock Place, London WC1H 9RT
58. Hinton, J., *The Family in Transition,* NACCCAN, 1982
59. Hinton, op. cit., p.5
60. Tiller, op. cit., p. 75
61. Winter, G., *The Suburban Captivity of the Churches,* Doubleday, New York, 1961
62. *Times Educational Supplement,* 6/1/84, p.4
63. eg. Martin, D., *A Sociology of English Religion,* Heinemann, 1969; Gilbert, *Religion and Society in Industrial England,* op. cit.
64. Gilbert, Ibid., pp.138-143
65. Kent, op. cit., p.119
66. Kerkhofs, op. cit., p.18
67. Stark, W., *The Sociology of Religion, vol. III The Universal Church,* Routledge and Kegan Paul, 1967, p.403
68. Kent, op. cit., p.80
69. *North-South: A Programme for Survival,* Pan Books, 1980, p.16
70. Newbigin, op. cit., p.34
71. Bethge, op. cit., p.155
72. Ambler, R. in Musgrave, R. (ed.)., *Theology in the Making,* NACCCAN, 1982
73. Bethge, op. cit., p.162
74. Gilbert, The Making of Post-Christian Britain, op. cit., p.153
75. Ibid., p.124
76. Gill, R., *Prophecy and Praxis,* Marshall Morgan and Scott, 1981, p.44
77. Ibid., p.46

III: BREAKTHROUGH?

1. Lloyd, R., *The Ferment in the Church,* SCM Press, 1964
2. *The Charismatic Movement in the Church of England,* Church Information Office, 1981, p. 7
3. Ibid.
4. *Renewal,* Crowborough, East Sussex
5. Ibid., no. 104, April/May 1983, p. 29
6. Ibid.
7. *Renewal,* no. 58, August/September 1975, p. 4
8. Charismatic Movement, op. cit., p. 11
9. Ibid., p. 23
10. Ibid., p. 18
11. Ibid. p. 29
12. Michael Harper in correspondence with the author, 27/9/82

13. England, E., *The Spirit of Renewal,* Kingsway Publications, 1982, p. 118
14. Michael Harper — correspondence 27/9/82 and 18/10/82
15. Charismatic Movement, op. cit., p. 46 and Tom Smail in correspondence with the author, 3/11/82
16. Charismatic Movement, op. cit., p. 1
17. Ibid., pp. 12-19
18. Harper, M., *This is the Day — A Fresh Look at Christian Unity,* Hodder and Stoughton, 1979, pp. 66-75
19. Ibid., p. 37
20. Charismatic Movement, op. cit., p. 39
21. Ibid., p. 39
22. Ibid., p. 16 and England, op. cit., p. 146
23. Harper, op. cit., p. 10
24. Harper – correspondence, 18/10/82
25. Smail – correspondence
26. Charismatic Movement, op. cit. pp. 15, 29, 14, 17
27. Smail – correspondence
28. Mason, D., Ainger, G. and Denny, N., *News from Notting Hill,* Epworth Press, 1967
29. Jeffrey, R.M.C., *Areas of Ecumenical Experiment,* British Council of Church, 1968
30. Stacey, N., *Who Cares,* Anthony Blond, 1971
31. Croft, P., *A Primer for Teams,* One for Christian Renewal, 1979, p. 14
32. *What is a Team?,* CCLEPE broadsheet, British Council of Churches, c1982
33. Croft, P., *The Collaborative Church,* One for Christian Renewal, 1979
34. *Community,* no. 3, Summer 1972, pp. 9-11
35. Tiller, J., *A Strategy for the Church's Ministry,* Church Information Office, September 1983, p. 135
36. Hammersley, J., *TAP Handbook for Teams and Groups,* British Council of Churches, 1981, p. 21
37. Croft, Primer, op. cit., p. 14
38. Ibid., p. 3
39. Croft, Collaborative Church, op. cit., p. 147
40. *Conversations between the Church of Fngland and the Methodist Church: a Report,* Church Information Office and Epworth Press, 1963
41. *The Guardian,* 23/11/82
42. *The Final Report,* Anglican-Roman Catholic International Commission, SPCK, and Catholic Truth Society, 1982
43. *Unity Begins at Home,* British Council of Churches, 1964, p. 79
44. Ibid., pp. 77 and 78

45. *Local Councils of Churches Today,* British Council of Churches, 1971, p. 42
46. Ibid., p. 9
47. Ibid., p. 35
48. Hammersley, J., op. cit., p. 10
49. Ibid., p. 100
50. Templeton, E., 'Spring in Rome' in *Vision One.* British Council of Churches, October 1983, no. 52, p. 7
51. *The Guardian,* 8/7/82
52. *The Methodist Recorder,* 17/10/82
53. Ibid
54. Gilbert, A.D., *Religion and Society in Industrial England* Longman, 1976, p. 59
55. *The Guardian,* 14/7/82
56. Vision One, op. cit.
57. *Moving into Unity,* British Council of Churches, 1977, p. 10
58. Hugh Cross in correspondence with the author, 15/12/82
59. *The Guardian,* 23/11/83
60. Moving into Unity, op., cit., p. 8
61. *The Guardian,* 23/11/83
62. *Progress in the NIE Strategy,* NIE, March 1982
63. *Prospect for the Eighties,* Volume One, MARC Europe, 146 Queen Victoria Street, London EC4V 4BX, 1980; *Prospect for the Eighties,* Volume Two, as op. cit., 1983
64. *PR9,* NIE, 1/10/79
65. *PR19,* NIE, May 1981
66. *The Methodist Recorder,* 14/10/82
67. *The Guardian,* 24/10/83
68. Paper, NIE, 7/11/80
69. See e.g. Progress, op. cit.
70. *PR19,* op. cit.
71. English, D., *NIE – a Brief Assessment,* (unpublished) November 1981
72. Ibid.
73. Ibid.
74. *The NIE Strategy,* NIE, July 1980, p. 3
75. *Church 2000,* Catholic Information Services, 1973
76. *A Time for Building,* Catholic Information Services, 1977, p. 41
77. Hornsby-Smith, M.P. 'Two Years After: Reflections on "Liverpool 1980", in *New Blackfriars,* no. 63, June 1982, p. 252
78. See *Responses,* Catholic Information Services, 1980
79. *Congress Contact,* no. 6, May 6th 1980
80. *The Easter People,* St. Paul's Publications, 1980
81. Congress Contact, op. cit., p. 3
82. Ibid., p. 6

83. Ibid. p. 3
84. *Congress Contact,* no.1, February 1980, p. 3
85. Jones, P., 'The Church the People Want', in *New Life,* vol. 36, no. 1, Winter 1980, pp. 6-9
86. Congress Contact, no. 6, op. cit., p. 4
87. Easter People, op. cit., p. 9
88. Ibid., p. 13
89. Ibid., p. 71
90. Ibid., p. 13
91. Hornsby-Smith, op. cit., p. 256
92. Ibid., p. 259
93. *Mid-Term Report,* National Conference of Priests, February 1982
94. Hornsby-Smith, M.P., 'What sort of Catholic? (2)' in *The Tablet,* 15/5/82, p. 475
95. Ibid.
96. *In the House of the Living God,* Catholic Information Services, November 1982
97. *The Bishop's Conference of England and Wales – The Review of its Structures and Procedures,* Catholic Information Services, 1983
98. Ibid., paragraph 46
99. Ibid., para. 47
100. Ibid., paras. 3 and 10
101. Ibid., paras. 38 and 40
102. Ibid., para. 39
103. Ibid., para. 20
104. Ibid., paras. 4 and 31

IV: BASIC CHRISTIAN GROUPS

1. Halvorson, L., 'Where Two or Three . . . The Human Scale' in *Word and World,* vol. II, no. 3, Summer 1982, p. 249
2. Halvorson, L., *Primary Enterprise,* Luther Northwestern Seminary (typescript), 1983, p. 82
3. Knowles, D., *Christian Monasticism,* Weidenfeld and Nicolson, 1969, p. 48
4. Cohn, N., *The Pursuit of the Millenium,* Paladin, 1970
5. Stark, W., *The Sociology of Religion, vol. III The Universal Church,* Routledge and Kegan paul, 1967, p. 355-356
6. Newbigin, L., *Your Kingdom Come,* John Paul The Preacher's Press, 1980, p. 28
7. Cox, H., *The Feast of Fools,* Harvard university Press, Cambridge, Massach., 1969, p. 97
8. Davies, J., *Jesus and the Prophets,* SCM Publications (Birmingham), 1983, p. 8

9. Ibid., pp. 5 and 8
10. Ibid., pp. 23 and 30
11. Bethge, E., *Bonhoeffer,* Fount paperback, Collins, 1979, p. 246
12. Halvorson, Primary Enterprise, op. cit., p. 60
13. Metz, J.B., *The Emergent Church,* SCM Press, 1981, p. 62
14. Rahner, K., *The Shape of the Church to Come,* SPCK, 1974, p. 108
15. Haughton, R., *There is Hope for a Tree,* (unpublished), 1980, p. 23
16. Kirby, P., 'Basic Ecclesial Communities' in *Doctrine and Life,* vol. 30, November 1979, p. 588
17. 'Basic Communities in the Church', *Pro Mundi Vita – Bulletin,* no. 62 Brussels, September 1976, pp. 9-10
18. Marins, J.P., 'Basic Ecclesial Community' in *UISG Bulletin,* no. 55, International Union of Superiors General, Rome, 1981. See also Beeson, T. and Pearce, J., *A Vision of Hope,* Collins – Fount Paperback, 1984 for the most comprehensive and up-to-date survey of the situation of the churches in Latin America yet available.
19. See Marins, P.J., 'Basic Christian Communities' in *Concilio,* Madrid, April 1975
20. Pravera, K., 'The United States' in *Christianity and Crisis* (on Basic Christian Communities), vol. 41, no. 14, September 1981, p. 251
21. Ruether, R., 'Basic Communities: Renewal at the Roots' in Christianity and Crisis, op. cit., p. 236
22. Berryman, P., 'Latin America' in Christianity and Crisis, op. cit., p. 241. See also Torres, S. and Eagleson, J., *The Challenge of Basic Christian Communities,* Orbis Books, Maryknoll, New York, 1981
23. See papers on a visit in 1982 by Ian Fraser
24. Pro Mundi Vita, op. cit., p. 13
25. Ibid., pp. 13-20
26. Leech, K., *Youthquake,* Sheldon Press, 1973
27. Clarke, T., 'Communities for Justice' in *The Ecumenist,* Ottawa, vol. 19, no. 2, January/February 1981
28. Grace, E., 'Italy' in Christianity and Crisis, op. cit., p. 244
29. In a lecture given at Woodbrooke College, Birmingham, 6/9/83 (tape available)
30. Grace, op. cit., p. 245
31. *The Bridge* is available from the Italian Ecumenical News Agency, Via Firenze, 38-00184, Roma – Italy.
32. Ibid., p. 246
33. 'The Netherlands' in Christianity and Crisis, op. cit., p. 249
34. Grace, op. cit., p. 244
35. *Community,* no. 36, Summer 1983, pp. 11-12

V: HOUSE GROUPS AND HOUSE CHURCHES

1. Pravera, K., 'The United States' in *Christianity and Crisis* (on Basic Christian Communities) vol. 41, no. 14, September 1981, p. 251

2. Jagger, P.T., *A History of the Parish and People Movement,* The Faith Press, 1978
3. Perman, D., *Change and the Churches,* Bodley head, 1977, p. 105
4. Adair, J., *The Becoming Church,* SPCK, 1977, p. 59
5. Southcott, E., *The Parish Comes Alive,* Mowbrays, 1957
6. *Local Councils of Churches Today,* British Council of Churches, 1971, p. 42
7. Mitton, C.L. (ed.) *The Social Sciences and the Churches,* T. and T. Clark, 1972, p. 72
8. Clark, D., *Basic Communities,* SPCK, 1977, pp. 148-149
9. *Congress Contact,* no. 6, May 6th 1980, p. 3
10. Schillebeeckx, E., *Ministry – a case for change,* SCM Press, 1981, pp. 135-136
11. Ibid.
12. Smith, A., *Tomorrow's Parish,* Movement for a Better World, Mayhew McCrimmon, 1983, p. 36
13. *The Easter People,* St. Paul's Publications, 1980, p. 42
14. Ibid.
15. Hollenweger, W.J., 'The House Church Movement in Great Britain', in *The Expository Times,* vol. 92, no. 2, November 1980, p. 46
16. Ibid., p. 47
17. Ibid., p. 45
18. Williams, D., 'Denominations – the End of the Road?' in *Crusade,* vol., 26, no. 8, January 1981, p. 23
19. Hollenweger, op. cit., p. 46
20. Williams, op. cit., p. 24
21. Ibid., p. 23
22. Tom Smail in correspondence with the author, 3/11/82
23. *The Charismatic Movement in the Church of England,* Church Information Office, 1981, p. 37
24. Ibid
25. *Update,* Teamwork, 413A Linthorpe Road, Middlesbrough, Cleveland TS5 6JN, October 1983
26. Michael Harper in correspondence with author, 18/10/82
27. Update, op. cit.
28. Harper, op. cit.

VI: THE BASIC CHRISTIAN COMMUNITY MOVEMENT – BACKGROUND

1. Leech, *Youthquake,* Sheldon Press, 1973
2. Cox, H., *The Secular City,* SCM Press, 1963
3. Robinson, J.A.T., *Honest to God,* SCM Press, 1963

4. Robinson, J.A.T., *The New Reformation?* SCM Press, 1965
5. Davis, C., *A Question of Conscience,* Hodder and Stoughton, 1967
6. Abbott, W.M. (e.d.) *The Documents of Vatican II,* Geoffrey Chapman, 1966, pp. 24-37.
7. Ibid., p. 144ff
8. Hibblethwaite, P., *The Runaway Church,* Collins, 1975, p. 42
9. Levin, B., *The Pendulum Years,* Johnathan Cape, 1971, p. 95
10. Gibbs, M. and Morton, R., *God's Lively People,* Fontana, Collins, 1971
11. Rigby, A., *Alternative Realities: A Study of Communes and Their Members,* Routledge and Kegan Paul, 1974, and Rigby, A., *Communes in Britain,* Routledge and Kegan Paul, 1974
12. Shipley, P., *Directory of Pressure Groups and Representative Associations,* (second ed.), Bowker Publications, 1979
13. *Community,* no. 10, Winter 1974, p. 2
14. Palmer, P.J., *A Place Called Community,* Pendle Hill Pamphlet 212, Pendle Hill Publications, Pennsylvannia, April 1977, p. 15
15. Where in the following section quotations have no reference, they are taken from one of the following:
    Clark, D., *Basic Communities,* SPCK, 1977; *Community,* NACCCAN: *Directory of Christian Communities and Groups,* NACCCAN, 1980 (second edition published May 1984); or the *New Christian Initiatives Series,* NACCCAN, 1982 and 1983. The National Centre for Christian Communities and Networks (NACCCAN) is at Westhill College, Selly Oak, Birmingham B29 6LL (021 472 8079). See also Ellis, I.M., *A Directory of Peace and Reconciliation Projects in Ireland,* April 1983, and Crichton-Stuart, N. (ed.), *New Christian Communities in Scotland,* from Falkland Palace, Fife, Scotland
16. *Community,* no. 30, Summer 1981
17. Hinton, J., *The Family in Transition,* NACCCAN, 1982, pp. 32-37
18. Ibid., p. 35
19. Ibid., pp. 50-51
20. Ibid. p. 50
21. Ibid., pp. 51-53
22. *Community,* no. 33, summer 1982, pp. 13-14
23. See *Christian Community and Cultural Diversity,* NACCCAN, June 1982
24. Dammers, A.H., *Life Style – a Parable of Sharing,* Turnstone Press, 1982
25. Clark, op. cit., pp. 140-141
26. Ross, E. (ed.), *Christian Initiatives in Community Education,* NACCCAN, July 1983
27. Bird, A., *The Search for Health: A Response from the Inner City,* University of Birmingham Department of Theology, 1981

Well!
Well!

28. For a symposium of case-studies and resources, see Eggleston, B., (ed.), *Christian Initiatives in Peacemaking,* NACCCAN, October 1983
29. *Community,* no. 20, Spring 1978, p. 1
30. Ibid., pp. 1-2
31. Ibid., p. 2
32. For brief notes about the many apostolates of religious orders see the *Directory of Christian Groups, Communities and Networks,* op. cit., (second edition published May 1984)
33. Weston, W. and Leachman, J., *The Vauxhall Project,* Nashdom Abbey, Burnham, Bucks., 1981
35. Pravera, K., 'The United States' in *Christianity and Crisis* (on Basic Christian Communities) vol. 41, no. 14, September 1981, p. 251
35. Metz, J.B., *The Emergent Church,* SCM Press, 1981
36. Marins, J.P., 'Basic Ecclesial Community' in *UIGS Bulletin,* no. 55, International Union of Superiors General, Rome, 1981
37. See Gilbert, A.D., *Religion and Society in Industrial England,* Longman, 1976, on the convergence on the main religious bodies
38. *CORA Report – Collaboration of Religious,* Conference of Major Religious Superiors of England and Wales, 1980, p. 10
39. Halvorson, L., 'Where Two or Three . . . The Human Scale' in *Word and World,* vol. II, no. 3, Summer 1982, p. 247
40. Jagger, P.J., *A History of the Parish and People Movement,* The Faith Press, 1978, p. 127
41. Clark, op. cit., p. 255
42. Ibid
43. Ibid., p. 231
44. Ibid., p. 135
45. Ibid., p. 236
46. *Community,* no. 3, Summer 1972, p. 2
47. Rigby, A., *Alternative Realities,* Routledge and Kegan Paul, 1974, p. 97
48. *Community,* no. 30, Summer 1981, pp. 14-15
49. *Towards Community – some experiences and visions,* The Towards Community Group of the Religious Society of Friends, 1980
50. Sabbath, B., 'A Community of Communities' in *Sojourners,* Washington D.C., January 1980, pp. 17-19
51. For example, Abrams, P. and McCulloch, A., *Communes, Sociology and Society,* Cambridge University Press, 1976
52. Palmer, op. cit., pp. 21-22
53. *Community* is now published by NACCCAN (see 15 above)
54. Clark, op. cit
55. *1980 Community Congress,* NACCCAN, 1981
57. Directory, op. cit.
58. See 15 above – all obtainable from NACCCAN

59. *The Visit to Britain of His Holiness Pope John Paul II,* a meeting with the religious of England and Wales, Conference of Major Religious Superiors, May 1982, p. 23
60. *Encounter and Exchange,* The Journal of the Communities Consultative Council, Summer 1983, p. 22
61. *Community,* no. 15, Summer 1976, pp. 1-3
62. Ibid., Spring 1983, p. 20

VII: CLARIFYING THE MESSAGE

1. *Community,* no. 37, Autumn 1983, p. 2
2. *Community,* no. 26, Spring 1980, p. 8
3. Ibid., pp. 8-9
4. Harrison, A., *Bound for Life,* Mowbrays, 1983, p. 50
5. *Community,* no. 32, Spring 1982, p. 11
6. *CORA Report – Collaboration of Religious,* Conference of Major Religious Superiors of England and Wales, 1980, p. 14
7. *Community,* no. 26, Spring 1980, p. 6
8. Metz, J.B., *The Emergent Church,* SCM Press, 1981, p. 58
9. *Community,* no. 1, Autumn 1971, p. 2
10. Ibid., *Community,* no. 24, Summer 1979, p. 10
11. Clark, D., *Basic Communities,* SPCK, 1977, p. 81
12. Ibid., p. 83
13. *Community,* no. 37, Autumn 1983, p. 17
14. Clark, op. cit., p. 266
15. *Community,* no. 19, Autumn 1977, p. 1
16. *Shaping Tomorrow,* Home Mission Division of the Methodist Church, 1981
17. A full list of titles of the booklets is available from the Liverpool Institute of Socio-Religious Studies, Christ's College, Woolton Road, Liverpool L61 8ND.
18. *Community,* no. 26, Spring 1980, p. 8
19. Vanier, J., *Community and Growth,* Darton, Longman and Todd, 1979, p. 183
20. Ibid., p. 149
21. For a full discussion see Clark, op, cit., pp. 32-36
22. Ibid., p. 104
23. *Community,* no. 33, Summer 1982, pp. 12-13
24. Harrison, op, cit., p. 47
25. Ibid., p. 104
26. Haughton, R., *There is Hope for a Tree* (unpublished), 1980, p. 31. On this theme see also Parvey, C.F. (ed.), *The Community of Women and Men in the church:* the Sheffield Report, Fortress Press, Pa., U.S.A., 1983
27. *Community,* no. 26, Spring 1980, p. 9

28. Fordham, F., *An Introduction to Jung's Psychology,* Pelican, 1956, p. 52f
29. *Community,* no. 26, spring 1980, pp. 8-10
30. Palmer, P.J., *A Place Called Community,* Pendle Hill Pamphlet 212, Pendle Hill Publications, Pennsylvania, April 1977, pp. 1-13
31. Harrison, op. cit., p. 72
32. *Community,* no. 34, Autumn 1982, p. 14
33. *Community,* no. 32, Spring 1982, p. 12
34. *Prospectus,* William Temple College, Rugby, (undated), p. 3
35. *Community,* no. 26, Spring 1980, p. 11
36. Clark, op. cit., p. 51
37. *Community,* no. 30, Summer 1981, p. 10
38. Clark, op. cit., pp. 21-57
39. *Community,* no. 33, Summer 1982, p. 15
40. *Community,* no. 30, Summer 1981, p. 10
41. *Community,* no. 26, Spring 1980, p. 7
42. *Community,* no. 7, Winter 1973, p. 8
43. Vanier, op. cit., p. 77
44. Harrison, op. cit., p. 35
45. Hinton, J., *The Family in Transition,* NACCCAN, 1982
46. *Community,* no. 36, Summer 1983, p. 18
47. *Community,* no. 30, Summer 1981, p. 7
48. *Community,* no. 26, Spring 1980, p. 12
49. *Directory of Christian Groups, Communities and Networks,* NACCCAN, May 1984
50. Duckworth, R., 'Ecumenism in Community' in *Encounter and Exchange,* no. 20, Winter 1977, p. 2
51. Wilson, K., 'Theology and Philosophy' in Davies, R. (ed.), *The Testing of the Churches 1932-1982,* Epworth Press, 1982, p. 202
52. Wallis, J. *The Call to Conversion,* Lion Publishing, 1981, p. 125
53. Holland, J., 'Probing the Crisis of our Modern Civilisation', in *Centre Focus,* Issue 52, January 1983, Centre of Concern, Washington D.C., pp. 1-2
54. Berger, P.L., *The Heretical Imperative,* Anchor Books, Doubleday, new York, 1980, p. 58
55. Ibid
56. Musgrave, R. (ed.), *Theology in the Making,* NACCCAN, 1982, pp. 6-7
57. Ibid., p. 34
58. For a full account of the Christian feminist movement see Maitland, S., *A Map of the New Country – Women and Christianity,* Routledge and Kegan Paul, 1983
59. Musgrave, op. cit., p. 30
60. Ibid
61. Jenkins, D., *The Glory of Man,* SCM Press, 1967

62. Ecclestone, A., *Yes to God,* Darton, Longman and Todd, 1975, p. 125
63. *Community* no. 26, Spring 1980, p. 6
64. Halvorson, L., *Primary Enterprise,* Luther Northwestern Seminary (typescript), 1983, pp. 147-148
65. *A Society of Lay People,* The Grail, 1974, pp. 9-11
66. *Newsletter,* no. 7, NACCCAN, January 1984, p. 2
67. Potter, P., *General Secretary's Report,* (typescript), WCC, Vancouver, 1983, p. 15

VIII: THE MISSIONARY STRUCTURE OF THE CHURCH

1. Williams, C.W., *Where in the World?,* National Council of the Churches of Christ, New York, 1963 and *What in the World?,* National Council of the Churches of Christ, New York, 1964
2. See Davies, J. on the increasingly corporate nature of prophecy since New Testament times: *Community,* no. 37, Autumn 1982, pp. 1-3
3. From the title of the book about the possibilities of lay renewal: Gibbs, M., and Morton, T.R., *God's Lively People,* Fontana/Collins, 1971
4. Metz, J.B. *The Emergent Church,* SCM Press, 1981, p. 113
5. Sheppard, D., *Bias to the Poor,* Hodder and Stoughton, 1983, p. 221
6. Tiller, J., *A Strategy for the Church's Ministry,* Church Information Office, 1983, p. 53
7. Ibid
8. Ecclestone, A., *Yes to God,* Darton, Longman and Todd, 1975, p. 107
9. Tiller, op. cit., p. 71
10. The terms 'local' and 'cosmopolitan' have a particular sociological designation for which see their first use as such by Merton, R.K., *Social Theory and Social Structure,* New York, The Free Press, (revised ed.), 1957, pp. 387-420. I have developed this theme further in a number of articles – see especially, Clark, D., 'Local and Cosmopolitan Aspects of Religious Activity in a Northern Suburb', in Martin, D. and Hill, M. (eds.), *A Sociological Yearbook of Religion in Britain,* vol. 3, SCM Press, 1970, pp. 45-64; Clark, D., 'Local and Cosmopolitan Aspects of Religious Activity in a Northern Suburb; Processes of Change', in Hill, M. (ed.), *A Sociological Yearbook of Religion in Britain,* vol. 4, SCM Press, 1971, pp. 141-159; Clark, D., *Basic Communities,* SPCK, 1977, pp. 1-20
11. *Involvement in Community – a Christian Contribution,* William Temple Foundation, Manchester, 1980 , p. 82

12. Foy, N., *The Yin and Yang of Organisations,* Grant McIntyre, 1980, p. 117
13. Sheppard, op. cit., pp. 223-224
14. Foy, op. cit., p. 115
15. Ibid., p. 142
16. Ibid., p. 120
17. Ibid., p. 122
18. Ibid., p. 120
19. Ibid., p. 121
20. Ibid., p. 120
21. Ross, E. (ed.), *Christian Initiatives in Community Education,* NACCCAN, July 1983
22. Kerkhofs, J., 'From Frustration to Liberation?' in *Minister? Pastor? Prophet?,* SCM 1980, p. 18
23. Newbigin, L., *Your Kingdom Come,* John Paul The Preacher's Press, 1980, pp. 40-41
24. Schillebeeckx, E., *Ministry – a case for change,* SCM Press, 1981, p. 60
25. Ibid., p. 58
26. Ibid., p. 77
27. *Advices and Queries,* Society of Friends, 1964, p. 11
28. Vere, E., in *The Friend,* 20/8/82, p. 1046
29. Punshon, J., in *The Friends' Quarterly,* vol. 23, no. 2, April 1983, p. 53
30. Brown, Tony, in The Friends' Quarterly, op. cit., p. 77
31. Ibid., p. 74
32. Palmer, P.J., *A Place Called Community,* Pendle Hill Pamphlet 212, Pendle Hill Publications, Pennsylvania, April 1977, p. 27
33. Ibid.
34. Advices and Queries, op. cit., p. 15
35. Brown, Tony, in The Friends' Quarterly, op. cit., pp. 76-77
36. Cross, F.L. (ed.), *The Oxford Dictionary of the Christian Church,* Oxford University Press, 1961, p. 477
37. *What we believe,* Evangelical Alliance paper, undated
38. *Idea,* Evangelical Alliance, Spring 1984, p. 4
39. Ibid., p. 9
40. Bruce, S., 'The Persistence of religion: conservative Protestantism in the United Kingdom' in *The Sociological Review,* University of Keele, vol. 31, no. 3 new series, August 1983, p. 461
41. Ibid., pp. 459-460
42. *The Guardian,* 29/7/83
43. Brierley, P. (ed.), *UK Christian Handbook, 1983 Edition,* Evangelical Alliance, Bible Society and MARC Europe, 1983
44. Bruce, op. cit., p. 465
45. Ibid., p. 464

46. Ibid., p. 462
47. Idea, op. cit., p. 4
48. Ibid., p. 1
49. *Evangelicals at Vancouver – An Open Letter,* Vancouver, August 1983, typescript, p. 2
50. Sider, R.J. (ed.) 'General Preface' to a series on *Contemporary Issues in Social Ethics,* The Paternoster Press, 1982
51. *Grass-roots,* March/April 1984, p. 3
52. Idea, op. cit., pp. 6-7
53. Evangelicals-Open Letter, op. cit., p. 4

IX: ONE IN CHRIST

1. Whitelock, D., *The Beginnings of English Society,* Penguin, 1952, p. 160
2. Ibid., p. 161
3. Ruether, R., 'Basic Communities: renewal at the Roots' in *Christianity and Crisis* (on Basic Communities), vol. 41, no. 14, September 1981, p. 234
4. Stark, W., *The Sociology of Religion, vol. III The Universal Church,* Routledge and Kegan Paul, 1967, p. 402
5. *Community,* no. 31, Autumn 1981, p. 2
6. *The Witness of Basic Christian Communities and Groups – Seeing Britain* in a World Perspective, (typescript), NACCCAN, October 1983
7. Tiller, J., *A Strategy for the Church's Ministry,* Church Information Office, 1983, p. 137
8. Ibid., p. 82
9. Hodge, M., *Non-Stipendiary Ministry in the Church of England,* Church Information Office, 1983, p. 86
10. See *The Church Army, Report of the House of Bishops Review Group,* Church Information Office, 1983, especially pp. 47-50
11. Tiller, op. cit., p. 76
12. Hinton, J., *The Family in Transition,* NACCCAN, 1982
13. *Exodus,* issue 3, February/March 1984, p. 6
14. *Community,* no. 26, Spring 1980, p. 9
15. Halvorson, L., *Primary Enterprise,* Luther Northwestern Seminary, (typescript), 1983, p. 120
16. Fromm, E., *Fears of Escape from Freedom,* Routledge and Kegan Paul, 1942
17. See for example, Rupp, G., *The Old Reformation and the New,* Epworth Press, 1967
18. Palmer, P.J., *A Place Called Community,* Pendle Hill Pamphlet 212, Pendle Hill Publications, Pennsylvania, April 1977, p. 15

19. Vollebergh, J.J.A., 'Religious Leadership', in *Minister? Pastor? Prophet?,* SCM Press, 1980, p. 54
20. Tiller, op. cit., p. 157
21. Rahner, K., *The Shape of the Church to Come.* SPCK, 1974, p. 114-115
22. Kent, J., in Ambler, R. and Haslam, D. (eds.) *Agenda for Prophets,* Bowerdean Press, 1980, p. 81

APPENDIX

1. Marins, José, 'Basic Ecclesial Community', reprint from *UISG Bulletin,* no. 55, International Union of Superiors General, Rome, 1981, p. 4
2. Ibid.
3. Boff, Leonardo, 'Ecclesiogenesis: Ecclesial Basic Communities Re-invent the Church', in *Mid-Stream,* vol. X. no. 4, October, 1981, p. 448
4. Smith, Adrian, B.., *Tomorrow's Parish,* Movement for a Better World, Mayhew McCrimmon, 1983
5. Beeson, Trevor and Pearce, Jenny, *A Vision of Hope – The Churches and Change in Latin America,* Collins – Fount Paperback, 1984, p. 39
6. *Pro Mundi Vita,* 'Basic Communities in the Church', no. 62, Brussels, September 1976, p. 7
7. Lernoux, Penny, *Cry the People,* Doubleday, New York, 1980, p. 394
8. Beeson, op. cit., p. 44
9. Beeson, op. cit., p. 92
10. Grollenberg, Lucas et al., *Minister? Pastor? Prophet?,* SCM Press, 1980, p. 9
11. Berryman, Philip, 'Latin America' in *Christianity and Crisis,* vol. 41, no. 14, September 21st 1981, p. 238
12. Ibid., p. 241
13. Grollenberg, op. cit., p. 9
14. Berryman, op. cit., p. 238
15. Marins, op. cit., p. 9
16. Beeson, op. cit., p. 39
17. Pro Mundi, op. cit., p. 8
18. Berryman, op. cit., p. 239
19. Beeson, op. cit., p. 93
20. Marins, op. cit., p. 6
21. Pro Mundi, cop. cit., p. 7
22. Boff, op. cit., p. 432
23. Pro Mundi, op. cit., p. 7
24. Ibid.
25. Beeson, op. cit., p. 48

26. Ibid., p. 10
27. Kirby, Peader, 'Basic Ecclesial Communities' in *Doctrine and Life,* vol. 30, no. 9, Dominican Publications, Dublin, November 1979, p. 586
28. Beeson, op. cit., p. 174
29. Pro Mundi, op. cit., p. 10
30. Kirby, op. cit., p. 588
31. Boff, op. cit., p. 432
32. Beeson, op. cit., p. 39
33. Lernoux, op. cit., p. 390
34. Pro Mundi, op. cit., p. 7
35. Lernoux, op. cit., p. 390
36. Berryman, op. cit., p. 239
37. Boff, op. cit., p. 442
38. Pro Mundi, op. cit., p. 7
39. Beeson, op. cit., p. 94
40. Lernoux, op. cit., pp. 391-392
41. Marins, op. cit., p. 14
42. Torres, Sergio and Eagleson, John (eds.). *The Challenge of Basic Christian Communities* (Papers from the International Ecumenical Congress of Theology, Sao Paulo, Brazil, February 20th – March 2nd, 1980), Orbis Books, Maryknoll, New York, 1981, p. 111
43. Pro Mundi, op, cit., pp. 8-12
44. Beeson, op. cit., p. 174
45. Beeson, op. cit., p. 201
46. Boff, op. cit., p. 433
47. Ibid., 433-434
48. Berryman, op. cit., p. 239
49. Marins, op. cit., p. 16
50. Torres, op. cit.
51. Berryman, op. cit., p. 241
52. Beeson, op. cit., p. 39
53. Marins, op. cit., p. 21